Utopics:
The Semiological Play of Textual Spaces

Also available in Contemporary Studies in Philosophy and the Human Sciences

Series Editors: Hugh J. Silverman and Graeme Nicholson

Before Ethics
Adriaan Peperzak

Beyond Metaphysics
John Llewelyn

The Deconstruction of Time
David Wood

Dialectic and Difference:
Modern Thought and the
Sense of Human Limits
Jacques Taminiaux

Elucidations of Hölderlin's Poetry
Martin Heidegger
Translated by Keith Hoeller

God and Being:
Heidegger's Relation to Theology
Jeff Owen Prudhomme

Heidegger and the Question of Time
Françoise Dastur
Translated by François Raffoul and David Pettigrew

Heidegger and the Subject
François Raffoul
Translated by David Pettigrew and Gregory Recco

History of Hermeneutics
Maurizio Ferraris

Illustrations of Being:
Drawing upon Heidegger
and upon Metaphysics
Graeme Nicholson

In the Presence of the Sensuous:
Essays in Aesthetics
Mikel Dufrenne
Edited by Mark S. Roberts and Dennis Gallagher

The Incarnate Subject: Malebranche,
Biran, and Bergson on the Union of
Body and Soul
Maurice Merleau-Ponty

The Language of Difference,
Charles E. Scott

Language and the Unconscious
Jacques Lacan's Hermeneutics
of Psychoanalysis
Hermann Lang

Martin Heidegger's Path of Thinking
Otto Pöggeler

Michel Foucault's Force of Flight:
Toward an Ethics for Thought
James W. Bernauer

The Paths of Heidegger's Life
and Thought
Otto Pöggeler

Political Philosophy at the
Closure of Metaphysics
Bernard Flynn

The Question of Language in
Heidegger's History of Being
Robert Bernasconi

Rationalities, Historicities
Dominique Janicaud
Translated by Nina Belmonte

Sensation:
Intelligibility Is Sensibility
Alphonso Lingis

Structuralism:
A Philosophy for the Human Sciences
Peter Caws

Texts and Dialogues
Maurice Merleau-Ponty

Translating Heidegger
Miles Groth

Utopics:
The Semiological Play of Textual Spaces
Louis Marin

UTOPICS:
The Semiological Play of Textual Spaces

Louis Marin

Translated by
Robert A. Vollrath

an imprint of Prometheus Books
59 John Glenn Drive, Amherst, New York 14228-2119

Published by Humanity Books, an imprint of Prometheus Books

Inquiries should be addressed to
Humanity Books
59 John Glenn Drive
Amherst, New York 14228–2119
VOICE: 716–691–0133, ext. 210
FAX: 716–691-0137
WWW.PROMETHEUSBOOKS.COM

16 15 16 15 14

Library of Congress Cataloging-in-Publication Data

Marin, Louis, 1931–
[Utopiques. English]
Utopics : the semiological play of textual spaces / Louis Marin ; translated by Robert A. Vollrath.
p. cm. — (Contemporary studies in philosophy and the human sciences)
Translation of Utopiques.
First published in 1984 as Utopics: Spatial Play by Humanities Press International, Inc., Atlantic Highlands, N.J.
ISBN 13: 978-1-57392-504-4
ISBN 10: 1-57392-504-7 (alk. paper)

1. Utopias. I. Title. II. Series.

HX806.M3818 1990
355'.02—dc20 90–31499

Printed in the United States of America on acid-free paper

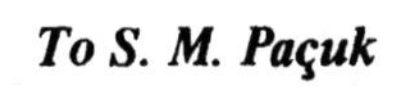
To S. M. Paçuk

Table of Contents

List of Figures

Illustrations

Preface

The present work has two parts. The first is a study of More's *Utopia*, where the noun "utopia" appears for the first time. It attempts to provide the elements for a theoretical reflection on utopic signifying practice. The second part can be seen as an application of the first: it is an analysis of utopic and pseudo-utopic spaces. The whole is preceded by an introduction that examines two generally valuable concepts...the neutral (or the indefinite) and the plural (or the field of dispersion of utopic discourse)...put to work by utopic practice and by the considerations on this practice by means of a *second* discourse.

The "thesis" of the project has three levels. The first is of a "categorical" or conceptual nature. Utopic discourse occupies the empty–historically empty–place of the historical resolution of a contradiction. It is the "zero degree" of the dialectical synthesis of contraries. It edges its way in between the contraries and thus is the discursive expression of the *neutral* (defined as "neither one, nor the other" of the contraries). Here is one example: More's *Utopia* is neither England nor America, neither the Old nor the New World; it is the in-between of the contradiction at the beginning of the sixteenth century of the Old and New Worlds. The *theoretical* expression of utopic discourse can be found in Kant near the end of the eighteenth century in the position of the third term, neither positive nor negative, of each group of categories. There one can read the zero degree of the Hegelian synthesis.

On a second "schematic" or imaginary level utopic discourse "works" as a schema of the imagination, as a "textual" figure, despite the antinomic nature of these two terms. It is a discourse that stages–sets in full view–an imaginary (or fictional) solution to the contradiction. It is the simulacrum of the synthesis. From this the remarkable connection between narrative and descriptive modes can be seen. These modes can also then be tied to the utopic discourse's relation to both myth (ritual) and theater (in its synoptic, closed, and centered form).

On a third, "aesthetic" or perceptive, level the utopic schema (or the signifying practice that stages the discourse) engenders *spaces* in the unity of a same project. It is a plural organization of spatiality. Within this discourse, which has been closed off by the synopsis of a totalizing (or totalitarian) gaze, this multiple production is signified by the incongruity of the produced spaces. This is a spatial play that can be defined as both imaginary (a productive figurative schema) and nonsuperimposable (multiple spaces), all within the most rigid *coherence* of a totalizing *discourse.*

These three levels will be explored from the basis of a double methodological preoccupation: structural and historical.

1. The structural analysis of texts tries to illuminate their narrative and descriptive modifications. It entails the hierarchic organization (surface and deep syntaxes) of the transformational procedures of the immanent semantic elements so that they become evident. This kind of analysis allows for the most rigorous exposure of the productive function of the figurative schema and the meaning effects resulting from the play among the spaces produced.

2. Historically, utopia functions as a twofold discursive practice—poetic and projective. At a precise moment in history utopic practice sketches out and schematizes, unconsciously, by the spatial play of its internal differences (incongruities), the empty places (topics) of the concepts social theory will eventually occupy. The play of spaces utopic practice produces (in both senses of the word "play") constitutes its particular historical mode of being, the "aesthetic" mode of its historicity. And thus we note the remarkable relationship utopic practice maintains with ideology. It is an ideological critique of the dominant ideology.

The historical moments for the application of this "thesis," texts from the sixteenth to eighteenth centuries, can be historically justified by analyzing them as the natural breaking point between the feudal world and its transformation into the world of capitalism. The contemporary examples have solely a "fixation" value, and thus are ideologically regressive. In other words the term "utopia" is used in a sense that is historically restricted to the formative period of Western capitalism.

I would also like to add here that the following texts are the result of a group effort that spreads over time and space, at Nanterre, Montreal, Oxford, and San Diego. I would hope that the participants find in these pages my personal gratitude for all that they have contributed. I also would like to thank Jean Piel for allowing these studies to be included in his collection, and for patiently waiting for their imperfect maturation.

Second Preface
The Neutral: Playtime in Utopia

A new examination of the neutral is not my only intention here, even though it is true that a reflection on the neutral opened my study of utopia and even affected its title. Instead I will speak of a deviation from and a critique of that study. There will be paths that cross over ones already cut by me or by others, but my new ones will contain other detours and switchbacks. I will try to point them out in passing. This new route may seem like a simple perversion of those already travelled; this time, however, the digression sketches out a bolder conclusion than that of its correlary, the principled discourse of just consequences. Here the perversion may constitute the essential element of what can be said.

This is a deviation from my own discourse on utopia and on the neutral; it is also an attempt to create a discourse of deviation and of the neutral, the place of "no-place" Utopia inhabits. I propose a utopic discourse within the discourse on utopia which will examine what is in the saying. I offer, in other words, a critical discourse.

The notion of the neutral finds its roots in my fascination in the signifier "U-topia" and in the detailed tension inscribed in this name that More accorded to the blessed isle, situated somewhere beyond England and the American coast back in the early years of the sixteenth century.

Because of its Greek etymology, the noun "utopia" is obviously inscribed in a geographic, or rather "thalasso-graphic," reference. But there is also a play on words inscribed in this marine writing and in this name: OU-topia is also EU-topia. This word play is to be found in the margins of the book entitled *Utopia.* But given what has just been said about digression can the book's borders point toward its center? Substitution of the first letter changes ou-topia to eu-topia. This word play prefigures the spatial play I tried to analyze previously as the very crux of utopia. It is spatial play in another sense, too. As writing play, a play of letters, one can interpret it as another play on words which, this time, points out the essential element in the book.

My first step toward the deviant path of perversion would be this: assume that the topographical, political and other spaces of utopia *play*, just as one thinks of the play between parts of a mechanism. They play in the same way that the elements in a system of the parts of a whole play. Imperfectly adjusted, empty spaces exist between the cogs and workings. My discourse about utopia had tried to adjust the spoken spaces. The utopic text signified them by filling the empty spaces with its own signifying substance. By explaining these different moments of play, the discourse on utopia froze them solid. The quasi-system of utopic construction thus became a true system: a structured whole in which, precisely, no more play occurred.

I would now like simply to restore play to the utopic text. I would like to *let it play*, first by displacing the play of the utopic quasi-system, of its inconsistencies, incoherencies and absences, toward simple fantasy: a playfulness of the text. I would then like leave to play with it, to extract every possible pleasurable benefit it gives with no speculative or practical interest in later asking of what this pleasure is the ephemeral manifestation.

Outopia—Eutopia: I would like to indulge in these terms. If on the way a number of allegories arise, consider them as part of our game. The no—the negation—inscribed within the name is *also* the most transcendent of values, the Good, because of the transparent inscription of an epsilon over an omicron. The name on the page's white space, here inaugurating the modern world, initially and simultaneously writes the monogram of nothingness and that lying beyond all being, of nothingness and of the good, of the good within nothingness.

Omicron, the circle. Epsilon traces out a fracture over it. If we let Democritus speak, as Aristotle reports, we can hear the rhythmic play: *ruthmos* was first a play of lines in a written letter. A graphic bar in movement created either a lambda, an alpha or a nū. If we let epsilon turn within omicron, omega will appear pointing toward a center in the circle, one which omega opens and omicron closes.

O: a fractured circle in the micro-space it enclosed by epsilon-omega. The O is also an open mouth and expiration of breath through this opening, and of which the omega is only an excess: surprise, astonishment and admiration, but also interference, noise and disorder. Recall the servant's noisy cough: it covered over Raphael's words, the very words which were to indicate the precise geographic coordinates of the unrecuperable loss of that place, because More forgot to have Raphael repeat his directions.

Both closure and opening, or opening within closure itself by means of a play in writing and in speech. All this is repeated in the interruption of a dialogue to which the most extreme attention was given. Forgetting was produced.

The O is also the center and the letter of the center designating the point around which, and from which, the circle is generated. The letter reproducing it also anticipates it in its inscription, even before the rule is applied to generate it. O is a letter which designates the central hole around which the compass traces; the hole weighs on the paper, and never fails to pierce it.

Let there be a center circle O: omicron. a well-named center which relates to the hole the movement of its trace, the wake of the force by which a space becomes drawn up and enclosed.

And into this elementary geometry epsilon inscribes the infinitesimal quantity, the negligible. Here we find a kind of limit, the surplus of a nothing. I speak here of geometry, and of elementary geometry, at that, only because the name into which utopia was inscribed and named—for the very first time in the history of the West—was space. It was the writing of space contained within a play of lines and points. Utopias, as you know, continually play between the figures of the circle and in the elements of circumferences and centers. In fact their destinies are *played out* in these images.

Now the supreme value beyond being, the *Good*, needs only the infinitesimal letter in order to be inscribed in the omicron of the negation, and of utopia's very name. By pointing toward and turning around the center, omega appears: the letter for the final goal and the infinite. Omega is the letter of excess within the designation of the infinitesimal.

This is a play on words, but also on letters because the most serious play, "*serio ludere*," is on the surface, and like Nicolas of Cusa we can also extend it to infinity, beyond totality. I would like to quote the fragment from Bloch, "the Rococo of destiny," in turn also breaking it up to follow the plural measure of my quotations: "Everything is a sign, and of course the sign is realized only in the infinitesimal. *First*, a unit of measure is agreed upon, a well connected series ...therefore...measure exists and as soon as the measure has been met, a minute drop suffices to make it overflow. This is the *mechanical* function of the infinitesimal with respect to measure. It may make one think wrongly of a container, a measured bourgeois rationing...it transforms the infinitesimal—a sign—into the cause of a goal. Much more important is the qualitative mode of the infinitesimal, that it is the end of a process...it has nothing to do with a ration gone beyond its limits, but rather the limit of a form... This infinitesimal is not the kindly appearance we have already seen. It is not...the refined force of a "loophole," even less the magical land and true sign after which change is interrupted... Here there is no sign of an authentic "end" as with certain imperceptible experiments during which joy and terror are overcome by simple astonishment. The sign of the authentic "end" opening into nothingness is perhaps this: the pipe lying there, the light on the road from an electric bulb, or whatever. This feeling of abyssal depth, this sign instead immobilizes the pendulum. It is the absurd movement on to another series. The "infinitesimal" is not the forerunner of a new series; it leads out of the series, but not far. In any case, it is hardly possible to know where... There is no mistaking it, these have something to do with the infinitesimal of the true end, implied ahead of time in any true beginning, giving to this end its direction, inciting it to go in *our direction*...These signs...reveal that we have left the series and that we join the possibility of the non-fatalistic, or we at least enter into a modifiable destiny...The "rococo" and the astonishment in front of the barely imperceptible share at least the infinitesimal of the "end," whether it be revolution or completion." Thus the Good, transcending the transcendency of Being itself, is by means of the letter of the infinitesimal inscribed in the hole of the center, O, the perforated center of the circle. The Good is broken up within itself and through the rhythm set up by the letter points to the omega of infinity within this hole. Both the infinitesimal and the infinity of the end are to be found in the hole of the center: ou-topia–eutopia.

In fact, when I suggested the ideal of the neutral, I wanted it to aim at the fracture of totality by the infinitesimal–infinite of the Good, also called contradiction, distancing the parts of a totality from themselves. This is the differentiation that produces difference. Ou-topia: in the nominal signifier, the name creating it brought about a place and a distance, but neither before or after negation or affirmation. This is the place of the limit on which depends the disjunction that founds knowledge, or that is at the base of the founding of knowledge: either true or false. The Greek negation *ou* is coupled with the space the name designates. It is joined to the space of a name and opens up a whole field of possible aims, but which are not the possible terms of truth: neither yes nor no, true nor false, neither one nor the other. We acknowledge this place, rather than have knowledge of it. But even here this acknowledgment is practically imperceptible because it is only a line, containing neither width nor surface. It has only modal reality, as Descartes would say; diacritical, it is fathomable only from that which disjoints, "relatio" inseparable from its "relata." The "position" is, notwithstanding, unable to be occupied as such. "We" cross it to move from one to the other, from true to false, from false to true. How can we stop the swing of which Bloch speaks? In motion since the dawn of Western knowledge, this is also the movement of nature and science Pascal described in the same terms, by a single letter's play, capital and small, the first and original letter, A. According to him, it repeats unending as the ebb and flow of the ocean. The omicron with its center hole, with its zero's O, and the neutral have nothing in common with origin and end, and even less so with authority and power to which they so easily become attached. This "position" has nothing to do with the neutrality of institutional power, even if representative of common truth; nor is it associated with the obvious imaginary disconnection where utopic representation unfolds the architecture of its perfection by freeing itself from historical ties. The neutral could be the name given to the signal for exiting the series and for entering into a modifiable destiny, in Bloch's words. The neutral is the *threshold* limiting the inner and the outer, the place where exit and enter reverse and are fixed in this reversal; it is the name for all limits, provided by the thought of the limit: contradiction itself. Now it seems that dissolving and resolving contradiction in a change which would cancel and go beyond it is the destiny of knowable thinking and its action, at least when it doesn't confuse contradiction with the frozen logic of truth and falsehood. Then totality is reconstituted in another way, but identical to itself at every synthesized moment. The criss-cross of contradiction is perpetually effaced, the wound cauterized, the traces of differentiation's passage emerging only as the determining lines of the whole which has capitalized on them as its *own* treasury. This is the propriety of totality, and the differences are established and connected and combined in the growing complexity which totalizes them. This totalizing movement may be seen as the internal movement of the totality of being and of history. Totality may also be seen as an unending totalization. Neither of these interpretations affects the discourse of thought and of being. In their gathering up of differences, and in this very act, both of them cancel productive differentiation and contradiction by means of integration.

Is it possible to think and to tell of the contradiction aimed at by use of the name neutral? Can a supplement that a synthesis fills be actively affirmed? It is a fiction rather than a concept or an image; it is a fiction that a play of letters brings out in a word, or a joke reveals as undecidable (this could be the only way to modify the destiny of the logos in which all is gathered up). The undecidable is lodged within a text where we read within a non-place of happiness, and in the place of happiness, the non-place. Conceptual discourse will transform the undecidable into a well formed proposition: happiness is not of this world, the end of this world is happiness. Thus we encounter despair, or the opiate of the people.

If the present text is self-critical, it is so precisely in the sense that I had forgotten to give the original letter its play at the beginning of my former text, from the very beginning of its discussion of the neutral. I had forgotten to let it play, so that as a result I had repeated the recuperation that all of utopia dragged along with it. I had neglected to isolate the other within the exposition; then the unending contradiction would have been 'present': of course, it is nowhere more obvious than through word-play in language, or a play of letters in writing or a stutter or a quick flutter within signifying linearity. The fiction that utopia transformed into representation was transformed by my discourse on utopia into theory. The benefits of pleasure the textual word play triggered were capitalized into analyses and theses. An authoritative power settled at the very spot of what is not capable of interpretation; in the guise of a truthful objective position, the limit and knowledge took hold of the play and differences already existing among the surface elements. If ou-topia is also eu-topia (playing here with the monogram to divert it toward the logic of the neutral and its fiction, toward the theory of contradiction), the movement whereby thought and discourse regained its power showed up precisely in the place they forgot, forgetting its starting point and where I will again try to return now. But a new failure is inevitable, as it perhaps is with all discourse on utopia, just as were these descriptions which unfolded the spectacle of a perfect society right on the scene of the limit. It may simply be impossible to write and speak about utopia. Because both acts—writing and speaking—must be uttered or traced in the empty and white space-time I called the neutral, and thus they build semantic bridges between the 'relata' of the differences, endlessly conjugating them in order for them to be heard, read and understood. When spread out in discourse's representation, the structure (but is it really a structure?) of double negation that characterizes the neutral semantically becomes the double conjunction relating the formerly negated terms. Look at only one example of contradiction More invests into the utopian paradigm: the double negation of wealth and poverty produces the harmonious picture of a society both rich and poor, rich to corrupt and dominate its imagined outside, but poorly able to look after virtue and to raise citizens up as mortar, into the ethical and religious monument which is the State.

It is very possible that a discourse on utopia can construct, as I have done, the edifice for the critical analysis of the book *Utopia.* It may be able to discern within that totalizing and synoptic image—one born of aesthetic story-telling—the power of a pure schema of the imagination, and within the matrix of the schema, the communication of the concept and of history. A discourse on utopia can perhaps strive to reveal by what vertical relations, presented in the terms of recognition and misrecognition, these textual levels of utopic thought are engendered and create what J.-F. Lyotard has called a figure in discourse. As a figurative mode of discourse, utopia as a textual product of utopic practice is in turn produced by the critical discourse at the place of the limit as the figure of this empty place, a place where the productive difference of the possible synthesis will be read. It is here that the future reconciliation of a working contradiction will be seen. As a figure in discourse, utopia is written and imagined within the discourse which criticizes it. It is a discourse located within its own truth, giving it power and authority—but always after the fact—to show how a representation could be produced from the negative side of its contemporary history by discursive rhetorical and poetic operations. History is the absent term of the figure which refers to it. The utopic figure cutting through the textual levels of utopia to join them together is therefore not without a referent, but rather has an absent referent. The figure is projected into a reality that is not said; it is not itself taken into the figure as its signified. Rather critical discourse will provide it for a figure at the end of its historical moment as its true signified. It is in this way that this critical discourse could write: utopia as figure within discourse refers to that which is not discourse. It opens out onto its conclusion. It does not signify reality; it rather indicates it as its absent referential term. It is the figure of a practice that produced it but which dissimulates it by means of representations within which it is formed: social aspirations, imagined musings, political projects, and so on. These are various models whose criteria will always be the impossibility of their realization.

My present discourse could then culminate in the following questions: Of what utopic practice and of what fiction, of what pure contradiction is theoretical and discursive discourse the product and representation in turn? To what reality or to what absent term does it finally refer? What figure—fraught with incoherencies of its own—traverses it? What discursive conclusion opens up as soon as the thesis of historical truth, from whose posture it speaks, is lacking? What happens if the authority and power giving it its "truth-end of history" thesis comes up short, or is simply put into question? What occurs if its foundation is not firm ground but, as Bloch wrote, an abyssal depth? Nothing, except that we then are put to take seriously the game started by the first letter of the name outopia-eutopia. The game of pure contradiction must be played; the stakes are nothing less than the metalinguistic and transmetalinguistic status of Western philosophy and its political and ideological implications: the discourse of truth over ordinary languages, finding its starting point as a decision, one of radical mastery, being posited as its starting point from which it can be raised as such.

What then does this monogram of the first letter of utopia signify? What does this inscription of two letters into one single and unique letter mean? A contradiction is traced out here, and is always being traced out, between a no (a nothing), both point and circle, hole, closure and a whole that is the infinitesimal, the imperceptible but also the infinite. It is a unique and double letter that must be read in a single *instant*; it is the permanence of an irreducible number that must be written while it is read and traced. This is utopic practice, introducing the sudden distance by which contiguities and continuities of time and space are broken in historical narrative and in the contemplation of geographic space. It is by this fracture that we catch a glimpse—as if illuminated by a flash of lightning—of the free force of unlimited contradiction.

How can pure contradiction be thought, unless by fiction? There the question of an infinite polemic cannot be seized better than in the minute scratch or imperceptible fracture in the concrete totalities of current situations, instantaneously present where absolute difference occurs? How can we get a glimpse of this "between" of two contrary terms, unless we look at contradiction as an antagonism of forces, and its pure difference or opening as struggle and conflict?

Let us return to this game, and instead of considering it as a systemic strategy totalizing all possibilities, *uno intuitu mentis*, think of it as a game that is played in this space. Each "turn" of the game whose rules describe the system allows the conflict between the players to be reinvented and superior to it. With every turn, or throw, the whole system is brought into being; each turn nonetheless surpasses the system and its strategies. But if we ask the question in these terms, we then pose utopia in temporal terms. What exactly is the connection between utopia and time?

My work—down to its very name—had considered utopia in spatial terms. If utopia is a fantasy on the limit, a staging of the neutral quality of the limit which plays out in the imagination the contradictory terms it separates, the critical distance revealing this surprising construction is also constituted in a system of hierarchical levels or moments that a central vertical figure articulates. As a limit between two spaces, such as the old and new Worlds in More's geography, the island of Utopia was born on this limit, within the window or framework that these spaces sketched out. Its very name calls up the spaces surrounding it by indicating that it is between them, in the separation it fills out by its imaginary presence. By speaking critically about the "neutral" spatial quality of the limit, the theoretical discourse was formulated within the terms of a "topic;" the future it revealed was only so in order to create a coherence from a spatial incoherency that the representation organized into its own totality. It is a "topic" of the utopic fantasy, but here I do not need to press the point because all the terms I used to characterize this space directly refer to it: frame, limit, representation, stage and staging. But it is also a fantasmatic "topic" within theoretical discourse because it had only been constituted—like a screen-memory in the dream—to fill the gaps, to articulate the empty spaces and holes and to produce those empty places in the space of the text *Utopia* and within the text of the utopic space, the systematic elements indispensable to its intelligibility. There are production, constitution and articulation which, as we just saw, could only be uttered after the fact from a place which is supposed to be true knowledge with the end of history in mind, and as a matter of fact also the end of utopia. Both the "topic" of the utopic fantasy and that of the fantastic critical and theoretical discourse on utopia are both anchored here.

Thinking about utopia dynamically is equivalent to thinking about the neutral of the limit, about pure contradiction, in temporal terms. It is perhaps surprising to learn how different this task is when the very existence of utopias lead directly to it. Don't they aim toward the future of human society, toward the parousia of a perfect reconciliation between man and the world? Critically speaking, don't they come up with a future that has no previous example? Don't they fabricate a future of desire with pieces of a nostalgic past? Whether we speak of the futurology of utopia or of its archeology, utopia is nonetheless seized and shot through with the category of time. We can perhaps try to provide a clarification for this surprising difficulty; this in turn may open up a way to reflect upon it. When we think about utopia in terms of space, it could be said that we are thinking about its essential nature "imaginatively," its present. The "hic" of utopia unfolded into its "topic," clarifying and systematizing it according to the conditions described, is its "nunc," that is, the insistence in the text and in discourse of its "now." Its map whose viewpoint is everywhere and nowhere sketched out by an observer everywhere present, nearby and far off, simultaneously here and there, may perhaps provide a sign that will indicate this unique point of conjunction between time and space, the *now* that is *here*. And if this here is actually nowhere, it is because the now when it is unfolded is a moment having nothing more to do with the "temporal," linear representation of time than does the site of the blessed island with geographic space.

What then is this utopic now? I feel impelled here to recall the cry raised several years ago on the Pacific coast. It was an insensed cry expressing everything I have mentioned up to now, "Paradise now."

It is clear that the text of utopia is in the present with respect to the narrative that founds it: it is the "present of description," as one says, the present implied in the imaginary map. It is also clear that utopia knows nothing of time, and the only time it knows is the rhythmic cycle of rituals, celebrations and accomplishments. These are immobile times and temporal images of eternity. Utopia knows nothing of change. It is constituted by the representation of the identical, of the "same" of repetitive indifference. There is no going beyond, no "supersession," because even at the beginning of the game, utopia is either origin or end; it is immobile representation and repetition compulsion.

But at the same time—if indeed I can use this expression—there are absolutely surprising events and utopic moments in both past and present history. Absolutely new moments do occur: they seem both unexpected and unthinkable. This moment or event can leave its trace in the text. As Bloch writes: "an already present indication uses small events as traces and examples; they indicate a more and a less which are to be reflected upon..." This is the passage, at this moment and point, of an intensity-sign, or rather of an exiting out of the series. "Utopias" can retain the markings of this passage: this would be the instant of difference emerging here and now. Thus in More's text, we find the moment that Raphael, the mysterious traveller, speaks in the Antwerp garden, no matter what he says or how surprising is More's description of him, making an attempt to cover over this unsettling wound in the text; we find the same moment in Cyrano de Bergerac when the window opens up to receive the emissaries of the other world, and who have also escaped from a page of a book by Cardan. This is the instant of pure difference; quoting Bloch again, it is the indication of a presence traced in the event: the signal of the imminence of a fracture, an imminence which is immanence. It is present, but of an already arrived future.

What then is this "utopic" now? It is an instant of difference and indifference of what is permanent. The neutral limit, here to be thought of temporally, moves from one to the other. Something perhaps more difficult to say, this utopic time has little to do with the time of delaying or deferring, still less with an approaching, maturing time of the ideal. It is true that this is time, but within it we get a glimpse of a particular problem which is aligned with the two non-temporal dimensions, that of the instant and of permanence. A number of Freud's texts, as well as a number of profound Eastern ones, have doubted the *a priori* form of intuition, or the category by which we think time within time as rational causality. It is similarly that the Moslem perceives the laconic pronunciation of God's judicial decision over his birth; its status will be announced when Justice arrives. This time is not one of duration, but rather a sprinkling of instants whereby each time *all* of time is uncovered. Greek thought provides the moment of the *kairos*. Gorgias inscribes this unforeseeable and unexpected figure at the base of the "divine," this latter may be simply a name given to this very unexpectedness and unforeseeability. We also encounter the *éxaiphnès*, the "sudden" which is not *nûn*; it is rather that which is inscribed into a temporal line only to interrupt it. Then again there exist *occasions* of desire, those found in the spiritual texts of Port-Royal. They punctuate a unique existence by their undecidable singularity. Fallen from grace or pushed from concupiscence, these occasions reveal history only at the very last "occasion" of death, even though it is then not truly possible to know the meaning of it.

This is a force of disruption: an absolute difference, but one which is always there. Imminence-immanence, we discover a moment of antagonistic contradiction which in turn reveals the neutral of the opening between time and non-time. It can be described as a game, or rather one throw of the dice in the game of contradiction. Each throw is situated between the structural balance of the positions and the unbalancing effect of the throw itself, of the event or act whereby a double strategy is contained and invented, despite the fact that a diagram of possible choices eliminating the force of contradiction of the rational struggle of contradictory elements cannot be sketched out. This throw or move opens up the whole field of possibilities, but the field itself cannot be controlled because it is nothing but indetermination, what the "no" designates in the utopic no-place. This throw is the general instance of the particular example of the game between the first and second letter of utopia. Here a certain emptiness is fractured by an infinitesimal epsilon, occupying it without filling it, leaving it its emptiness.

Utopia is both the product of this play and its detour into representation. It deadens the move in its tracks, and loses it by producing its image. Utopia attempts to enclose the immanence of what the instant of difference indicates, within the quasi-system it constructs. The non-temporality of time is thus unfolded within utopic representation. And here we encounter a sort of reverse-image negative of time and the generation of time in the intensive instant that I referred to in my study as fictive praxis. The contemplative theory utopia offers to the totalizing gaze of thought is utopia's end. The "becoming-sign" of the symbolic object turns into sign, representation. How could it be otherwise? How can we repeat the once, the only once? How can we repeat it in a memory or represent it without the event being forgotten?

Signs and representation and memory, memory which is representation and representation which is memory: these can only be the most necessary, ineluctable forgetting because they can only lose that radical and permanent exception, difference itself, as time sets up its institution of mastery (even if time is articulated negatively). What representation-memory and utopic discourse negatively formulate is the insistent necessity of a non-memory. The event must be forgotten; it must not be represented, for it always comes back to a memoryless being. Thinking and speaking about utopia means thinking and speaking in this necessary space between the representation and recollection of what takes place only once (the event, the notice of a coming difference) and forgetfulness, the loss that this representation carries with it and produces. Utopic representation would only *indicate*, and not signify, that the forgetting of difference and the new event is, in knowledge and in theory, the form of its memory, that indifference is the form of its difference. The a-temporality of utopic representation which signifies constant space, a perpetual now, permanence of the identical, indicates the instant of difference, the blessedness always takes place, ceaselessly "takes instant," but as if always and without fail pushed aside and repressed. To live utopia means constructing the representation which will speak its impossibility and simultaneously indicate it as that which it excludes. It is the empty space bordering and framing representation. This is the space of blessedness in representation, the permanent instant of happiness, all in one moment loss, limit and the neutral. Now we can understand the despair that accompanies all utopic representations: the instant of prediction, the moment of good news and time outside of the time of pure difference is broadcast in the time of mourning. We know ahead of time that we can only forget what we mean when saying it. It must also be clear that accepting this empty dead time is the only way within representation to trace the utopic now as the empty spaces and silences which punctuate discourse. The a-temporality of utopic representation and of its discourse of knowledge, the imaginary completion of mastery, points out the temporal disinterest in the place of the limit between inside and outside, past and future, fantasy and the possible.

Louis Marin, Paris 1982

INTRODUCTION

CHAPTER ONE

Of Plural Neutrality and Utopia

From Event to Book

Two circumstances gave birth to this book. They are seemingly unrelated, and their import is unequal: May 1968 and a colloquium organized two years later by the University of Montreal devoted to neutrality in higher education and in the student-teacher relationship. The former event, it has been said repeatedly, is directly linked to the question of utopia, if not in the specific demands that surfaced, at least in its more universal nature as a revolutionary festival. For a few weeks historical time was suspended, all institutions and laws were again challenged in and by discourse, and networks of communication were opened among those immersed in one way or another in the experience. May 1968 was not only a liberating explosion and an extratemporal moment of overthrow; it was also the seizure of every opportunity to speak.[1] Subjects and objects were exchanged so that suddenly discourse seemed to conjure up its referent. It appeared to make manifest, through its verbal expression and by its images, desires. Both roaming in reality and fixated in words, these desires could not have been accomplished by discourse itself. Rather, it brought those who spoke to such a point of excess that they could do nothing but misjudge the discourse that animated them. They consequently found themselves beyond themselves, beyond what they thought or believed.

But then, almost simultaneously, the global and radical "dispute" came to a sudden end through the restoration of order; the overthrow reinstalled institutions and laws. Street festival and the diverse freedoms of its discourse and images gave way to electoral representation and to the stock slogans and formulae of its speeches and banners. This "return" of events left no structural traces, except perhaps in a few social spaces, such as the University. In a lightninglike crossing of May and June 1968, from Nanterre to the Latin Quarter, to Flins and Beaujon, there lingered a feeling of an experience lived at such an instantaneous chronology that it seemed necessary to reflect calmly on it and to provide it with theoretical instruments. The experience was seemingly devoid of these, despite the remarkable inflation of practical and theoretical discourse. Lived as a strong and vivid challenge, the "movement" seemed to have been steered toward certain goals, then to have disappeared without informing those swept up in it whether these goals had been won. This is the direct experience of a utopic practice: discourse and situations were produced. In order to control a possible next tactic, the experience needed to be conceptualized by possessing its strategy and its systems. It was necessary to construct the theory of the practice that had preceded, which must have been linked to concealed movements in the social processes and relations of society's production.

Thus we consulted utopia to understand utopic practice. How can we make practice possible without establishing its corresponding theory? We also had recourse to a dialogical situation in order to set up a "properly" utopic space in the very place that the event had left some trace: the University. Wasn't this the place where the relationship between teacher and student, authorized and institutionalized, could be deconstructed through this relationship's very content? After all, this relationship was its medium of transmission. If utopic practice is the overthrow of law by discourse, wouldn't it be possible to discover the theory of this practice by proposing utopia as an object of "study" from totally within the clutches of an institutionalized authority? Shouldn't this content then have created of its own accord a corresponding resurgence in the educational space and within the educational relationship? In short, shouldn't it have created "noneducation"[2] as the only utopic practice possible in the University, which had been marked with its signs a few months previously? Didn't we believe it to be, if not separate from the exterior world, at least sufficiently independent and "autonomous" in relation to the rest of society that the attempt could be made? This was the tactic we drew up, the rational trick whose critique in and against the university institution we tried to lay out. Such was the detour we thought could, if not "overturn" the University, at least be introduced practically into the questioning of its essence.

In fact we had much to learn about utopia in order to master its circular paths and the work it produces: this book is also proof of the project's failure. For it is nothing more than a book *written*—alone—four years after the event that was its source, a book destined to a solitary reading, maintaining only the traces of its origin: the "movement" is neither contained in the "volume" of a book nor described through written signs. Utopic practice, a trial moment, got caught in the institution of the book, in the law of writing. But utopias have never been just books. What, then, is the relationship between utopia and utopic practice that the tactics of deconstruction of the institution reveal to us?

The other event at the source of this text was a reflection on neutrality in the University. It was jostled the world over by student revolt, "politicized" even in the most gratuitous and disinterested domains of culture. Transmitting knowledge, pursuing scientific research, shaping and educating future "managers" of society: all these functions of the University were challenged. Wasn't it but the vehicle and space for unfolding the dominant ideology—that is, the dominant class ideology? Was it institutionally linked to the most insidious forms of cultural exploitation?

Despite the fact that the University was an instrument and product of modern industrial society, its "cultural" function had seemed to predominate until this point. For a long time it had appeared to be relatively independent from the economic and social base of society, even as an institution of the superstructure. It selected its students from certain social classes and offered them a knowledge that did not seem immediately determined by the social structure. The student's goals did not seem to be directly controlled by the State's political and ideological authorities. This independence and freedom were nowhere more appreciated than in the departments of literature. In France the course crowning these courses was philosophy: a universal knowledge that was abstract, totalizing, and separated from the society over which it ruled. It was mastered only by its own decisions and, as such, was all the more faithful to the ruling class's ideology because its form and content were distant from it.

Henceforth it seemed that the University was one element in society among so many others. It lost its privileged positions and became subservient to industrial society and the reproduction of capital. Fluctuations in the job market began to determine its response; its cultural function became subordinate to its social function. As it began to resemble the capitalist industrial system more and more in form, it was to respond increasingly better. If ideology can be defined as "the representation of the imaginary relationship individuals of a specific society maintain with their real conditions of existence"[3] —i.e., with the existing productive forces—the University stopped belonging to the ideological level because it was clearly integrated with the productive forces.

Conversely, resistance to this subordination did stem from ideology. The University's declaration of independence from political and economic authority originates from ideological factors insofar as it translates the imaginary representation individuals have with their real conditions of existence. Two contradictory declarations emerge: the utility of the University, with its close ties to the infrastructure as a moment in the productive process, and its *independence* with respect to this domain and to political authority, one of the productive process's determinations. The very question the Montreal colloquium wanted to study, neutrality in higher education, stemmed from ideological factors because it considered the possibility of the University's independence in space and time from the rest of society. But it was exactly here that educational ideology became academic utopia. Are not the separation from "society" and the creation of "another world" the initial gestures of utopia? Education and utopia seemed to strike the same pose: to exist in a state of independence with respect to the culture surrounding it, to live in a position free from institutions and existing laws, and to circumscribe a separate space that benefits from its external, independent position. Each wants to be determined only by its own definitions and radically autonomous demands; each wants to "reproduce" in complete independence. The term "neutrality" applies to both.

We were then able to discover analytically the ideological trappings in the educational institution's neutrality; several symptoms of ideological leanings appeared. There exist the social legitimization of knowledge, passed down in form and content, and the conservation of the forms and instruments of this transmission. Social selection results from this procedure. These are signs of dependence on the interests and values of society's ruling class: "The educational system never fulfills better its social and ideological functions (as a mask for its real social functions) as when it seems to pursue its very own goals."[4] In other words neutrality as independence is outwardly the detour of goals and inwardly the disguise for a logic and a dynamics for the realization of these goals. The trap and deception consists not only in an inert screen hiding a deeper phenomenon. The deception is one that those very modes meant to bring about. It is a force the ruling class uses in order to ensure its mastery.

However, while reflecting on the University's neutrality and its relationship with ideology, another external tie between neutrality and utopia occurred to us and eventually led us to the "other world." If the very soul of education and its practice were necessarily to repress theoretical and critical consciousness (and conscience) for reasons internal to this discourse, the "utopic" thrust should produce within this very discourse a critical and theoretical awareness of its own production. It should henceforth be cognizant of its dependence on the ruling class's values and interests. If the essence of this activity requires the censure and repression of awareness in this very activity, don't we have to move outside of it and even outside the institution to produce this theoretico-critical work as a separate cognizance? But what is this "outside," this "place out of place"? Where can we utter a discourse on discourse that would avoid becoming the object it critiques? From what point can we theorize its contradiction and think out, circumscribe, the circle that encircles? How can we constitute a theory of the neutral and of neutrality, a theory of utopic practice that would critique the ideological trappings of institutional neutrality?

First Front of Attack: The Neutral

The signifier "utopia" fascinated me from the beginning. Of course the negation is an integral part of the word "u-topia." It therefore has no negative function because it comes before judgment or even a position one might take. Does it not set up, inside the nominal signifier, neither before nor after affirmation or negation but *between* them, a space and distance prohibiting them from terminating the possible paths of truth? Neither yes nor no, true nor false, one nor the other: this is the neutral. Of course this is not the neutral as neutrality, the ideological trick played by institutions propped up by class rule. Neither is this the neutral as the utopic figure that seems to be freed from society as it is historically and geographically positioned but all the while constructing its perfect representation. Rather, this neutral is the span between true and false, opening within discourse a space discourse cannot receive. It is a third term, but a *supplementary* third term, not synthetic. This term has ties to fiction and questioning but not to the imaginary, the doubtful, or the possible. Along with a theory of the neutral other theories should develop: of a pure critique, of infinite polemics. The theory of the neutral would permit placeless contradiction in discourse to have limitless force. And yet it upholds its productive power, forever shifting and impossible to mobilize in one single figure. This theory, finally, would entail utopic practice, introducing into narrative history and geography the sudden distance that breaks apart closely held spatial and temporal surfaces. Lightninglike, before coming to a hard and fixed image in the utopic figure and "ideal" representation, the *other* appears: limitless contradiction.

This is why this book keeps something of the name "utopia," marking out the path and movement of contradiction before it is caught, immobilized—but that is its risk—in a figure. The neutral can be conveyed by forcing the adjective "utopian" into a new form, "utopic," and using this adjective as a noun to free it from its substantive anchoring.

Second Front: The Plural

I will come back to the tension created between these two ways of approaching the neutral as neutrality and as contradiction, one a force reflected into a neutralizing violence, the other the differentiation of contraries held in a polemic movement. I would just like to justify, once more, the book's title, its subject, and the exposition of the discursive procedures that make it up. Utopic practice reveals to us a neutral as a third term in a supplementary and not synthetic position. This means that the utopic resulting as its textual product would necessarily disguise or dissimulate this supplementary position of the neutral, because once it was modeled into discourse, it would have that spot of logical mediation between contradictory terms. This would be tantamount to transforming it into a synthesis totalizing the opposites into an affirmation more advanced than the yes or no it would simultaneously deny and affirm. It would become a concept. However, as a textual product of utopic practice utopia would reproduce them by exposing its construction procedure. How, and in what form?

Utopia is a discourse, but not a discourse of the concept. It is a discourse of figure: a particular figurative mode of discourse. It is fiction, fable-construction, "anthropomorphized" narratives, "concrete" descriptions, exotic, novel, and pictorial representation: these are all of its nature. It is one of the regions of discourse centered on the imaginary, and no matter how forceful or precise, how correct or coherent, are its theses, utopia will never become a concept. It will always stay wrapped in fiction and fable-making. There will always be much speculation concerning these "ideas" about utopia's discourse. The exegetic commentary will continuously be confronted by the polysemy of the utopic figure. It floats, variegated, on the ether of the imaginary with phosphorescent, multiple impressions. Its nature and properties are secondary qualities. Recall how the ideological philosophy of representation has warned us about attributing to it truth or the affirmation of being.

Utopia is a figurative mode of discourse, a textual product of utopic practice; as such it sits somewhere between yes and no, false and true, but as the *double of figure*, the *ambiguous representation, the equivocal image of possible synthesis and productive differentiation. It points to a possible future reconciliation and a present acting contradition of the concept, and of history.* As such, utopia masks and reveals the fundamental conflicts in ideology between developing productive forces and social conditions of production formed into judicial and political institutions. It also does so between theory and practice, the practice of theory and the theory of practice as a possible resolution. But utopia performs this masking *diversely*; it works at multiple levels. As the wandering center of utopia, the imaginary, the *sensorium commune*, is broken apart and decomposed. It is at work in the fiction and gives it *play*. The wandering figure works on the model and allows its roles to change in a necessarily plural configuration. But this plurality cannot appear until the effect of fiction's play has been demonstrated; utopic fiction's discursive procedures need to be exposed. This is the goal of my analysis. And this is why my title is pluralized: not utopia, but utopic; not utopic, but *utopics.*

Third Front: Play, Space, Monogram

Let me offer a final preliminary justification: utopia produced as text by utopic practice in the multiple play of utopic fiction figures equivocally the conceptual synthesis of contradictories and the historical differentiation of contradiction. In addition it develops this play as space, as an "*a priori* form of external sense."[5] Utopia develops its "utopics" as spatial figures, but within discourse, its sole means of bringing them about. Utopics are discursive spatial figures: discursive *places* or *topics.*

Utopia is a discourse whose text, a complex and hierarchical system of levels of articulation for meaning, constitutes a space of discursive places, *topoi*, multiple and widespread. Its plurality and spread follow certain specific rules. Structurally defined in this way, the utopic text carries out a twofold operation: it performs the semiotic transposition of a spatial organization (its goal—even if "negative"—is a total "habitation" of the world[6]) into an organization of language, a discourse whose most obvious feature is its temporality, whether it be verbal-oral or linear-written.

Actually, every text performs an equivalency between space and discourse. The utopic text, however, is a remarkable form of it because it places the performative definition of text in general next to its own project, its own specific signified. The "content" of utopia is the organization of space as a text. The utopic text, in its formal makeup and operational procedures, is the constitution of a discourse as space. In other words utopia brings about an interesting equivalency between its referent—that about which it speaks, its particular project—and its emitting, receiving, and transmitting codes. The contents of its message is not the transmission of the message but the code for transmission. Along with this come the codes for the speaker and interlocutor. When talking about the Perfect Island, the Lunar States, or the Austral Continent, utopia talks less about itself or the discourse it has on the island, moon, or lost continent than about the very possibility of uttering such a discourse, of the status and contents of its enunciating position and the formal and material rules allowing it to produce some particular expression. Utopia does not of course speak about these things as such. Rather it speaks *symbolically* of these things as it speaks of the island, the star, or the cave. A utopic is thus a "symbolic," in fancy, in the imaginary. It is an activity of "shaping" having to do with the procedures at work on the imaginary. Utopics show how utopic fiction gives rise to the play of figures in utopia in its text and as text.

The production of utopic practice is also evident on another level, that of the discourse's referent. Utopia is both the total organization of the world-space as text and the exhaustive organization and complete system of discourse. Formal logic is its referential signified. Utopic practice is an architectonics, an art of systems. The explicit utopias show only monograms of this art, however. Each utopia is the "figurative" product of possible architectural production. It is a particular product of this production, but it also figures in its layout all production in general. The metaphor of the monogram is presented by Kant in the theory of the schematism of the pure concepts of the understanding.[7] It is somewhat related to these matters because the monogram is *an* inscription, *but* plural. But in the single form that a line traces in the space of the imaginary *several letters* are inscribed; several signifying spatial circumscriptions play off each other and make up the *figure* of a name. This is the code allowing us to decipher a larger unit of signified within a single inscription. This unit is given there, but as dissimulated. It is the origin and productive source, but it is also absent from the signifier's literal quality. "An art hidden in the depth of the human soul, the true secrets of which we shall hardly ever be able to guess and reveal," utopic production is inscribed within the figurative space of the text; it comprises the symbolic play of fiction. Utopia is space organized as a text and discourse constructed as a space. But it is produced by the utopic practice revealed and masked there in the form of a play of lines to decode. Time is summarized, accomplished, and annihilated in this play of spaces, which is also a play of *letters.* Spatial play but also signifying play in a textual system: this is utopia—utopic practice—utopic(s): spatial play.

I would like to briefly outline the projects that make up this book as the title refers to them. For the concept the utopic discourse occupies the unoccupiable place (theoretically because blocked by ideology; historically empty because "times had not yet come") of the historical and theoretical resolution of a contradiction. It is in the place of the neutral, the replacement as supplement-replacement.[8] As a discourse at the "degree zero" of materialist-historical synthesis within the distance of contradictory elements, it is a product of contradiction and of the productive differentiation of differences. Here I must turn to one of Kant's texts in the *Critique of Pure Reason* which could serve as theoretico-ideological background for utopic discourse. This critique of metaphysics finds neither resolution in a totalizing Hegelian dialectic nor completion in a return to a Marxist practical critique. Rather, it remains in the gap between antinomies—at least speculatively. The problems I will raise center on the critical force of utopic practice in the discourse it produces in the place of the neutral, and on its procedures and instruments.

In the imagination utopic discourse functions not like an icon, but as a schema. Utopia is signaled out as a figure. Produced in the distance between contradictory elements, it is the simulacrum of the synthesis, while yet signifying the contradiction that produced it. It stages the fiction of reconciliation and offers it up for view in the text. I will also need to question the complex connection between utopia, the neutral and fiction. Their seeming relationship has been assumed until now, and their respective level, status, and position must be clarified. For this Husserl's research on the modification of neutrality will provide analytic means for defining the relationship between the neutral and fictional representation in utopic discourse as figure. We must be sure to understand how, simultaneously, utopic figure is caught both within the general ideology of representation (an ideology rooted historically to a precise moment, from the quattrocento to the nineteenth century) while exhibiting a deconstructive and critical *force* within the schema of the imagination by the fictional procedures giving it life. From this emerges the remarkable relationship between the discursive and narrative modes within utopic discourse and, in turn, its relation to mythic narrative because of the typology of textual forms. Utopic discourse comes closest to mythic narrative in its ritual "realization." It is also closely tied to theatrical and pictorial representation in its centered and closed—legitimate—synoptic form.

On the level of the visible and readable the utopic schema is a "producing product," an activity of fiction that is marked out and inscribed in the space of a discourse tied to spatial organization. By textually staging contradiction as a distance between contradictory elements, it engenders a plurality of spaces in the totality of one project. It is an organization of spatiality as a production of spaces. But this production is fundamentally plural. In the discourse-text whose referential space is closed off by the synopsis of a totalizing gaze, this multiple production is signified by the incongruity of the spaces produced. This lack of perfect coincidence in the referent discourse speaks about and the dialogic and intermittent structure of the text outline the places of enunciation in the enunciated expression. It provides a glimpse of the implicit codes and fragmentary coded elements used by the split subject of totalizing discourse. These spatial interactions—spatial play—in the text and its referent, both imaginary and plural, fictional and spreading, indicate—no, symbolize—in the imaginary the theoretical and practical procedures of history-making.

Propositions for a Pure Analysis of the Neutral: Definitions

As a point of departure we need an abstract definition of the neutral. Etymologically ***ne-uter***, neither one nor the other, grammar defines it as neither masculine nor feminine. It is, rather, outside gender; neither active nor passive, but outside voice. In botany or zoology a flower or insect is "neuter" if it lacks organs for reproduction, unable to mate or reproduce itself. In grammar "neuter" verbs are intransitive verbs expressing an action by themselves, without object and without the possibility of an objective case—i.e., "to walk" or "to die." These verbs express an action applicable to the subject that produces it.

The neuter is intransitive. This means two things. First, it is the expression of a pure action. (All infinitive verbs are neuter.) Second, it indicates the closure of a subject by his own circularity. He is himself his own object, and his actions are his passions: self-consciousness.

On the one hand the neuter is an indefinite action lacking subject and object. It is a "to think," a "to speak," knowing neither whom nor of what; it is pure virtuality from which the discursive act will cut out its figures, simultaneously permitting and founding them. It is not, however, their sole necessary condition or even less their condition of intelligibility in the meaning process. A "to speak" and a "to think" mean nothing, in one sense. It is where meaning is accomplished because the infinitive verb neutralizes this "accomplishment" by referring to the power of the noun. It does not identity with it, however, because the verb is here the expectation of a subject and object, whereas the substantive must be included in the act of a process, then passing on to a higher level of discourse, where meaning is actually accomplished.

On the other hand, conversely, the neuter is no longer this relatively indefinite and insignificant base from which significations are brought about, lifting off from it and masking it. It is instead a doubled being introducing distance into itself only to annihilate it in a presence, whose acts spring up outside of itself, only to return immediately to their source. This is self-consciousness but not yet any consciousness of something; rather, it is consciousness that all the figures of consciousness as *extasis* in the world *conserve* in order to find root in an origin, in truly productive activities of a subject, and *forget* as they are accomplished diversely here and there, now and tomorrow, in objective independence.

In its excessive commentary grammar surely designates the zone of the neutral by the double negation of the one and the indefinite gap or break of the other.[9] Using grammatical play, the following definitions will serve us: both the two negations and the distance between this conjunction are in play, as if the neutral were an "other" place (neither one nor the other) but also the "other" of place (nonplace, utopia). History's tribunal would hand down this verdict with respect to the truly neutral. What remains after crossing out the reciprocal negation? What is the logical, ontological, and semantic reality of this "nothing" without a name? It is indicated by the play of this double-negative procedure, but not reduced to it.

1. *Chemistry:* "That element is called neutral which is formed through the chemical combination of two acid and base elements whose specific properties mutually cancel each other out."[10] Here the neutral is the place where mutual "neutralization" occurs between contrary properties. The material is exposed in the mutual destruction of its qualities. The result remains on this side of any formal composite because of this destruction: neither acid nor base; neutral.

2. *Politics:* "A neutral party is that party taking no part in a debate, and especially taking no side among those engaged in war."[11] This definition is fraught with the very difficulty of the indefiniteness indicated in it. The neutral is that party not taking part. It is not completely estranged from, nor lacking in relationship with...The neutral party must entertain relations with that party with whom it remains neutral without becoming involved in the conflict or war. In the same way "no-man" is indefinite, not in general, but with respect to "man," which constitutes the anchoring pole in the determination. It is indefinite relative to "man" and admits, therefore, in an empty form the first determination—the one that permits, and founds, all the others. Thus the Pascalian zero from his treatise "Of the Geometric Spirit" is calibrated to a specific size, number, time, movement, and space and to the dynamic pole of reduction—the

term of divisibility but not an element of the divisible. It is calibrated to a particular size but not necessarily on the same order, transcendent to it, external and tied to it. But what would this relationship be? It is at this precise, unlocatable point that discontinuity strikes, like a bolt of lightning. Here the whole of Pascalian epistemology is affected. This zero has its own force. With this nothing of time, movement, number, or space, science determines one of the *fundamental* properties of its object and simultaneously annihilates itself to make way for another kind of matter.[12]

Arbitration of Synthesis and War of Difference

The pure analysis of the notion of the neutral can be glimpsed from these first dictionary definitions. The neutral could henceforth be defined as in a relationship of dynamic totality whose parts are ***in opposition, in a position of marked difference.*** The nature of this relationship, however, would exclude it from this totality, ***in a position of difference with respect to the internal difference of the totality.*** The neutral thus creates the paradoxical idea of a part of a whole, but outside of the whole, of a part that would be a supplement to the complementary parts of the totality whose sum exhausts it. A difference is added to the closed system of difference.[13] Just as was the relative indefinite, so too this idea is very difficult to come to grips with. But perhaps there is a way to think about it and to write about it. The neutral must be grasped as the transitory and passing term that allows movement from one contrary to another, but it would be the mediator between one and the other because its nature would be neither (for) one nor (for) the other. In the logic of myth, for example, it would act like the instrument and reiteration of the original contradiction as well as its displacement toward a final conjunction (its end and goal).[14] How do we go from prohibited sexual relations to prescribed sexual relations unless we use a term that will gather together, by means of a double negation, nonprohibited sexual relations and nonprescribed sexual relations?[15] To speak of a neutral term here would substantialize a process, a movement from the same to the other. The neutral term will be the one that is no longer one and not yet the other, a logical attempt to say (rationalize) the passage. By means of this attempt it is no longer impossible to say the unthinkable of the neutral—the surplus of the system belonging to it, essentially.

If the neutral term functions logically as the instrument of conjunction for contraries, it is from and around it that the contraries find an equilibrium in their contrariety. As its organizing principle it is the center of the structure and the rule for its coherence. It allows for the elements inside the whole system to be substituted. This term designates the process at the very same time it comes into being between the contraries. It ontologizes this duration in the synchrony of an opposition it henceforth masters and orders. The neutral will constitute the *principle* of the conjunction of contraries; it will join them in their very opposition. While being the mark of their opposition, tying them together and dominating them, it is the very contrariety of contraries. It allows each of them to be contraries and at the same time escapes from this relation that founds them.

"The great and small have the same accidents, problems and passions. The one is higher on the wheel, the other closer to the center and less bothered by the same movements."[16] The axle-center of the wheel is nothing other than the king; he is the immobile center around which the great and small turn, according to the same movement, its speed depending on how close or how removed they are from him. They are interchangeable and substitutable elements in a circular dynamics ruled and organized by the center. It belongs to this circular dynamics, yet is outside it. But between the founding indifference of the play of differences and the difference that is added to the differences as a supplement excluded from their system, difference is itself indiscernible and total. The center of the wheel is of course in the wheel and outside the wheel. It is in the paradoxical situation of the reverse of a difference supplementary to the system of differences; the neutral, however, this "reverse-side," is unthinkable, imponderable. This reversal, nonetheless, is essential because it is the condition of possibility for producing and giving birth to *the other side of the royal position of mastery and domination*, the other side of the violence contained in the structure's central administration: a gratuitous freedom of the play of differences, an open-sided infinity of the production of differences. All this is produced through the introduction into the system of differences of gratuitous difference, thereby breaking every rule. This reversal, however, is as difficult to come to grips with, as imponderable, as were the neutral and supplementary differences. One of the most efficient means of coming to grips with it is to think it negatively within the critical thought of the neutral as the structure's intransitive center, but brought to the pure verbal position of a movement between contraries.

The neutral term appears between one and the other, neither one nor the other, as the third missing term yet to come. The neutral is not the third term; it is the weakest form of it (= 0). In this case it is less the lack of the third term than the lack of either two terms sketching out the profile of an empty term the third term would occupy. It is the zero degree of the synthesis; it is the synthesis of the contraries reduced to a state of pure virtuality. If the synthesis of contraries is one and the other, both denied and conserved, the neutral would mark out its empty place, waiting to be filled. Neither one nor the other, waiting to be one *and* the other, it has the power (for it is no longer simply passage from one to the other) to allow both to recognize the figure of their superior unity and mastery. The neutral is also the sign of the absolute "polemicity" and the mark of their mutual destruction. Polynices and Eteocles will confront each other and die on this battlefield. The neutral exists in a name turned into sign where the third term no longer is awaited; it is the deserted space of contradiction and the proof of its power—death's trace. Confronted with a future organizing power and the violence contained in the reconciliation of contraries, another violence acts as a counterweight. This violence is neither the stasis of logical incoherency nor the inertia of principles of noncontradiction and of the third excluded term as the immobile conjunction of the two opposing terms needed to be thrown out in order to recapture the real and the rational. This other "counterviolence" is contradiction caught in the productive dynamics of the difference of contradictory elements, in the movement that brings it about by breaking up continuities and separating the terms all peacefully tied to the whole. It creates their reciprocal negation by giving it the power of death. "War is the father and king of all; some he designates as gods and others as men. Some he makes slaves, others, free."[17]

The Institution and Differentiation

Henceforth my analysis of the neutral must take a new and fundamental step. With respect to the two parts of the whole that are both in conflict, the center occupies a position of potential reference. Through and because of its absent presence the conflict stops being a strict face-off and acquires the empty possibility of opening up. This position of potential reference is related to the contrary and reciprocal neutralizing elements in a state of tension: a real zero of opposition.[18] The position of the third term as neutral (neither one nor the other) is thus the projection of the dynamic neutrality of conflicting forces, of opposing values and sizes. It indicates the equilibrium of tension between forces and receives from these forces its own force. These forces are in a state of reciprocal neutralization: parts of a whole in conflictual tension which *are*

neutralized in a referential neutral that is indicated negatively by their tension. The third neutral term designates this neutralization before controlling it. And here appears the source for the paradox of the neutral, both inside and outside the whole: the neutral as an object of thought points toward the neutralization of contraries or toward contrariety as the reciprocal annihilation of forces. It offers it as a movement of annihilation of one by the other. It shows it in this guise before returning to the conflict, whence it originates, as *judge* and *arbiter.* It will thereafter assume it under its authority.

At this juncture two possible routes open up in the critical analysis of the already recognized ambivalence in the utopic figure, but also here in the pure analysis of the neutral. There is a certain reflexivity evident in the conflictual neutral, allowing us to focus in on the judicial force of the neutral in its ties to the forces in conflict. This analytic movement on the critical level institutes the general form of institutional ideology, the external and transcendent arbiter between the opposing or contrary interests it brings into harmony. This is justice: the institution, supreme judge, paternal authority, and state of law ruling conflicting situations of fact. Next follows the problem of the genealogy of institutional authority. The notion of the *contract* attempts to resolve it by a gesture both transcendent and mythic of a generalized and instantaneous giving up of absolute and specific rights. In truth these are antagonistic forces knowing no limits other than those resulting from the factual polemical situation. A general and common law is thus posited, but it is in reality an effect, or "empirical" consequence of the conflictual situation.[19] The schematic and abstract formula for this ideological operation is the following: the oppositional tension in the conflict, the real zero of opposition characterizing the dynamic equilibrium, confers on the third term a force equal to zero, granting the right to intervene. This force equal to zero (which is not an absence of force) is the position in a third term of the true zero of opposition. In this case it creates play where might and right, force and law, find their juncture. It is a legal force resulting from rules and regulations that can be perceived in the real and reciprocal annihilation of contrary forces in a state of tension. In other words it is an *effect* of the neutralization of terms in a conflicting situation.

In this kind of structure the third term creates an asymmetry that reveals, as Lévi-Strauss maintains, the possibility for a hierarchy, an institution—even the underpinnings of a state—that presents itself of course, as neutral. It will be proposed as the arbiter between different groups; it is the judge and moderator for class struggle. It is clear that the State occupies the paradoxical position of this third term, both part of the whole and outside it. Perhaps the essential function of this neutral term—force equals zero or real zero—is to create the possibility of a hierarchy for which it marks out the empty spot, the "floating" signifier waiting for its signified. Thus certain institutional forms of this kind of zero exist, "lacking any intrinsic property unless it be to introduce the preliminary conditions for the existence of a social system on which it depends but which in itself is devoid of signification."[20]

From the neutral State to neutral discourse we see that by overcoming the conflicting oppositions through the use of a synthesis whose discursive neutrality allows for the neutralization of the opposites, a position of judicial force *is reproduced.* An authoritative position of speech and ideological organization are created that subject the conflicting parties or polemical discourses; yet this position is the simple "hypostatized" reflection of them. These present parties would seem to turn on themselves, unrecognizable, to display the mirror image of their oppositon, as if they suffered such a fear that they would abandon the task to the just and transcendent principle that the law holds. Of course this law may only be the disguised reflection of their force and antagonism, seen as violence. "Children frightened by the face they have scrawled out are only children..." but, Pascal adds, "the means by which what is weak becomes something so strong with age is just a change of fantasies..."[21] The misrecognition occurring in childhood also affects the founding of institutions: it is force *justified*, violence, the figure of the neutral. We see how utopic discourse constructs the figures of the social contract instituting the State as neutral judge. In a way that is not entirely innocent it provides the figures of the social contract. It originates a civil society of private property from the fiction by *its expression* of a conflicting, antagonistic situation where the historical contradiction is sketched out and in which the subject of enunciation is caught.

But the movement of the contradiction can also be seen in the neutral. We can observe the operation whereby the one is annulled by the other, the other by the one in a conflicting, polemical, and symmetric opposition to infinity. This does not describe a fall into indifferentiation,[22] but rather an unlimited movement and infinite production of differences: differentiation. The utopic discourse, in its figure, is the circuitous expression of this movement insofar as it brings into play through its textual structure the ideological organization by which it is itself caught.

I will attempt to show how this works in several examples and comparisons later.

Quotations: Kant, Infinite Judgment, and Limitation

One of Kant's texts provides a theoretico-ideological formulation of the ambivalence that the pure analysis of the neutral has shown us: a place of synthesis for contradictory elements as they are fulfilled and a dynamic route of contradiction. I do not want to bring in the whole of the Kantian text here; for us it simply will be a striking indication at the end of the eighteenth century of the complex critical movement of which utopic discourse has been the symptom since the Renaissance. As I previously said, the neutral is the third absent and supplementary term of the opposition, of affirmation and negation. It enters between yes and no: there is an unoccupiable "place" that the neutral occupies. When Kant questions the functions of unity in judgments in the "Transcendental Analytic," he brings them under four groups: quantity, quality, relation and modality, "each of them with three subdivisions."[23] Under the subdivision of the quality of judgments Kant specifies that along with affirmative and negative judgments a third moment is included, the infinite judgment, about which he has an important observation. This interests me because of the neutral term, neither positive nor negative, and because of the specific articulation of the signifier u-topia, itself positing an in-finite.

Kant notes that in general logic infinite judgments are classed with affirmative ones: "Now it is true that, so far as the logical form is concerned, I have really affirmed by saying that the soul is non-mortal, because I thus place the soul in the unlimited sphere of non-mortal beings."[24] Why then does transcendental logic, and along with it a critique of knowledge, have to distinguish between infinite and affirmative judgments? Why does the judgment, "the soul is non-mortal," have to be distinguished both from the affirmative judgment, "the soul is immortal," and from the negative judgment, "the soul is not mortal"? Because "transcendental logic...considers a judgment according to the value also or the contents of a logical affirmation by means of a purely negative predicate, and asks how much is gained in the affirmation, with reference to the sum total of knowledge." It also foresees the contents of the affirmation made by a negative predicate. Kant makes the following remark:

> As the mortal forms one part of the whole sphere of possible beings, the non-mortal the other, I have said no more by my proposition than that the soul is one of the infinite number of things which remain, when I take away all that is mortal. But by this the infinite sphere of all that is mortal is excluded from it, and that afterwards the soul is placed in the remaining part of its original extent. This part, however, even after its limitation, still remains infinite, and several more parts of it may be taken away without

> extending thereby in the least the concept of the soul, or affirmatively determining it.[25]

When I affirm the nonmortality of the soul, I do not affirmatively determine the concept of the soul; I simply exclude the soul from all that is mortal. I do not endow it with the property of immortality; this would exhaust through its extension all other possibilities.

In fact Kant presents a third neutral term. Between affirmation and negation, between thesis ("the soul is mortal") and antithesis ("the soul is immortal"), comes the affirmed nonmortality of the soul. The logical infinite is thus articulated as a transcendental limit, the reverse or "other" of the metaphysical stance. "The soul is non-mortal"—the logical infinite is the abstraction made from all contents in the predicate. It points out the pure limit for the concept of the soul as the line excluding the group of possible mortal beings. This limit is itself the negative of the metaphysical stance of immortality by which the soul is determined affirmatively. Because the infinite has no specific place, according to general logic and because infinite judgments are "properly classed together, and do not constitute a separate part in the classification,"[26] transcendental logic—critical philosophy—grants it the position and status of the limit which, far from being the synthesis of the affirmation and the negation, of reality and nothingness, in a hierarchically superior affirmation that would cancel them and conserve them in a final reconciliation, is, as Kant writes, "reality connected with negation."[27] The production of a third concept from the union of the first two "requires an independent act of the understanding"[28] different from that required for the first and the second, but not leading to a consequence or derivation of the first two. Through close analysis of infinite logic of the transcendental level, and with the negative predicate, the productive operation of the limit thus gives the neutral a status. As Kant emphasizes at the end of his observation: "These judgments cannot therefore be passed over in a transcendental table of all varieties of thought in judgments, it being quite possible that the function of the understanding exercised in them may become of great importance in the field of its pure *a priori* knowledge."[29] The neutral is after all the operation whereby the difference between positive and negative—union of one and the other—is considered. The neutral cannot be taken in the sense of the synthesis by Hegelian *Aufhebung*, but on the contrary, of the reciprocal distancing of one from the other: this is the productive operation of the limit, a differentiation between complementary elements of a whole by which the metaphysical enterprise is turned upside down by the critical act, to reveal its other side.

The operation that is revealed theoretically at the beginning of the "Transcendental Analytic" by assigning a transcendental function to the purely negative predicate in the affirmative judgment (the critical work of the neutral as contradiction's own power) will be unfolded with the great polemical metaphor of the "Transcendental Dialectic." There it will take up the aspect of an antagonistic space where the thesis and antithesis of metaphysical antinomy endlessly lock horns, with no peace or victory possible. Reason remains with the struggle, however: the neutral operation takes on the name "the sceptical method."[30] "This method of watching or even provoking such a conflict of assertions, not in order to decide in favor of one or the other side, but in order to find out whether the object of the struggle be not a mere illusion, which everybody tries to grasp in vain, and which never can be of any use to any one, even if no resistance were made to him, this method, I say, may be called the *sceptical method*.... The sceptical method...aims at certainty, because, while watching a contest which on both sides is carried on honestly and intelligently, it tries to discover the *point where the misunderstanding arises*.... The antinomy which shows itself in the application of laws, is, considering our limited wisdom, the best criterion of the original legislation (nomothetic)...."[31] The point where the misunderstanding arises is the neutral point of the antinomy, the place of the contradiction and the differentiation between the contradictory elements. When Kantian philosophy here moves toward the foundation of a nomothetic, we see that Kant diverts the ambivalence toward the synthesis of the law. It is no less true, however, that with abstract speculation, the limit, antinomic differentiation and the neutral, critical philosophy's force was displayed. It is in this very space that the utopic discourse, a product of the utopic practice of the neutral, unfolds the multiple figures of its fiction. These figures reveal, both obliquely and variously, the critical work of the neutral (of contradiction). They also provide a picture of their seizure by ideology, which in turn will have to become the object of a critique in order to achieve its fullest force. This critique, it is true, will no longer be of a philosophic nature.

Husserl: Neutrality and Imaginary

With that I return to utopia and its own form of discourse, now that its place has been determined with its theoretico-ideological ambivalence. I come back to it in order to constitute one of the operating elements of the analysis, the level of utopic fiction. Utopia is not at the level of the concept, but neither does it belong to the level of the image. It is a figure, a schema of the imagination, a "produced and productive" fiction whose polysemic forms can be focused in on only through the imaginary. This takes place while showing how utopic signifying practice—the work of the neutral—continues to affect this level through and in the same ambiguity. We must tackle the problem posited by the relation between the neutral and the imaginary on the level of utopic fiction. At first my plan for this analysis had received most of its foundation from Kant's texts on schematism, as one might expect. Isn't the schema's role that of producing an operation and providing a space of articulation between the pure concept of understanding and the multiplicity of perception? It thus occupies in the imagination the positive ambivalence I sought to describe concerning the discursive figures of utopia. It does occupy it while also displacing it with a critical philosophy of theoretical knowledge. In fact the utopic figure seen as a schema "iconicizes" the theoretical concept following certain complex procedures. It prepares and delimits in the form of a lack its place of appearance; but simultaneously it signifies the force of the *historical* contradiction in which it is caught and from which it receives its contents—its intuition, as Kantian language would have it. In light of our preceding analysis one can see how important this displacement is. Utopic fiction demands it as it pursues its analysis. Contradiction, recall, was seen as the differentiation of contraries; it hastened the fulfillment of the metaphysical antinomy. Now it reappears in the position of the schematism of the imagination between the concept and intuition, but as historical content shown as the figure and as space of divergence produced by and producing the scientific elements meant to understand and resolve it.

"The Knight, Death and the Devil"

My analysis progresses if we use certain key elements in the articles from Husserl's *Ideas: A General Introduction to Pure Phenomenology*. Husserl has an important chapter on neutrality modification[32] and, more importantly for us, on its ties with fancy, the imaginary.[33]

These passages treat precisely the contemplation of a world depicted by a portrait (*abbildlichen*) on a perceptive figuration (*perzeptiv dargestellt*). We are dealing here with the contemplation of a Renaissance engraving: Dürer's representation of "The Knight, Death and the Devil." Husserl's analysis goes straight to my question, "What is utopia as a figure?" but by turning it around, "What is figure as a utopia?" or "in its utopia?" What types of connections exist between utopia, the productive fiction of a representative figure, and neutrality?

In a world of fancy, the imaginary, to what type of object does utopia as figure belong? For the moment I prefer to avoid the special conditions of utopia as a text. In the consciousness of the picture-object "Dürer's engraving" Husserl distinguishes two different perceptions: the first is the "normal perception of which the correlate is the '*engraved print*' as a thing, this print in the portfolio." This perception is positional: it is the certainty of belief whose correlate is the real. It is a thetic act belonging to the general thesis of the world. "For instance, a perceived object stands out there at first as a plain matter of course, a certainty." This is true even when "we are doubtful whether we have not been made victims of a mere 'illusion,' whether what we see or hear, etc., is not 'mere seeming,'" or "else that which appears preserves its ontical certainty, but we are uncertain with regard to some one or other of its sets of qualities."[34] Modifications take place in the characterization of being as well. These changes take their effect at the general base of the position of being, of the natural thesis.

To what in discourse corresponds all these forms of affirmation and negation, from absolute belief to suggestion or presumption, all aiming for something in being, a determination of meaning with reference, exhausting it in the referential movement? Discourse speaks of something there; it is discourse because of that, even when it speaks of this "something" in order to put it into question: "The certitude of belief is in its plain and simple form, belief in the pregnant sense of the term. As a matter of fact, as our analyses have shown, it holds a highly remarkable and unique position among the variety of acts which are all included under the title 'Belief'—or, often under the title, here very misleading though used by many, of 'Judgment.'" It is here that Husserl introduces the expression of *Urglaube*—primary belief—and protodoxa to get rid of "the popular tendency to place certitude on a level with the other modes of belief."[35] Husserl then arrives at the notion of the *position* of an object in general in the consciousness of belief.

From this point of view negation is a modification of the protodoxa, whose noematic function is to "cancel" its corresponding positing character. Its particular correlate is the "canceling," the "not." In contrast to negation affirmation "underlines"; it confirms a position by "accepting" it instead of "removing" it as negation does. But, just as negation is a modification, so is affirmation; it is a determination of the protodoxa on the noetic and noematic levels. Note how in Husserl's analysis there is a relationship with the previous Kantian text presented here. In the infinite judgment (the judgment with a purely negative predicate) and its transcendental correlate in the notion of the limit a hierarchical articulation of negation and affirmation, and more generally of all "judgment" modifications, is discovered. We perceive in the infinite judgment and its transcendental version a relationship to a fundamental position, an earlier thesis, the certitude of belief, whose neutrality will be exactly the opposite, or reverse, of the phenomenological critique.

Representative Figure

This radical modification or switching of the protodoxa into its "other" position comes up in the perceptive consciousness of the representative figure. We do not see the "***engraved print***" as a ***thing*** "aesthetically," all the while totally perceiving it in the position of being characteristic of the certitude of belief.[36] It is the small, colorless figures, "knight on horseback," "death," and "devil," that appear in the black lines of the picture, but "in aesthetic observation we do not consider these as the objects." We have our attention fixed on what is portrayed "*in the picture*"—more precisely, in the "***depicted***" realities. These realities are not so much the knight in flesh and blood, etc., but insofar as they are objects of the act of depicting, the end term of the operation of portraiture. What is the status of these little figures, for they are not actually being because they do not benefit from a position of full, rightful being. Vision does not stop with them, and contemplation does not go exactly hand in hand with them. Nonetheless, they are necessary conditions for it to take place.

"That which makes the depicting possible and mediates it, namely the consciousness of the "picture"...is now an example for the neutrality-modification of the perception."[37] It is very precisely, might I add, the consciousness of the utopic-fiction toward which utopia is constituted. In the example of Dürer's figures, whether we are talking about the noetic aim or the noematic object, the reversing force of the protodoxa in the modification of neutrality is made manifest in the imaginary. The figure is literally the product of the utopic figure. It does not "cancel" the other thing it depicts while positing it in the certitude of the "not." But neither does it affirm it completely in the stronger reality of acceptance. When I contemplate aesthetically "The Knight, Death, and the Devil," I perceive the figures neither as the negation of the objects they depict as positing them as not being, nor as the affirmation of their very being, in the way psychologizing or objectifying thought might do regarding Death and the Devil. I perceive them as objects depicting *other* things, as this by which something else is depicted, as the replacement implying "presence and absence" of what is figured, using Pascal's terminology, excluding both reality and nothingness.

The figure is a "picture-object." It "stands before us ***neither as being nor as non-being***, nor in any ***other positional modality***; or rather we are aware of it as having its being, though only a quasi-being [*gleichsam seiend*], in the neutrality-modification..." In fact, it is not ***this*** knight, ***this*** devil, or ***this*** death that is taken as ***reproduced*** in the engraving. Neither is it a generic reality of the Knight, the Devil, or Death as they are ***translated*** by allegory in the artist's sketch. I do not posit a transcendent being whose image would be the copy. The end term of the contemplation of this engraving does not have the being of a referent, but a reference. It is the simple pole of the "portraiture" relation, the figured of the figure, and not *what* the figure represents. It is not the "direct object" of the image, but the "reflection" of the figure back on itself, the intransitive–neuter –relation constitutive of it. It is a reference without referent, if such a paradoxical expression can be formed. Thus utopia, the figure produced by fiction (the specific mode of utopic signifying practice), is the perceived neutralized "thing," neither being nor nothingness, negation nor affirmation; it is the fictional product of this operation that, contrary to Urdoxa, turns the natural thesis of being against itself.

The Force of the Neutral

This is definitely a fundamental operation in Husserl, because it is through it and in its universal opposition to positional consciousness that philosophical knowledge in its full theoretical sense can deploy its methodological strategy: the *épochè*. Although negation "shows in the negated a positive effect, a non-being which is itself once more being," the belief-modification that Husserl seeks to isolate does not cancel or perform anything. "It is the conscious counterpart of all performance: its *neutralization*."[38] Its power comes from its ability to *remove* force from any position and to introduce performance in the simple thought of performing it, to convert procedures and qualifications of the verb into the infinitive, into "'merely thinking' what is performed without 'helping to bring it about.'" Simultaneously, belief and its modifications stop being "seriously" a belief.[39] Its correlates appear in the void and in simple thought without any thetic activity; this is utopic practice, a critical force whose fiction converts the historical given in the world into ironic figures.

It makes no difference to the fundamental orientation of these analyses that the discourse is modeled in the form of a text. The object in question implies only that the particular procedures by which a text can be the vehicle for a figure be revealed. We must clarify how a representation can be inscribed there, in written signs and in the words and phrases of discourse as it is offered in imaginary space, having the same neutralizing force we saw as the picture-object in Husserl's text. So it is that in the first moments of his analysis of the picture and the "thing portrayed in the picture," Husserl adds:

> Finally, the sign-furnishing presentations with the analogous contrast of *sign* and *thing signified* offer a type of modifying noematic characters (to which there correspond, as everywhere, noetic parallels), which is closely related to the preceding, but nonetheless new; and here again presentative groups, and as correlates of their peculiar unity as sign-furnishing presentations, *pairs* of noematic characterizations that belong to each other, appear in noematic pairs of objects....One also observes that just as the "image" in itself, in virtue of its meaning as image, presents itself as the modification of something, which apart from this modification would be there in its corporeal or represented selfhood, so it is precisely with the "sign," but likewise in its own way as the modification of something."[40]

Back to the Book

I will conclude by making a last remark concerning the final level of my analysis: utopics are spatial play. The major themes of my project have been sufficiently evident to warrant not returning to them. The seminar on utopia with its strategies and tactics, emerging from theoretical and ideological origins, was thought to be a failure in 1968, both on the practical and speculative levels. The reasons have been provided by means of Pierre Bourdieu's theses in *La Reproduction.*[41] The statements made in Montreal concerning the University's neutrality came up against the incomprehension and opposition of those who, undergoing ideological and political pressures in the Eastern-bloc countries, believed that an adequate response could be found in the University. The apology for academic neutrality, in its "formalism," was in reality an attitude couched in the mask of ideology and politics indirectly linking them with a certain economic system of exploitation and violence. As time went by, the original events that led me to want a reflection on utopia changed into reasons, not so much to interrupt it, but rather not to signify it by running it through the discursive and textual mode. It was not for having found certain forms of utopic life somewhere on the edge of the Pacific that I abandoned—even forgot—the project. Even if a certain existence blossoms there and lives are lived, it does not reach, even after much frustration, the theoretical comprehension of the ideology that urged these people to flee to places that geography and historical time ignore. In these utopias dream and reality, desire and political struggle, are

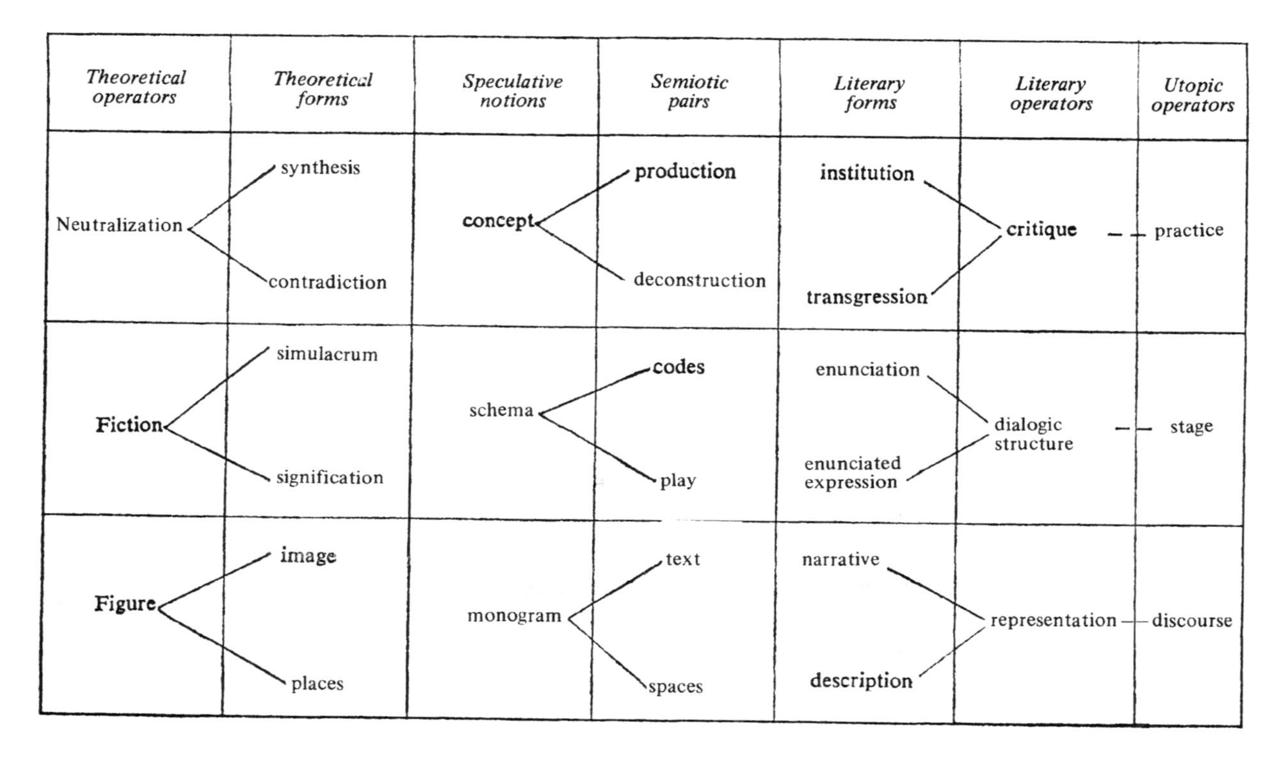

Figure 1. Table of concepts

magically mixed—and confused. Let it simply be noted that the original trigger for my own movement of writing and discourse was offered by a colloquium of semioticians, mathematicians, and architects.

It was in the presence of scientists and artists, both familiar with geometry and the sign, that a critique of contemporary ideology and architecture took place. While we sought a theory, a practice in which these two activities could be allied harmoniously, it occurred to me, to my pleasant surprise, that the analysis of the divergent spaces of the text and its "referential" in Thomas More's *Utopia* met with our current preoccupations. The book was in no way foreign to the theory and practice tied to our society of 1972. The critical force of the utopic figure More presented *in a book* at the beginning of our modern times remained relevant, even if we now had at our disposal a scientific theory, even the practical means, not to realize its objectives (utopia is not a social or political project), but to accomplish in a concept what had previously been variously traced out and figured. The book, you see, had a mediated, indirect critical force, although still in the grips of ideology. This is all the more reason that a book on the book could turn over its figures and construct or deconstruct them. My first critical task is not primarily the theoretical critique of signs and symbols. I wanted to write a book—a utopic instrument—that tried to find the means for reflecting on utopia and utopic practice today.

If it is true that a foreword or introduction—a preface to the reader—is always written *after the fact* and that it attempts to provide a diagram, even one that is speculative or provisional, of the work's concepts and working notions, it also tries to place *the* place from which it speaks and is written and to define the one who is its author. I have tried to present a diagram of the notions in *Figure 1*. It is the projection within the larger syntagm that becomes a book of a final phase of my thoughts as they conclude this Introduction. In other words nothing less than a whole book was needed to mark and measure the itinerary of terms in their relationships and reciprocal limitations. This is a coherence constructed from various routes and tactical manipulations. It is the *temporary* immobilization in a diagram of multifarious research continually in a state of dispersion.

Notes

Chapter 1

[1] See Michael de Certeau, *La Prise de la parole* (Paris: Seuil, 1969).

[2] To be faithful to the dictates of the signifier "u-topic": no-place.

[3] Louis Althusser, "Ideology and Ideological State Apparatuses (Notes toward an Investigation)" Lenin and Philosophy and Other Essays (New York and London: Monthly Review Press, 1971), pp. 127–186.

[4] P. Bourdieu and M. de Saint-Martin, "Conscience de class et excellence scolaire," *Les Annales E.S.C.*, 1971.

[5] To adopt Kantian terminology.

[6] See Heidegger's texts concerning this, quoted in F. Choay, *L'Urbanisme, utopies et réalites* (Paris: Seuil, 1965).

[7] Kant, *Kritik der reinen Vernunft* (Riga: 1781), p. 142. [*Critique of Pure Reason* (Garden City, N.Y.: Anchor Books, 1966)]

[8] Jacques Derrida, *Of Grammatology* (Baltimore: Johns Hopkins University Press, 1976). My whole development on the neutral owes its basis in great part to the work of Derrida.

[9] Aristotle gives it this accent in *On Interpretation*, 16a 2, 30: "'No-man,' however, is not a name. No name has been imposed to designate this – for it is neither speech nor a negation – but let us call it an indefinite name."

[10] "Neutre," Littré, *Dictionnaire de la langue française.*

[11] Littré.

[12] Pascal, *Lettres et opuscules*, "De l'esprit géometrique," (Paris: Aubier-Montaigne Lafuma, 1955), pp. 138–39.

[13] J. Derrida, *Writing and Difference* (Chicago: University of Chicago Press, 1978).

[14] See Louis Marin, *Sémiotique de la Passion, topiques et figures* (Paris: Desclées de Brouwer, 1971). See especially the Introduction and p. 140.

[15] Algirdas Julien Greimas, *Du Sens* (Paris: Seuil, 1970), pp. 141–145.

[16] Pascal, *Pensées* (Paris: Delmas, 1955); second edition, fr. 258 (Brunschvicq Minor, fr. 180).

[17] Heraclitus, fr. 53. Hippolyte, ref. IX, 9, 4, trans. J. Bollack, H. Wismann (Paris: Minuit, 1972), p. 185.

[18] Kant, *An attempt to introduce the concept of negative quantities into philosophy.*

[19] As in Rousseau, *Social Contract* (Book 1, Chapter VI).

[20] Claude Lévi-Strauss, *Structural Anthropology* (New York: Basic Books, 1963).

[21] Pascal, op. cit. fr. 153 (Brunschvicq Minor, fr. 88).

[22] As René Girard seems to feel in his *Violence and the Sacred* (Baltimore: Johns Hopkins University Press, 1977).

[23] Kant, *Kritik*, p. 70.

[24] Kant, p. 72.

[25] Kant, p. 73.

[26] Kant, p. 73.

[27] Kant, 1787 edition, p. 111.

[28] Kant, 1787 edition, p. 111.

[29] Kant, 1787 edition, p. 98.

[30] Kant, 1787 edition, pp. 451–452.

[31] Kant, 1787 edition, p. 451 (my emphasis).

[32] Edmund Husserl, *Ideen zu einer reinen Phänomenologie und phänomenologischen Philosophie*, Part 3, Chap. X, p. 109–*General Introduction to Pure Phenomenology* (London: George Allen & Unwin, Ltd.; New York: Humanities Press, Inc., 1969).

[33] Husserl, p. 111.

[34] Husserl, p. 103.

[35] Husserl, p. 104.

[36] Husserl, p. 111.

[37] Husserl, p. 111.

[38] Husserl, p. 109.

[39] Husserl, p. 109.

[40] Husserl, p. 99.

[41] P. Bourdieu and J.-C. Passeron, *La Reproduction* (Paris: Minuit, 1970), see especially pp. 230 ff.

MOREANA

CHAPTER TWO

Narrative and Description

A brief comparison between utopia and myth – one that will see recurrent development in the following pages – will lead us into the very interrogation of the utopic *text*.

Myths

Recall three of the essential characteristics of the definition of myth: first, myth, upon its immediate reception, is a narrative or story. It is a linguistic ensemble combining simple units in accordance with the temporal categories of before and after. Second, depending on the particular story or narrative myth is the narrative place of contingency and event: anything can happen there; the most extraordinary acts, the most exceptional adventures, and the wildest situations occur in myth. I believe that this surprise and eruption of events, this irreducible newness on which our attention hangs, must be related to narrative's form at its most superficial level. Because narrative occurs in time, is said rather than read, told instead of pursued through the spatialization of the printed page, it is a form of waiting and expectation. Third then, its mode of reception, like its mode of emission (both obeying the law of succession), always implies the possibility of the unexpected. Narrative is always more or less an expectation of the unexpected.

Temporal duration as it controls the narrative's events is not simply a form, for the story's content is also affected. This oral-aural emission and reception, the narrative's formal expression, is connected to the form of its content by a strict semiotic function. *What* the narrative will say – the very signification of what will be told – is necessarily related to the very specific mode of saying and listening – that is, of expectation and possible surprise. It is in this way that narrative space is the contingency of events par excellence. The same would apply to discourse in general. Discourses that are judicial, political, etc., function in the same manner in that they are pronounced before a group of listeners and combine memory and expectation in the unfolding of arguments, proofs, and exhortations. Contingency is thus not only related to events; its goal is not simply reference to an accident, a miracle, or an unfortunate occurrence. Tempered by rational necessity, logical coherence, and objective detail, this contingency reveals under its successive emission of words a willful law and the formation of things, beings, and actions. This cannot be myth, however, because it seems entirely dedicated to the repetition through speech of the surprising evolution of events. It seems completely controlled, even in its mode of expression, by what is outside of it. This first characteristic of narrative in general and of myth as a type of narrative hinders our ability to analyze it. In so doing, doesn't our analysis attempt to dominate the successive and contingent occurrence of elements that reshape it into a necessary order? Doesn't it try to master, through accurate and uniform rules, the gratuitous coupling of episodic elements? In fact, doesn't it actually constitute these units as transformable, capable of being shifted and combined into seemingly new groups?

Structures

One aspect of myth has interested a number of readers. Again a superficial aspect, it finds its origin in another kind of structure. It does not belong to narrative as the act of telling a story, as the ability of evoking and provoking speech; rather, it comes from the knowledge of mythic narratives gathered together in the form of larger units that can be grouped. They are classed in the hope of revealing comparisons for theoretical understanding. Our viewpoint thus changes. The second characteristic of mythic narrative is not homogeneous with the first; it obeys another perspective. No longer a question of listening, it is rather one of knowledge. All myths are similar, as if, untiringly, they combine among themselves the same units according to the same rules and laws. They appear to displace and transform them following the same operations along narrative's temporal line, the same that a moment ago we tried to label as the very place for the eruption of events into speech.[1]

It is obvious, however, that such a structural characteristic of mythic narrative can be discovered only through systematic comparison of numerous myths. The first gesture of this theoretical inquiry would involve constituting myth as an object of knowledge. One would first compare similarities and, even more so, similarities of the differences among myths. Reduction and condensation of the expressive form of the material would then allow one to construct narrative units in the form of groups of predicative relations. These relations would also be articulated into correlations whose distinction consists in escaping from temporality. These correlations would be of a logical order. The semantic proportions and the equality between them reveal not a succession but an order; not a juxtaposition of events but rational connections between them. They are a-chronic. Claude Lévi-Strauss was able to provide the general formula of mythic narrative, which accounts for "newness" in narrative. He expresses it in the form of a transformation obtained through the ordered presentation of the functions and terms of the initial situation.[2] P. Maranda and C. Kongas have shown that this formula, despite its generality, expresses the law of complex and complete mythic narratives, and that all real or "possible" myths do not precisely obey this law but, rather, limited or incomplete versions of it.[3]

Nonetheless, order was introduced where confusion had reigned. Instruments of knowledge demonstrated their functional nature; a science of myth had been constituted. As theoretical knowledge myths display two characteristics: they are narratives and correlations of relations. Both a diachronic axis of their expression and telling and a synchronic axis of their logic and syntax exist. The diachronic sequences are perceived—*heard*—in their chronological succession; they are *read*, however, as organized synchronic relations in order to be understood. The two axes are thus perpendicular to each other. The second axis is not the exact expression or rigorous scientific transposition of the first. The telling and hearing and consequently their truth, are not accomplished through reading and understanding. There are two different approaches to mythic narrative; one takes place in its "existential" practice, the other in its theoretical knowledge. The one is irreducible to the other. They are the results of a choice; more precisely, the second results from a scientific option. It remains to be seen if the first deserves a science of its own.

Functions

There is a final characteristic that responds to questions of function and that, as well, is situated at the crossroads of these two axes: What purpose do myths serve? What role do they play? What is the nature of their social function within a specific culture? The origin of these questions is lodged in two long-standing interpretations: myths have been seen as social expressiveness and as explanatory instruments. According to the first interpretation myths would constitute the reformulation of fundamental feelings and social emotion into discourse or a symbolic projection narrated to a group. Instead of being transformed into aggressive actions that would endanger society itself, this social affect would find, in the form of narrative, a secondary and symbolic exteriorization. Language would take the place of action, speech the place of motor response, discourse the place not only of violence but of the direct or indirect, mediate or immediate playing out of this conduct in the grips of a real contradiction.[4] Of course, speech in itself can be the conduit for a violence and a power as effective as polemic action; accusation, blasphemy, insults, and curses are clear verbal channels whose effects are registered in the material presence of the situations in which they are uttered.[5] Mythic narratives would be both similar to and different from these examples. In their reciting and telling a world of oppositions, alienations, contradictions, and want symbolized by narrative is revealed. But this same world is also ordered through the myth's episodes, dramatic actions, and denouement. It is precisely because mythic narrative symbolizes and, in this very symbolization, unfolds as a story that it can reformulate a society's story—as history—and origin in order to transform it through its telling.

This *transformation-in-the-telling* of mythic narrative, and of narrative in general, is quite different from the transforming activity of oracular speech, blasphemy, or accusation. It does not create a new situation through its reciting as these other activities do by their sole performative power. Mythic narrative picks up a history or past, even one that precedes time, and gives it its own rhythm and order. It *transforms* by relating its symbolic history, and it therefore constitutes the history of the group, itself constituted through and by that mythic narrative. It explains and clarifies what normally, in lived experience, would remain opaque, dangerous, and full of anxiety. The original insurmountable antithesis of everyday activity is thereby explained. An internal transformation within discursivity, mythic narrative ensures the exchange of contradictory poles. They are unfolded along a story line that is history. They now are laid out in time that is the time of narrative discourse, where they were once, originally, felt and discharged as the immobile tension of contradiction. Through this movement of society's original contradictions society itself is brought into being and provides its own history by narrating the symbolic history of its contradiction in the temporality of speech.

History

Mythic narrative can thus be seen as the symbolic projection of important antinomies: Nature and Culture, Individual and Society, Origin and Presence, Life and Death. How can myth thereby become an explanation for them? In what way does it allow us to understand these oppositions better? Is it not precisely because, symbolically, within discursive time, it narrates the exchange between them, the passage from one to the other, the transformation of one into the other? By telling this story, this "history," it brings into being the story—and the history—of society. At the same time, through the open system created by shifting correspondences between each discursive unit at various levels of natural reality, the explanatory knowledge of this society's world is constituted. The signifying ensemble that creates order within it, and that regularizes it, is brought into being.

This is the immobile change that mythic narrative "realizes." In a sense the discursivity—narrative sequence—that intervenes through successive episodes is the repetition of a nexus of contradictions in which a specific society discovers its particular origin. But through the unfolding of contradictory terms along a temporal discourse, by displacing them into language's succession, by molding them into discourse and into common "spheres of action," narrative gives the impression of a sequential solution to the contradictions. They are the ersatz of a synthesis, a harmonious order of reconciliation. The a-chronic system of correlations of relations in mythic narrative constitutes a complex interchange of transformations between poles and contrary functions. The meanings of the structure of mythic narrative are clear when analyzed in its narrative form, whose oral-aural recitations and rituals of telling and listening are the expressions upon the surface of social experience.

Reading *Utopia* thus reveals simultaneously the adoption of narrative form and its abandonment. Book One opens as a historical chronicle:

> The most invincible King of England, Henry, the eighth of that name, who is distinguished by all the accomplishments of a model monarch, had certain weighty matters recently in dispute with His Serene Highness, Charles, Prince of Castile. With a view to their discussion and settlement, he sent me as a commissioner to Flanders....We were met at Bruges, according to previous arrangement, by those men put in charge of the affair by the Prince—all outstanding persons.[6]

The event in all its contingency erupts: a serious difference of opinion between Henry and Charles; Thomas More chosen to settle it; the meeting in Bruges.... Then comes the surprise of the accidental as our reading takes a detour:

> One day I had been at divine service in Notre Dame, the finest church and most crowded with worshippers. Mass being over, I was about to return to my lodging when I happened to see [Peter Giles] in conversation with a stranger, a man of advanced years, with sunburnt countenance and long beard and cloak hanging carelessly from his shoulder, while his appearance and dress seemed to me to be those of a ship's captain.[7]

And here we witness the suspension of our attention in the strange expectations of information created by the narrator; he makes use of it to continue:

> The moment I saw him, I was sure he was a ship's captain. 'But you are quite mistaken,' said [Peter Giles], 'for his sailing has not been like that of Palinurus but that of Ulysses, or rather, of Plato.' Now this Raphael – for such is his personal name, with Hythlodaeus as his family name – is no bad Latin scholar, and most learned in Greek. He had studied that language more....[8]

Referent

Thus, despite the questions and responses of the dialogue, or rather because of and through them, the narrative spins its web: events, incidents, and meetings rise up, one by one, from the surface of the text. They appear in the form of anonymous words and speech, the utterance of no one, as if things themselves were granted an anonymous voice so that the reader forgets its sonority and believes he is witnessing the true events themselves. This is the referential illusion that accompanies every narrative. One of the pure ways it presents itself consists in carefully effacing the traces and marks of its own production, thus appearing as the absolute equivalent to that of which it speaks. Our text would conform to this description were it not for two particularities that complicate matters somewhat. Two opposing poles of discourse, the position of a referent and the introduction of the enunciating subject, disrupt this otherwise perfect register. The initial gesture of Book One carries with it the traces of discourse other than the narrative itself: the second discourse consists of history, full of multiple references and diverse witnesses. The narrative we are about to read appears to rise up from this historical backdrop. "The most invincible King of England, Henry, the eighth of that name...His Serene Highness, Charles, Prince of Castile..." The proper names point to an exterior where beings (persons or places) are determined by them. The titles situate them within a system of hierarchical social relations, simultaneously synchronic and diachronic: the "eighth of that name... His Serene Highness, Charles, Prince of Castile...Is not the ambassador accompanied by Cuthbert Turnstal...[just] created Master of the Rolls to everyone's immense satisfaction"?[9]

Multiple Reverberations

A whole network of signals and references is set up that anchors the narrative in history. The narrative thus becomes the detached fragment of another silent narrative, exterior to the one we read. Its presence, however fragmentary in this text, grants it the authority of the pure and simple exposition of past facts. This "touch of the real" accompanies the preface-letter that More addresses to Peter Giles: "you know that I was relieved of all the labor of gathering materials for the work and that I had only to repeat what in your company I heard Raphael relate...the nearer my style came to his careless simplicity the closer it would be to the truth, for which alone I am bound to care under the circumstances..."[10] The narrative has a "witness" guaranteeing the authenticity of what is told, whose own narrative can join in and confirm More's narrative, the "true," "real" fact situated somewhere at the crossroads of these similar, yet different, narratives.

But we must advance carefully; this "touch of the real," this "effect of reality," here can also accomplish the opposite. It may "de-realize" the scene, for if More's narrative is to such an extent tied into the larger narrative of history and its various testimonials, far from benefiting from its authenticity, the one narrative may fictionalize the other, or at least—for we cannot even be sure of its status as fiction—draw attention to its narrative qualities. *Utopia* would then not be More's narrative anchored in historical reality, with this reality conferring upon it, through its network of references, an objectivity. It would be, rather, a system of narratives referring and reverberating among themselves. We would be aware of only one narrative made up of a system of reverberations between references, which in this case designate only other narratives. More would thus be informing us, here at the opening of *Utopia*, that history is nothing but a system of narratives that are interconnected and interreflecting. Reread the dedication to Peter Giles: "the nearer my style came to his careless simplicity the closer it would be to the truth..."[11] The truth or exactitude of More's narrative is measured only through Raphael's narrative, or through Peter Giles' potential narrative: "I have finished *Utopia* and sent it to you, my dear Peter, to read—and to remind me of anything that has escaped me."[12] The validity and truth of the narrative of history would thus be proportional to the number of possible reflections of which the narrative is made. The more densely they intersect, the closer it would approach that veracity. From here on in More's whole art will consist in making us believe that *Utopia* is history, so that finally we understand that the very center of history is, precisely, utopic: a place both empty and yet plural with absence *and* with relations where narratives are spoken, one against the other.

Subjects

Actually the other characteristic of *Utopia* as narrative should have aroused suspicion. The very nature of narrative in speech—which consists in rejecting the subject of speech out into forgetfulness and making the object of it its only subject—is here twisted;[13] the narrator's "I" already appears in the second sentence: "he sent me as a commissioner to Flanders...accompanied by Cuthbert Turnstal," etc. The presence of this narrator's "I" is constant, almost insistent. Even if the remark about "the most invincible King of England, Henry, the eighth of that name," opens the narrative with an explicit reference to history, the story we are told does not refer to history as it emerges in its anonymous generality or abstract objectivity. It is told by a voice that refers and points to itself through a precise marking in the text we read. It does so through a point of view that is indicated in the narrative itself ("Mass being over, I was about to return to my lodgings when I happened to see [Peter Giles] in conversation with a stranger...") and, to be complete, through a place and moment that are precisely determined in space and time ("One day I had been at divine service in Notre Dame...Mass being over, I was about to return to my lodgings..."). The indication of the enunciative operation has already been provided implicitly with the reference to the larger historical narrative: "The most invincible King of England, Henry, the eighth of that name, who is distinguished by all the accomplishments of a model monarch, had certain weighty matters *recently* in dispute with His Serene Highness, Charles, Prince of Castile..." The time of this diplomatic incident—and thus of historical fact—has been given only as reference to another time, which is that of the origin of the specific narrative we are reading, and where we read that the "most invincible King of England, Henry...had certain weighty matters recently in dispute with...the Prince of Castile..." Thus here exists more a subtle circularity than a simple "self-referential indicator" found at the beginning of our text: the "true" historical fact is inscribed in the text with reference to a temporal determination, which is none other than the origin of the text in which it is inscribed. The *recent* time of the historical event is recent only with reference to the time when a narrator's "I" produces it as inscribable in discourse; this is the introduction of an added referent in the simple instance of enunciation of the linguistic "I."

The Other Voice

In short, the whole system of narrative references, which had at first appeared to make up the historical narrative's objectivity, now, upon closer inspection, relies on the inscription in the text of the "I" that produces it. It is dependent on this other earlier text whose sole—but more fundamental—textual mark is this "I," simultaneously subject of all the adventures (things happen to "it") and participant in the entire story. It tells this story and even creates it in discourse. In other words, just as the system of narrative references ambiguously appeared to exchange history in general for utopia in particular so that *Utopia* would seem like a fragment of history, or that history would be concealing utopia at its very center, so also, at the other extreme and just as ambiguously, the producer of the story simultaneously is indicated as one of its elements. The subject is produced by the story and exists because articulated by it, though seemingly superior and transcendent to its products. The story is told through this narrator. He seems to be a simple voice or mouthpiece, just as this narrator within history is the mouthpiece for the invincible King of England, Henry.

In effect this double movement points out the complete ambiguity in historical narrative: just when we felt it was valid through the indication of an exterior referent, its objectivity became fragmented from its myriad reciprocal reflections and references. Conversely, however, when we were inscribing this narrative as one produced by a subject *hic et nunc*, we discovered that this subject was spoken by this story, thus becoming the simple specified place of its production. In this case the subject is not a product as if a complement in creative transitivity. Rather, it results from intransitive production, from the neutral process of a verb in the infinitive. But, hardly occupied, this position is given up periodically or, rather, shared. The author's narrative consists not in telling his story—I mean the story of events in which he has been involved—but in telling very special kinds of events, discursive events, speech incidents, dialogical meetings. In other words More, the author of *Utopia*, steps upon the stage only as subject of events in the text he writes, only to relinquish this position in discovering that the events that affected him are not weighty, "factual" events but discursive events that are weightless because they are the narrative of events that have happened to an "other." Thus the exactness More sought (and he says as much to Peter Giles) is not the referential exactness of a full signified; it is, rather, fidelity to another narrative, to the narrative of an other: utopia. In short, what happened to More and what he recounts to Peter

Giles is not a story, it is discourse as story, as one would listen to another voice.

Travel Narrative

Raphael's narrative is a travel narrative, a type of narrative where the story becomes involved with geography. The successive thread that connects it does not do so through a connection of events, accidents, or narrative actors. Rather, it ties together places that, as a circuit, constitute the narration. More precisely, it is a narrative whose events are places that appear in the narrator's discourse only because they are the various stops on an itinerary. These stops or stages can be marked out by incidents, accidents, or meetings (the other types of events that make up the material of historical narrative). But these events are not the essential elements; they are added only as signals of a possible "memorization." The essence of a travel narrative is this succession of places traversed by a network and punctuated by names and local descriptions. Traversing the network raises it from anonymity and exposes its unchanging preexistence. It is a geography in the sense of inscription. Names are written on and in a land that is the absolute reference system for all discourse. It is the world as ultimate horizon of all acts, of all conduct, of all behavior and fundamental experience. The travel narrative is thus the remarkable transformation into discourse of the map, that geographic icon. It is the discursive figure of the image that is itself the selection of relations of elements in the world, the construction of the world in the form of an analogic model that covers over reality with the network of its lines and surfaces. It also does so with its names, thus providing a transformed equivalent.

From Map to Narrative: Transformations

How, then, in turn, does travel narrative transform geographic inscription into discourse? What specificity does this transformation possess in the text of *Utopia*? The essential transformational operation consists in introducing a succession into the network of these names (whether expressed or as a periphrastic equivalent of the toponym). It consists in providing a form of temporality that is simultaneously that of discourse, in its syntagmatic linearity, and of narrative proper, by adding an actor. This latter anthropomorphizes the syntagmatic wanderings of the text; in this case the toponyms would be the simple marks of passage, the *topoï* of the simple function of travel. Here is the travel narrative, Peter Giles' intervention (in the narrator's discourse): "When after Vespucci's departure he had traveled through many countries with five companions from the fort [America], by strange chance he was carried to Ceylon, whence he reached Calcutta. There he conveniently found some Portuguese ships, and at length arrived home again, beyond all expectation."[14] Thus is constituted a first network of four names: America, Ceylon, Calcutta, and Portugal; we can add a fifth to the beginning of the series: Portugal. This last name, a few lines earlier, inscribes the itinerary's points of departure and arrival within the mobile identity of a circuit.

Here emerges the second characteristic of the transformation that sets up the travel narrative as a narrative equivalent of the geographical map: circularity. The beginning of the route coincides with its ending. The toponymic recurrence is the linguistic substitute for simultaneity. Repetition of the same name in the narrative equals the co-presence of the same elements in iconic space; the syntagmatic line of narration that folds over on itself through the repetition of the same name functions as the limit closing off stable space, differentiating an interior where mapped places are inscribed through names and an exterior which is, in discourse itself, the indeterminate white field of terra incognita. Interior and exterior are opposed as *A* vs. *B*, being contrary terms that the travel narrative transforms into contrary opposites, *A* vs. *non-A*, the "said vs. the nonsaid," the determined vs. the indetermined."

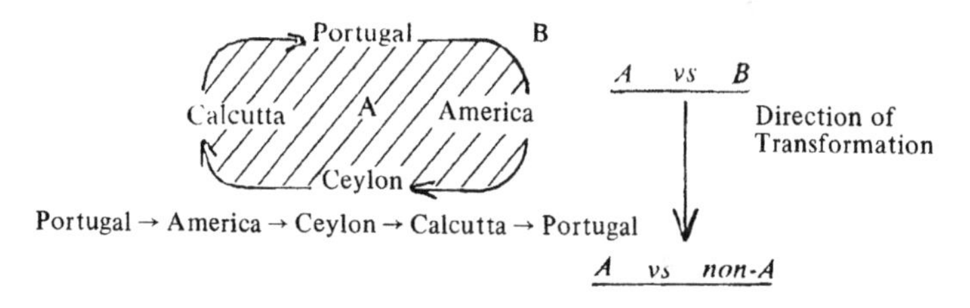

Figure 2. Schematic representations of Raphael's voyage

It would perhaps be possible to add to this transforming operation of map into discourse a certain number of explicit distances or relative quantities of distance distributed by means of signifiers along the syntagmatic line: then it would be clear that, while remaining with the analysis of Peter Giles' introductory narrative, Portugal is farther removed from America than from Calcutta, and Calcutta is very close to Ceylon, itself a good distance away from America. We thus have in Figure 2 "narrative" schema:

Portugal ⇒ America ⇒ Ceylon → Calcutta ⇒ Portugal

The map of this would be constructed in the paradigm:

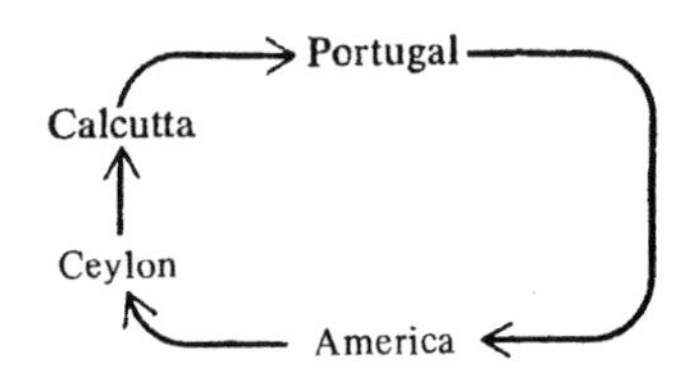

Figure 3. Modified schema of Raphael's voyage

Limits

We should return to the role the syntagmatic line plays in the transformation of map into travel narrative. Note how the series of names the narrator places on the narrative line seems to be, within each section of the series, the result of a binary selection between a marked and an unmarked term: "Portugal vs. non-Portugal," "America vs. non-America," etc. The narrative in question operates a differentiation within the set of differences that makes up the mapped icon, itself overlapping, analogically but selectively, the known world. Thus the second map we are constructing from the travel narrative conserves a mark of differentiation, *the* difference of differences, but everywhere within the totality of its route. In short, the travel narrative constitutes the map, but at its edge, through an operation of digital selection, all the while maintaining its nature as an analogic model within this limit. The narrative about the map constitutes the map, which is, as representation, the product of the narrative. The discontinuous nature of the units that make up the narrative is both conserved and negated. It is negated by the two ends of the discursive series through the repetition of the same unit that closes off discourse (thus creating a closed series), but it is also conserved in the model that is constructed in the series, because the circle is the representative figure of the geographic world, differentiated in a contradictory fashion from the nonworld, which is not named. We thus witness, it would seem, in an almost experimental way, the constitution in and through discourse of a representation that is the product and model of that representation. Travel narrative leads us from history to utopia. It shows us how narrative can be presented as the world's equivalent and how it can compose its order.

History-Geography.

Even more striking would be Raphael's travel narrative; it is actually contained within Peter Giles' narrative, even though the toponyms are not inscribed there, strictly speaking. But is it not true that the four names provided by Peter Giles sketch out the known limit inside of which the itinerary's language can develop? Indeed, this is where it will develop by establishing the equivalence between history and geography inside narrative's circularity. The description will accomplish this. Setting off from the fort where Vespucci had left him, Raphael and five other companions journey over land and sea, passing through "towns and cities, and very populous commonwealths with excellent institutions," through a zone of "waste deserts scorched with continual heat" all along the equator.

> But when you have gone a little further, the country gradually assumes a milder aspect, the climate is less fierce, the ground is covered with a pleasant green herbage, and the nature of living creatures becomes less wild. At length you reach peoples, cities, and towns which maintain a continual traffic by sea and land not only with each other and their neighbors but also with far-off countries.[15]

Figure 4 transcribes the syntagmatic line of the trip.

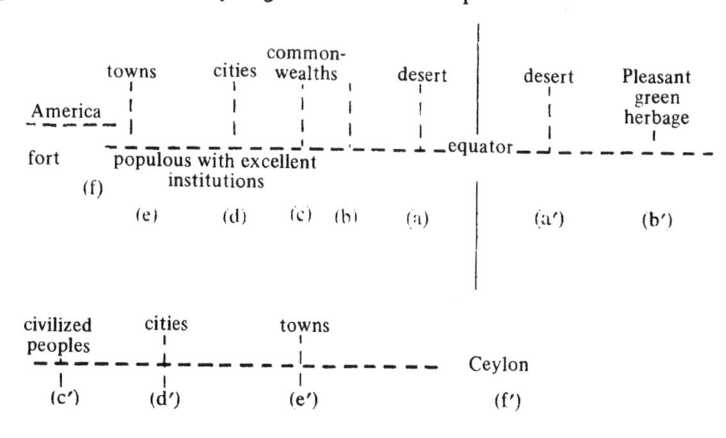

Figure 4. Diagram of Raphael's travel narrative

The diametrically organized structure is symmetric on both sides of the equator, with towns, cities, and commonwealths on one side, peoples, cities, and towns on the other. Within the circular structure enveloping the whole of the known geographic world by four toponyms—Portugal, America, Ceylon and Calcutta—Raphael's narrative sketches out a diametric line between America and Ceylon. This line crosses the equator and divides the geographic and narrative space into a world and an antiworld as if it were the invisible surface of a mirror. By constructing the map produced by Raphael's narrative and closely following Peter Giles' specifications, we get a diagram that combines the circular and diametric qualities of the two narratives (Figure 5).

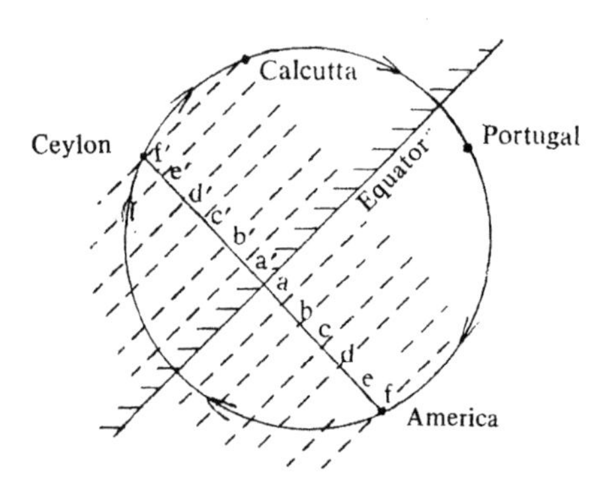

Figure 5. Multiple diagram of Raphael's travel narrative

Something else is also revealed by Raphael's narrative, as he describes the ships he has seen in the antiworld; first there were flat-bottomed ships with sails made of papyrus leaves stitched together, of wickerwork, or sometimes of leather. Then came pointed heels and canvas sails, and later those similar to Portuguese and English ships. The sailors of these latter vessels had a good knowledge of winds and tides; Raphael taught them the use of the magnetic compass, a modern invention.[16] The paradigm of the ship unfolded within the syntagm of his journey points toward historical progress through the setting up of a geographic space. There is progress in navigation techniques and generally in material, cultural, and political civilization. America and Ceylon have the same function in this diametric structure that Portugal has in the circular structure. Similar and symmetrical, like new and old exoticism, they are the final points of progress in the Orient and in the West, the final extremes of history inscribed on a geographic map of the world. It is a double projection of the Portugal Raphael had left, the equatorial deserts simultaneously constituting the zero degree of history's origin and the axis of symmetry of cartographic space, the inverse of Portugal, which in Raphael's narrative is the symbolic representation of England, the "place" of staging for this narrative directed by More.

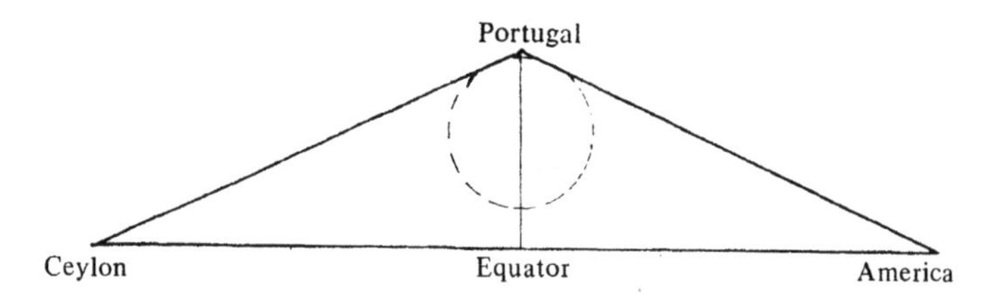

Figure 6. Structure of the toponyms of Raphael's voyages

Figure in the Text: Utopia

At the end of this double, internal-external trip a figure emerges between toponyms and descriptive moments. It is during this voyage that, on the formal, expressive level, narrative is converted into description; on the level of content, history and geography are brought to an equivalency. A figure emerges there in the text as a representation of the readability of this voyage. Its double mark is constituted by and woven into the fabric of the text by the double-transformable structure of circularity and diametric similarity. With this first figure of description another that we have been seeking can be perceived: the utopic figure. We know that the blissful island is found between Ceylon and America, but outside the toponymic circuit and the path leading from the world to the antiworld. It would also combine circle and diameter, time and space, history and geography, but *outside space* in a place that would be neither a moment in history nor a portion of the geographic map. It would be a separation—a neutrality—where it alone could be produced, once the perfect equivalency in distance between poles has been demonstrated through the travel narrative. Utopia is the homologue of Portugal and England belonging to the same hemispheres as Ceylon and America; it is a projection, but different. The island is not an antiworld or a new world, but an Other World. It is perhaps not by chance that Peter Giles chooses the two-faceted epigraph of Death to begin his evocation of Raphael's travel narrative: "He who has no grave is covered by the sky," and

"From all places it is the same distance to heaven."[17] Each voyage and every departure is an itinerary toward Death and the Gods. History and geography (the world's narrative and description) have protected the traveler through their variety and differences; these are the experiences of the world that have been offered by these two discursive modes. Yet there is another experience, identical, yet different and other. Utopia: the experience of a neutralized world, that of the same and yet Other World.

New and Old Worlds

As Raphael's travel narrative comes to a close, so does, in More's preliminary sketches, the preamble to Utopia: the reader thus enters the Other World after having traveled through this world and its other antiworld, after he has gone through the looking glass. It was only afterward that More added a first part containing the dialogue on the prince's council. And included in the dialogue are the three secondary utopias of the Polylerites, Achorians, and Macarians, each seemingly serving to illustrate different themes.

Let it suffice for our purposes to examine at the end of Book One the return of utopia after the double textual digression in the form of the dialogue. Note that its double quality is perceived both on the order of its reading and of its content. Here we will find the same desire to connect discourse to the history it describes and to make of the world one single world in space and time. It is another way to affirm that Utopia is not an "alibi" or an "elsewhere," but rather a same that is other, a neutral space. One of Peter Giles' questions about the Old and New Worlds, if we remain literally faithful to its qualifiers, once again raises the question of history: "It would be hard for you to convince me that a better-ordered people is to be found in that new world than in the one known to us. In the latter I imagine there are equally excellent minds, as well as commonwealths which are older than those in the new world."[18] Raphael responds with a paradox that is none other than the paradox of decentering and of the relativity of points of view and speech. The New World is, for those who live there, an old world; the Old World is new for them.

> "As for the antiquity of commonwealths," [Raphael] countered, "you could give a sounder opinion if you had read the historical accounts of that world. If we must believe them, there were cities among them before there were men among us...According to their chronicles, up to the time of our landing they had never heard anything about our activities (they call us the Ultra-equinoctials)..."[19]

Time did not rise in the New World at the same moment the Old World began its history. There are parallel histories that, year after year, century after century, are stored in cities' and commonwealths' annals until the day histories come together and converge. But through a strange anamnetic return, the ever-so-ancient history of the New World was born of the cultural and technical progress of the Old World's history.

> Twelve hundred years ago a ship driven by a tempest was wrecked on the island of Utopia. Some Romans and Egyptians were cast on shore and remained on the island without ever leaving it. Now mark what good advantage their industry took of this one opportunity. The Roman empire possessed no art capable of any use which they did not either learn from the shipwrecked strangers or discover for themselves after receiving the hints for investigation—so great a gain was it to them that on a single occasion some persons were carried to their shores from ours."[20]

Utopia is the daugher of Roman technology and Egyptian culture; history is one, and the Other World has been a tangent to a point on this world. Once the notion of parallel histories is evoked, it is immediately brushed aside. The relativity of the old and new from a decentering of cultural places is denied. Any suggestion bolstered by the travels and stories of our narrator tending to bring this constantly decentered center into play is quashed; rather, a filiation and cultural diffusionism that nineteenth-century ethnography will also develop is promoted.

Utopic Inscription and the Forgotten Memory

The same epistemological hypothesis will turn up in the very heart of Utopia—the Utopian language carries traces of it—in the ease with which the Utopians learn Greek. Proof can be glimpsed here of the most ancient origin within the pure origin of the unique civilization: Platonizing anamnesis of the idea of a Greek cultural humanity, of a Roman and Egyptian technical and practical mankind. It reaches toward the idea of humankind's Mediterranean and Western nature. Whatever they do or are, mankind of the New World will be the offspring of an older world, one of which we are the offspring if only because we are the first to provide the narrative of its former and new contacts, to keep the record of this history. Finally, written texts exist that store the events, incidents, and accidents, the meetings and contacts that *a* history inaugurates as a *single* history. This ensures to him who writes it down the advantage of filiation and ancestry. It provides the overwhelming advantage of memory.

But through a certain ironic reversal only the Utopians claim the privilege of being our descendants through this inscription. They are the only ones to assimilate the new; we Westerners, offspring of history, have systematically forgotten our reciprocal relationship to Utopia: "But if any like fortune has ever driven anyone from their shores to ours, the event is as completely forgotten as future generations will perhaps forget that I had once been there. And, just as they immediately at one meeting appropriated to themselves every good discovery of ours, so I suppose it will be long before we adopt anything that is better arranged with them than with us."[21] Yet, in what way are they "better arranged," if not in political matters? *Utopia*'s title is "Treatise on the Best State of a Commonwealth." Is this not the harmonious spatial organization of social and economic relations? Would this be the forgotten history? This would not involve so much the history of culture, science, and technical matters as the history of the city and of communal life. More picks up his pen as Raphael dictates in order to keep and transmit the event of this unique meeting; due to his effort our ancestors will know that Raphael went there and what he saw. But if the history of that other "reverse" contact has not been written, it is perhaps because its content cannot be written in the form of a history, in the form of a narrative. It could very well be that the Utopian contribution to Western Mediterranean civilization could not be written down as a record in the form of events, such as learning Greek or the art of printing. Surely Utopia is not of this world; and it is not precisely because it records and stores its relationship to Western society without having it be recorded by the West itself. Utopia, the perfect community, can never be recognized by it or by the New World. We can enter Utopia, but Utopia has no tie to our world, even though it has come from it.

Descriptions

"'If so, my dear Raphael," I said, '...give us a description of the island. Do not be brief, but set forth in order the terrain, the rivers, the cities, the inhabitants, the traditions, the customs, the laws...' 'There is nothing,' he declared, 'I shall be more pleased to do, for I have the facts ready to hand. But the description will take time.'"[22] Thus the mode of discourse proper to Utopia is description: to draw out a representation. It consists in projecting a perfect and total presence into language accessible to the mind. For that the proper disposition and the right amount of time must be available, for a hasty sketch will not do, if for the simple reason that the description of an image is never-ending. The visible will always be in excess of the "sayable." It is impossible to know all has been *said* about an iconographic image, whether it be the "presence" of a representation or a painting. Utopic discourse is perhaps this extreme pretension of language to provide a *complete* portrait of an organized and inhabited space. If it does manage it, however, it is perhaps because this portrait is constituted by its discourse and constructed through its language in order to serve as the origin and foundation for every map and every image. Utopia is a figure in discourse and subtends it. It is also in the narrative, but at the very place narrative pauses to allow another type of voice to come through. It no longer involves dialogue, staging, chance meetings, surprises, or discourses contained within narrative in the form of discourse. Rather, a unique and equalizing voice peaceably projects a full image onto the page. Progressively, as if on a screen, it gives birth to an iconic presence in the form of a representation; it is a "presence" that is but representation.

Synopsis

From this emerge the four aspects of descriptive discourse in *Utopia.* There is first its synoptic nature, which attempts to construct a particular type of reading. It does not follow the principle of the syntagmatic chain's linearity. Rather, it obeys a sort of synchro-diachronism, going from the whole to its part, from the general to detail. It is a type of reading which is precisely that of iconic representation according to the copresence of elements.

A close analysis of the beginning of Book Two will reveal this aspect of *Utopia*'s descriptive discourse. The first sentence defines the overall form of the island through its cartographic reality. Only the geometric and metric relations are conserved. Reading closely, we can watch the very process of the figure's construction ("figure" is here taken in its geometric sense). There is the precisely measured central area, then a gradual and systematic shrinkage of the configuration to its two ends, resulting in a first diamond-shaped diagram. A second operation consists in inscribing on this figure a second, circular figure, because "these ends form a circle five hundred miles in circumference and so make the island look like a new moon."[23] The island is thus constructed by two successive operations—one linear, the other circular, which a vivid comparison then obscures with its own presence, "a new moon," to suppress the diachronic linkage of the operations of construction. Henceforth this image will impose itself as the total figure representing the island of Utopia—a crescent moon. The chain of successive operations tends toward the emergence of the image where these operations become enmeshed by changing their very nature. An abstract, geometric generation, one of a precise and measured engendering process the tool of which Raphael specifies, the compass, is followed by a fixed, unified syntagm—a crescent moon. The textual process, a linear linkage of distinct units on the expressive level and a coherent succession of operations on the level of content, is in this way closed off. It is closed off not within its system or structure, but by their representation and figure within the text's manifestation.

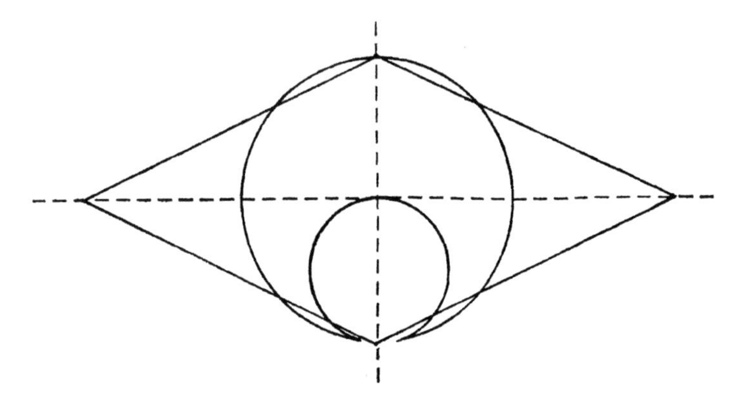

Figure 7. Construction of the representation of the island Utopia

Erasures

The figurative synopsis is also obtained through a double operation in the text: eliminating every enunciative mark on the one hand, on the other using the present tense for the description of every process. The first is indicative of narrative discourse; the text allows, not events or incidents, but the traits, crucial marks, and qualifying signs of them to appear themselves. It is not the event that seems to "tell itself" as it arises, but the determining qualities allow for its appearance, or appearing. From this it can be seen why the present tense is used: it implies the ***signified*** simultaneity of the "appearing" within the ***signifying*** succession of traits that appear on the textual surface. This of course signifies the timeless present of description, if this timelessness can be understood as a textual mark of simultaneity and co-presence, just as the signifier of the order of co-presences in visibility is always present. One is tempted to define the descriptive text as an iconic object, a space dominated and controlled by an absolute, outside of time and of any point of view. The present of description in its repetition all along the image's construction is the mark of pseudo-presence in representation. The whole is offered for inspection, without hidden surfaces or secrets. It can be examined as the "unfolded" surface of a map which is nothing other than the coherent ensemble of elements and relations it conserves. Nonetheless, this representation is told successively by the constructive and engendering operations the text assigns, as if they were the forms for the image's appearing.

Description in general (and utopic description in particular) is constituted by the group of processes that make up textual representation. Description is presented, or presents "itself," as if the echo of a visible object, of a transcendent and present referent it would carry along with it in the form of discourse; however, it actually constitutes this referent as such, through the operations described earlier. But isn't that what Raphael tried to say when he despairingly declared that "future generations [would] perhaps forget that [he] had once been [to Utopia]" and that luckily, he could easily answer their wishes to know Utopia because he had "the facts ready to hand."[24] Utopia is a forgotten memory, and as forgetfulness it is easily overcome in the obsessive desire to know. Utopic description is, at bottom, nothing but the construction of the multiple figure destined to satisfy the desire to know: ***it is the desire to know that creates for itself a figure in the text***, and the omnipresent gaze of the viewer contemplating Utopia's harmonious spaces is in fact the image, in the form of text, of a will to total knowledge of what the West, it seems, has forgotten: utopia of the human city.

Totality

The idea of utopic description as a harmonious totality comes directly from the representation's textual form: it is because descriptive discourse constructs a representation in Utopia that it is exhaustive and lacks any residue. Nothing will be in the representation that is not already in the discourse. Because description is thus, Utopia (simultaneously content and image in the text) will make itself a full totality, without anything missing or absent. It is because of this that it has a necessarily harmonious nature, not in the signifier, of course, because very often the omnipresence of viewpoint is situated simultaneously at the viewpoint of totality and of the minute element (these are, even on the first page, the reefs insidiously hidden in the entry of the bay, perceived only by Utopian pilots and the constructor's viewpoint).[25] Rather, it is found in the signified, for any disharmony, which implies incoherence and contradiction, risks upsetting the narrative process attempting to transform change and alienation into stability and fullness. It has often been noted that within utopic constructions there exist logical coherence and equilibrium within the ensemble. This state of equalization, whose general form is neutralization, not of difference or gaps, but the poles and edges of these gaps, tends toward a figurative representation, which, totalizing differences, is the complex space of the articulation of them. But this can be so only because in the initial operation the contradictory poles have been neutralized.

Fiction

This is why the nature of "artistic" or poetic fiction plays such an important part in Utopia. It is almost the distinctive characteristic with reference to political or social projects, strategies, and *ideal* republics. Fiction is essential, for it allows, on the one hand, a plural position of characteristics and differential signs within the same totality. Through the fictionalizing process the characteristics and signs have been de-differentialized, neutralized, and placed outside a logical system in which they could have been judged according to a true-false system. Fiction also makes it possible to give to this complex totality of neutral differences the density, force, and "presence" of a transcendent object or part of reality. Fiction is thus the instrument simultaneously of utopic neutralization (one of the fundamental provinces of utopic practice) and of totalitarian figurative representation, where differences come together in creating new effects of meaning. Utopia is thus the fantastic product of this creative practice. In other words utopic fiction explains, ambiguously, why utopic discourse is always presented as a description constitutive of a representation in the text, and why signifying utopic practice can construct such a product from a multitude of differences and contrary elements.

Utopia as a textual product can thus be seen as a figurative representation in the text; it is the metaphoric representation or projection of a system of signifiers into the descriptive object and of the system of signifieds into a system of equilibrium, a neutralized state of correlations or a complex totalization of differences. This definition would thus have the negative effect of burying the narrative discursive mode; utopia would be the event of a figurative representation in and through discourse. It would be a figurative mode of discourse the means of which would be description, neutralization, and totalization on the expressive level, on the level of content, and during different moments of production, as well as at different stages of the product. Narrative has disappeared from the representation: the dynamics of exchange, of repetition, and of displacement has yielded before the picture in the text, before the representation whose laws seemingly determine, from the Renaissance to the Enlightenment, the makeup of literary fiction.

Narrative in Description

Narrative discourse is not completely absent from the utopic text. On the contrary, it constituted the framework of our descriptive picture, the limit of figurative representation in the form of an initial staging allowing for the articulation between discourse and history and the constitution of history as discourse. It sets these two up in the form of travel narratives which raise the possibility of an equivalence between time and space, history and geography. From that point on the curtain can be raised on the monologue voice of Raphael building the figure of the island, of the city, of the perfect republic. The narrative, the frame for the representation and descriptive object, has thus provided the textual conditions of possibility, internally and externally, for the utopia. Nonetheless, the narrative level subsists with the descriptive itself as traces or pockets that mark—and thus our hypothesis for analysis—within the finished product the hidden processes by which it was produced. The short, fragmentary narratives rip through the picture of representation; they tear holes into the canvas which displays the figure of the most advantageous government and reveal, within the utopia, the work of utopic practice, its meaning, and its relationship to history and to the social and historical conditions of its production.

The structural analysis of a myth attempts to reveal the deep structure from certain similarities, differences, and correlations under the narrative in mythic language. This analysis provides the general law of how mythic narrative works in a particular culture and also provides the rules that specifically bring about resolutions in social contradictions and antagonisms. The analysis of utopia works in the opposite way. It must understand the function of these narratives, which the omnipresence of the figurative picture conceals and which the structure of representation that this picture offers for viewing in the text dissimulates.

Allow this narrative to speak again: this would be a sort of deconstruction of utopic representation. We would need to discover the painting, not as a simple surface where all is present, but as a hierarchy and *emboîtement* of texts at different levels; we would simultaneously need to discover the meaning of utopia's productive practice within that domain meant to cover it up.

The Hidden Narrative

These narrative pockets could perhaps be considered as simple examples of description or as anecdotes of illustration; if so, utopia would strangely enough reverse the relationship between narrative and description normally found in the epic form. Would it not be better to think of this relationship as a double text that is breaking up and becoming fragmented within itself? With varying propor-tions, that double textual space would be animated by changes and different arrangements whose natural function within utopia would reveal to us utopian practice. The analysis would consist in redefining the precise articulation of these large independent and individual narrative units. It would consist in re-establishing, at a certain level of meaning and textual organization, a narrative whose traces we never read. This analysis would show how a fragmentary narra-tive works within the utopic picture, simultaneously to deconstruct it and to force it to utter the historical meaning of this transforming practice from which the representation results.

The group of narratives making up *Utopia* is contained between two narra-tives of foundation. One is inscribed at the beginning of the text, the other at the end.[26] The first of these two narratives is affected by the arrival of the eponymous founding hero, Utopus, and takes place within a profane geographic, geological, and political space. The other is marked by a return into the sacred space of the religious. The first, opening the text, encloses the island by means of the ocean; the result is a homogeneous unity. The second, closing the text, opens up Utopian society to death and to religious tolerance. These mini-narra-tives have as a hero the Utopian people as a whole. They are woven into the figurative picture of the island and its institutions and can be divided into two groups. Each is valorized in a contrary way. The positive group of narratives describes contact with the Old World and show the Utopians assimilating the most valuable Western discoveries. The negative group of narratives recounts contact with other utopias—Anemolius, Alaopolitae, Nephelogetae, etc. Figure 8 sums up the large discursive narrative of which the figurative picture of *Utopia* reveals only the traces:

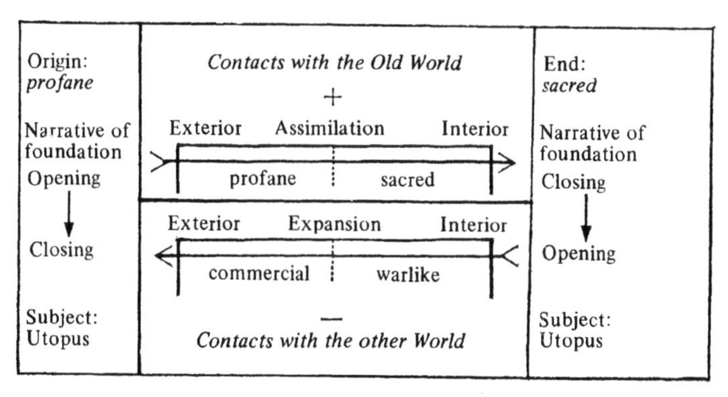

Figure 8. Diagram of the narratives in *Utopia*

What is the meaning and function of this larger narrative hidden underneath the descriptive picture? What signifying exercise does it reveal on the historical level? Two comments follow: the first concerns the utopic picture, the second the narrative it conceals.

The Story in the Picture[27]

Utopia as Raphael describes it through the voice of Thomas More, refers in a double way to the British Isles, England, the Old World, and the American continent, this last being the New World discovered by Amerigo Vespucci (Raphael having been his companion). But Utopia is the projection of neither. The referent, despite its double nature and its clarity here in the text, is not the origin, the model, or the goal of the text. This is because Utopia is first and foremost a text, a narrative that frames a description to which it ascribes its conditions of possibility. It is a text that points to a gap or difference that is active within historical and geographic reality: between England and America, the Old and New Worlds, misery and happiness, political analysis and the travel journal. Between history and geography this is an in-between space without place, lacking any geographical-historical coodinates that determine that a place is the trace of a tale, that a tale is first and foremost a scar left on the surface of the earth, an inscription to be added to a narrative. Utopia is thus the neutral moment of a difference, the space outside of place; it is a gap impossible either to inscribe on a geographic map or to assign to history. Its reality thus belongs to the order of the text; more precisely, it is the figurative representation that the text inscribes beneath its discourse, and by it.

This figurative representation will thus bring the double internal geographic and historical difference together in its fictional complexity: it will cancel out the "objective" difference displayed by historic reality, as picture and fiction in the text. It will do so by extending the limits of Western civilization, if not to the unlimited universe, at least to a space whose spherical nature excludes the notion of limits. The narrative concealed beneath the picture is the trace of this assumption and of this transcription of difference; while in contact, distance will be maintained. This textual spacing of the double text—figure and inscription, narration and history—creates the referential play by which Utopia finds its own reference within itself. This is how it is constituted as an autonomous referential system, all the while relating in a different way to the historical and geographic world whose contradictory consciousness produced it.

Such is the meaning of the narrative that the homogeneous descriptive painting masks. It symbolizes the absent synthesis, the work of negativity in history of which contradiction is the motor. The utopic painting is only the figure and fiction of what is revealed by it. The historical narrative, neither thought yet nor told, is at work on the semantic axis of interior and exterior, open and closed. This narrative has a dialectical name, but its very form denounces any ideological affiliation. It is the synthesis of the Old and New Worlds through the transforming assimilation of the sciences, of technology, and of moral and religious ideas. In short, it constitutes the synthesis of cultural "superstructures." The narrative affected by Utopia amounts to three centuries of historical relations between England, Spain, Portugal, and America, between the Old and New Worlds: war and exploitation, which will end in the larger real and historical synthesis as nineteenth-century Western capitalism, of the capitalism of the United States of America in the twentieth century based on internal and external economic exploitation. This "yet-to-be-thought" narrative thus offers a remarkable reading: the rejection of commerce and war into utopia, outside place, is the "coming trace," the projection of the real historical synthesis. It also shows us that the synthesis within utopia of culture, science, and technology is the rejection of the impious American savages into historical and ideological exteriority. As I will attempt to show through various examples, utopic signifying practice wields its critical force in the very moment it is joined to an ideology that prohibits it from being molded and completed into a scientific theory of ideology. This is precisely because it stops it from upsetting the position of utterance, of speech, from which it is made.

Such is the relationship that narrative and description sketch out in Utopia: between history in process in the very unconscious of its contradictory procedures and the building of the model where the contradictions cancel each other out. They thus form a representative harmony in which history is masked, but also obliquely revealed in the form of traces, the form of which my analysis has tried to reconstitute.

Notes

Chapter 2

[1] Cf. Lévi-Strauss, Ch. Xi.

[2] Ibid.

[3] Elli-Kaija Kongas and Pierre Miranda, "Structural Models in Folklore," *Midwest Folklore*, Vol. XII, No. 3 (Fall, 1962).

[4] See R. Girard.

[5] M. Détienne, *Les Maîtres de vérité de la Grèce archaique* (Paris: Maspero, 1967), pp. 51 ff.

[6] Thomas More, *Utopia*, edited by Edward Surtz, S.J. (New Haven and London: Yale University Press, 1964), pp. 9–10.

[7] More, p. 11.

[8] More, p. 12.

[9] More, p. 10.

[10] More, p. 3.

[11] More, p. 3.

[12] More, p. 5.

[13] Recall the page from Glotz's *Greek History* quoted and analyzed by E. Benveniste as an example of historical narrative in his *Problèmes de linguistique générale* (Paris: Gallimard, 1966), pp. 240 ff.

[14] More, op. cit., p. 13.

[15] More, p. 14.

[16] More, p. 15.

[17] More, p. 13.

[18] More, p. 55

[19] More, pp. 55–56.

[20] More, p. 56.

[21] More, p. 56.

[22] More, pp. 56–57.

[23] More, p. 59.

[24] More, pp. 56–57.

[25] More, pp. 59–60.

[26] More, p. 60 and pp. 133–134.

[27] Related to this, see G. Dragon and L. Marin, "Utopie et discours des origines," *Les Annales E.S.C.* (June, 1971).

CHAPTER THREE

The Utopic Stage

Utopia is a discourse. Better yet, it is a book or volume of signs disposed in a certain order. These signs owe their meaning to a system of which the book is one among an infinite number of possible realizations. In this volume are found sentences, words, and letters that realize, through their differential values, meaning. This definition is true for any book, process, or text. The differential nature of utopia is of a stylistic nature. It is based on a typology of genres that another syntax orders. With Thomas More's *Utopia* as an example, I have noticed that utopia, through its multiple and varied literary *spatial play* (historical narrative, travel narrative, description, illustrating narratives, etc.), is the textual place of production of a representative figure, of a picture within the text whose function consists in dissimulating, within its metaphor, historical contradiction–historical narrative–by projecting it onto a screen. It stages it as a representation by articulating it in the form of a structure of harmonious and immobile equilibrium. By its pure representability it totalizes the differences that the narrative of history develops dynamically. This representation is the project of a utopic practice that keeps inside of itself traces whose critical force remains in a neutralized area of historical contradiction, making possible the constitution of the figure.

This is the paradox of utopia as a *literary genre*: how can a text carry with it a figure, an almost *iconic* representation? How can it stage a historic contradiction by dissimulating, or more precisely, by playing it out in fiction? How, on the level of these larger literary units that are narratives and descriptions, can the letter, the printed type, be figured or figural? In other words, what new game is at work here in the text–yet another spatial game, by means of a metaphor that is not one of critical discourse about books but that is performed on the very letter of the text? We know from the previous chapter that the picture constructed in the text is not a simple "literary" artifice, a pure rhetorical "figure" or an ornament of discourse, but is its very essence and "objective" intention.

This is true because the goal of the representation produced in this way is to dissimulate and simultaneously to present the historical and ideological contradiction that, finally, brought it forth. How can a text be a representation? What sort of signifiers must it use to achieve this result, and what sort of syntax and grammatical rules must it follow in order to produce signifieds that escape from the order of the sign in order to appear on the order of symbols and icons?

There is thus a fiction in utopia, which is its necessary, but not sufficient, characteristic. We must question this, as well as the "spatial play" it implies, by laying out varied literary spaces that produce it. This is done through a sort of double confrontation between myth as ritual and theater as the scene of representation.

Mythic Ceremonies

I was saying earlier that myth is first and foremost a narrative. It is speech whose repetitive movement creates the antagonism in which society finds its foundation and also the conciliation in which it discovers its history, even if this history is immobile and does not coincide with a progressive accumulation of events. Ritual is the telling of history before history, through which mythic narrative is uttered in complete gesticulation. It is a telling that is simultaneously commemoration and reaccomplishment. It refers to a time that precedes time but that is also the return of this "original" time, its inaugural repetition. Myth cannot be evacuated of its ritualistic aspect in order to see it as a structure and "logical tool" of mediation in the original contradiction within society because, very simply, as ritual it accomplished the logical operation that structural analysis brings to the fore. The ritual is the "performance" of this operation; it comes to grips with social existence in order to regulate and order it. The mediation and reconciliation are not previously *in* the narrative's structure, the equation establishing the equivalence and exchange of contradictory poles. Mediation and reconciliation are instead a temporal process, one of speech and gesture that bring about this equivalence and exchange.

If it is not possible to reduce myth to an object of knowledge constituted only by structural operations that would express its general formula, we must assume a "performing utterance" of myth in two ways: not only does it perform the passage into reality of an adjacent intelligible structure, but it also constitutes this structure. It is the operation by which it is brought about and is repeated. There is a mythic practice irreducible to a theoretical practice, but which awaits its theory.

Ritualistic ceremony reaccomplished mythic narrative: it repeats it, but through this repetition it lays down within social time the order of another texture (and following a different rhythm) that narrative had laid down in its own time and mode. Something occurs during the present moment of the ceremony. This moment is not simply a pure "now" that is chronologically determined. It is the moment when this now and the temporal event of the origin are fused together. The present is the moment of a founding operation where the origin is not a beginning or a first past instant. It is a represence where "chronology" is simultaneously canceled and affirmed. It is constituted at every moment it is played out by a sort of "continuous mythic creation." In ritual the *practice* of mythic narrative is seen to be the ordering of social reality in its double temporal and spatial nature. At this same moment, then, this reality is realized outside of time by a return to the origin from which it is born, and in time by the repetition of original acts where it is unfolded and ordered, where it is made into social reality. It is an immobile time that is repetitive and mimes the origin; it is also the origin's represence in "history" in order to constitute it.[1]

The ritual stages mythic history, but with neither stage nor audience. History is accomplished and is told there but is not represented. If discourse is an element of the ritual, it is an integral part of it, like a hymn, a chant, or praise: narrative, if you like, but a special kind of narrative—a sort of incantation of the original events of which it speaks. In other words, the recitation is contemporaneous with the narrative it tells: an act of speech that is not discernible from other ritualistic behavior. It is an element of the whole ritual, inseparable from it.

Our Reading

In this respect we must compare ritualistic recitation to reading, which itself obeys the ritualistic to a certain degree. Indeed, reading a novel or short story or even a folktale or myth is the reactivation, evocation, and provocation of a specific form of existence that, before this act of reading, was a simple inactive trace. Avoiding a purely descriptive psychology, we could say that the act of reading projects upon an interior screen characters and events in a film with animated spectral doubles in order to reconstitute, as the reading progresses, the story insofar as it is read. This present reconstitution is not the written story, inscribed and enclosed within the traces on a page or in a volume. No one really knows what this is, in what place or space it is found, under what horizon of the pure existence of ideas without symbols, of signifieds without signs.

But such is the disturbing paradox of reading—in particular of silent, individual reading. It is always distant from its object and determined by its existence, be it in a space and ideal time, so much so that the distance in reading can never be determined by a term of reference by means of which its validity, its objective truth, can be measured. More precisely, the act of reading is determined with reference to an absent term whose existence is absence, but whose position as lack is absolutely necessary in order for the reading to take *place* and for it to have meaning. This absent story, these characters and events, places and things whose referential relation allows the story to be read, exists nowhere else than within the inscribed traces, which, however, do not contain it or enclose it because it must be read. We must retrace these traces through a sort of deciphering in order for the story to exist. From that moment forward it is a story read in that indeterminate distance by which it becomes a fantastic double, a pretext for every dream and possibility.

The imaginary aspect of reading and its product can only exist with reference to another object which it neither describes nor translates. It does not "verify" this always-absent object. In its place the imaginary content is offered as its double, a substitution that is indiscernible from it. This indiscernibility nonetheless assumes the essential condition of this absence to which it owes its absence. It is in this way that reading ushers us into the order of signs—in particular of alphabetical signs, where the same complementary nature, lacking any residue, joins the signifier and the meaning to the written trace. It subordinates it to the sign and integrates it into the system of differential values, where it encounters, as it vanishes, its truth. Reading, even silent reading, substitutes for the play of absence and repetition the indeterminate relation of an absent reference and an imaginary realm that repeats this relation in a representation. This latter is then the equivalence between *sound* and *meaning*, signifier and signified joined together without supplement or lack. The narrative presented to us in the book to be read is given as the reality it relates, all the while placing the reader at a bridgeless distance from the world it orders through the surprise of events it exposes. The book then makes us enter into the order of the sign as representation, and with this imaginary aspect substituting for reality and forgetting that reading is the reactivation of the trace, the signifier inscribes forgetfulness, which necessarily flows from remembrance because it was never anything but the image of an absence.

Utopia Is a Book

As far as our own subject is concerned, it must never be forgotten that, first and foremost, utopia is a book. Its productive practice makes us realize what reading books, since the Renaissance, has impelled us to forget: it is a text whose reality is nowhere. It is a signifier whose signified is not a spatial and temporal ideality or a rational intelligibility. It is the product of its own play within the plural space it constructs. Utopia is tied to the book and to the world of discourse as the articulation of the world and of history. It is tied to printing and to signs that the Renaissance visually substituted for the world of speech and listening.[2] It is a world of the written (or a writing of the world) as the ideal representation of history, a world of being that has been substituted for history or being. In the same moment, however, utopia is the book in which the book has been deconstructed by showing the processes that constituted it. It is, in a manner of speaking, the book of the book where the act of reading encounters its accomplishment and end. It is also the place where, through the very content of what is read, dissimulated substitutions that this act accomplishes between sign and symbol, between the imaginary and reality, are represented. This would also be one of the meanings of the figure that is produced by utopic practice beneath the text in the book.

Representation of Tragedy

With the theatrical representation of tragedy mythic narrative becomes performance, theater. A distancing gesture is thereby accomplished that is not exactly the same as for reading, distance with reference to an absence, but all the same the immediate contact with the ritual has been broken. With tragedy also appear knowledge and purification, contemplation and liberation by the very contemplation of what is known. "To understand, one must suffer," exclaims one of the characters in Aeschylus. Suffering is the condition for knowledge; theatrical representation is the contemplation of this suffering. It is its knowledge as well as its freedom (as a gas is freed from a solid after it is analyzed). The opposition contained within one aspect of the tragic, the relationship between the principal character and the chorus, has often been studied. A book aimed at studying the relationship between myth and tragedy claims that the elements of this relationship are "opposing elements, but at the same time solidly interdependent."[3] The opposition is one between mask and disguise, the individual and the collectivity, the mythic hero of the founding legends and the civic community, this latter expressing the feelings, hopes, and judgments of citizens as spectators.

Return of the Hero into the Performance

The representation of tragedy—tragedy in performance—brings about a double reversal precisely because it is representation. This reversal of complementary elements puts them at odds with each other without breaking them apart or denying their mutual linkage; the one is constantly worked on by the other. The first reversal concerns the mythic narrative on the level of its heroic protagonists. These characters are ***played***, not lived or relived, in their original actions that set the origin in the light of its founding presence. They are taken up within discourse uttered by a man whose profession is precisely to narrate. It is certainly true that the mask he wears casts him within a certain religious and social category. He is thus recognized by the spectators as Agamemnon or Oedipus, who will later appear in full presence before the community to repeat the contradiction out of which it springs. The tragic character is an ***other*** in every possible sense of the word: he is not only the "figure of a hero from another age, always more or less a stranger when it comes to the citizen's ordinary condition."[4] The reactivation of this figure before the eyes of the city is not the reapparition of the hero at its center. He is an other who, because of the mask, becomes other and presents as an object of contemplation the things whose constant presence the ritualistic ceremony had formerly affirmed through repetition.

It is at the very moment that mythic narrative and its characters and events come into visibility as representations or animated images that their identity is lost. They lose their immediate closeness by which the mythic story was the story and history of society, by which it was constitutive of the reality of the group, and whose telling—words and gestures necessarily unified in the same totality—cemented the community through the periodic representation of its origin. Mythic narrative placed on the tragic stage through its performance thus becomes vivid theater. It is surrounded by the full light of visibility. Both familiar and recognized, it is in the place of the other: a visible object and representation, not real presence repeatedly accomplished in corporeal and verbal gestures of the group that finds its identity by identifying with it and having this presence identify with it. It is a stunning privilege of sight and light, through which objectivity is placed at a distance and appropriated at this distance, shadowless and honest, but as other. Henceforth language as dialogue can lessen the distance between the protagonists and spectators by using a metric close to prose: a bridgeless distance has been set up in which speech itself has been caught, not only because it must cross that distance, but because it is heard from its far side.

The Representation of Theatrical Performance

But this first reversal of mythic narrative carries with it another one, which concerns the community's participation in the story visibly presented on stage through words and images. This second reversal, in a way, influences the first and, in another way, completes it. The other element of the tragic stage is the chorus—"collective and anonymous, it is incarnate by a group of citizens," disguised, not masked.[5] If the tragic heroes and their struggles are the mythic narrative made visible and represented in that other millieu, the chorus presents an element that does not belong to the narrative and places it right in the visibility of the stage. This element is foreign to the space of the first, all the while being connected to it. The chorus is the materialization of the representation inside that which is being represented; it is the relation of visibility constitutive of the tragic representation of myth on the stage. It is the other side of mythic narrative through which this narrative is constituted as representation, is brought to the watchful eye of the spectator in performance. It is the visibility of its reflection, the presence of the images intransitiveness brought under the spectator's gaze, the neutral element of the verbs: "to represent," "to stage." Through the chorus representation comes to be conscious of itself.

The presence of the chorus on the stage totally closes in representation around itself because it is included in itself in the form of one of its elements, the very act of representing. Nothing escapes the performance, this representation, and it henceforth contains within itself its audience. With the interjection of the chorus, however, theatrical representation is split in two because it does not represent only mythic narrative as visible play within the distance of visibility; this very representation is represented through the presence on stage of the chorus members, who witness the hero's struggles and comment on them. The stage is thus split in two, on stage: that of the visible, which is only seen, and that of the visible, which is simultaneously seen and seeing. This distance within the distance of representation would be only that if the chorus merely watched on stage. But these chorus members are actors—of another order, true—as they debate through their lines with the hero. They speak with ambiguity, actually, for they both chant and engage in dialogue. They perform a lyrical exultation and an active interrogation; their speech is on two levels as their double position is manipulated on stage. They are actors and spectators at the same time. These spectators are caught in the drama, although they are impotent to act on what takes place. The chorus members are actors in the drama, but on another level and at a distance from the action. They have the power of commentary, however; they hold the tool of discourse upon the action. They know, or rather feel, what is happening, while the protagonists of the mythic narrative are ignorant of, blind to, what is happening.

The Representation of the City

It is this disquieting shift resulting from the presence of the chorus and the representation of its discourse in the tragic spectacle that opens up the self-contained completeness of tragic performance into the outside. The members of the chorus, by their presence and their discourse, not only represent the representation, not only bring to visibility the visibility of the mythic narrative, but also represent the civic community on stage. They portray the citizens who have come to watch the performance and to take part in the tragic ceremony. The chorus members are the people's representatives and thus can comment on and explain the drama. They clarify it by anticipating the action, by predicting the consequences of a certain action, or by referring to ethical, judicial, or religious principles, which are, in short, interpretative rules of action.[6] But these representatives are there also to express the public's judgment, feelings, and thoughts through questioning. The choral members utter the citizens' discourse. By their presence and voices they represent the citizens' participation in the performance and in the tragic ceremony. The chorus makes this visible for them, and it gives them a voice in it. They are the discourse and visibility of public consciouness within representation. [This is a new dimension for the object of knowledge, which is not only constituted as an object in the light of otherness so that the beginnings of truth are established, but which also englobes the subject of this objectification as if it were one of its own dimensions, becoming an object for itself in the process by which knowledge finds its beginning.] *True* knowledge exists only in the consciousness of what is known. The luminous otherness in which mythic narrative is revealed echoes the knowing collective subject become aware of itself as subject in the knowledge it acquires of the narrative beyond the recognition of the archaic legend where the community discovered its original antagonisms and found its origins.

Tragic representation thus creates spatial play through the double reversal of narrative and of its representation. There, the primal contradictions, fundamental alienation, and archaic mysteries are objectified and told, told precisely because they are objectified, objectified because they are told. They are caught in the complex interchange of spectators' gazes and in the network of speech. Not simply represented but, indeed, represented within their representation, they are reflected and played out inside their spatial play. Play within play, this shifting of spaces on the same stage is what allows representation to become complete in its wholeness and to shift around inside. Henceforth the marvelous fascination escaping from repetition moves into knowledge and into the contemplative appropriation of contradiction as problems and as objects. This scenic spatial and discursive play, the levels where they come about and the articulations that bind them together, frees the participants from suffering through comprehension of suffering within the discourse of this other on stage. This other is myself, ourselves. This other is myself as this *other* that I come to know. It is society as *our* society, but within difference that allows for true judgment.

The Utopic Text: Space of Play.

Utopia is fiction: a fable skillfully woven by More with "true history," that of his embassy in Flanders and of his stay in Antwerp, Raphael Hythlodaeus comes back from another world situated somewhere beyond, in space and time, or else on this side of the New World. What is the function of this fable? In a way its function is very close to that of the staging of mythic narrative in a performance of tragedy: the fable furnishes a kind of space of representation in which contradiction can be figured and played out as a simulacrum so that it can be contemplated as an object of knowledge. But as we already have seen, utopia belongs to the world of the book and the sign in which, through a forgotten substitution, reality is created, brought forth in the discourse that utters it and in its inscription within the voice that silently reactivates it and constantly displaces it toward an absence. Is this comparison between utopia and theatrical performance—representation—justified, or is it nothing more than an ill-inspired metaphor? We saw earlier that description constituted a figure, a picture in the narrative text. We also saw that this figure dissimulated a latent narrative substituted in turn for an as yet silent history in the form of anecdotal inscriptions. Confronted with the myth as ritual practice and with tragic performance, we must ask ourselves if the utopic text constitutes a space of representational play and if some mythic equivalent is constituted as an object of true knowledge of its figure.

Tragic Text

We can begin to answer the first question by recalling this fact concerning tragic performance: it is first and foremost the text of an author—Aeschylus, Sophocles, or Euripedes—*before* becoming performance. Do not misunderstand this "before" and "after": they do not necessarily represent a chronology, only the presence of a specific operation ***between*** the mythic narrative and the theatrical staging. It is an operation that escapes simultaneously the ceremonial and ritual participation that defines the practical and functional involvement of the myth, and the contemplation, no less ceremonial, of this narrative as an object of knowledge conscious of itself and of the problems raised for the collectivity by this very narrative. It is an operation that allows for the transformation from one into the other and, with it, expresses and contributes to the production of a very real transformation of political society. It seems dangerous to consider the textual operation of literary creation, constitutive of tragedy, as a simple variant of mythic narrative. "Good" structural research on a specific myth would predict its tragic rewriting as a variant, a text granted the same rights as the other transcribed versions of the myth. The goal is to construct the general formula that regulates the circular transformations of the versions of the same myth: the myth discovers its identity in the regulatory law of its different versions.

My concern is different: the analysis of the transformations from the mythic "language" of ritual to the tragic ceremony must account for the intervention of a text in the transformation. Whether this text creates it or is an effect, a cause, or a result of it, is not a pertinent question. It suffices to note that the representation of tragedy is the staging of a text, a text closely linked to the social thought of the City, "especially judicial thought in its very elaboration."[7] It is as if historical change and the text were inherently connected, as if history—transformation in the event and the structure—could come about only through the possibility of being written, of being reactivated or revitalized in their traces.

But this text that finds its framework and structure in mythic narrative, the content that the City lives in its present "history," brings this experience to the consciousness of the community by exposing the mythic narrative on stage. The old contradiction, without ceasing to be one, is known as the current problem, all the while maintaining its relationship to the origin and its intense connection to the founding gestures. This reference receives from the text and from its representation another level of speech and, also, another function. It may very well be that this projection into the visibility of the stage, in the light of its representation, accomplishes the transformation of the profound solidarity with a mythic tradition into a problematic knowledge conscious of its ties to the origin and of its potential force of rupture. It may also very well be that this figurability refers to this intermediary discourse, to this text that performed the most radical transformation on myth by inscribing it as a signifying chain before staging it. It then becomes recognized and yet new, found again and yet discovered, because by it the misunderstanding that is part of all immediate experience turned up in the exposition and in the symbolic play of this very experience.

Textual Space

But utopia lacks this staging, the representation of its text. It is missing its performance one step beyond reading. It would be better to say that its representation is a figure that the text, in turn, unfolds as a space of language. The descriptive picture that constitutes it (Raphael's discourse in Book Two of *Utopia*) is sketched in a space of storytelling carefully outlined by More in Book One. We witness "a lively account, so animated with action and theater," that once the picture is made through the means discussed here, "we would actually think we were seeing it; we would believe ourselves present," in that Antwerp garden on the same bench as More, Peter Giles, and Raphael, hearing them give orders to "the servants that we should not be interrupted."[8] More attempts to liberate this space—and through reading, actually—because the preface he writes for the book *Utopia* (to be read *before* the book) contains every construction procedure for this space of play, in particular the author's request to seek out Raphael in order to verify, to check up on, or to correct a certain number of traits related to the "figure" and "details" of the picture.

> Therefore I beg you, my dear Peter, either by word of mouth if you can or by letter if he has gone, to reach Hythlodaeus and to make sure that my work includes nothing false and omits nothing true. I am inclined to think that it would be better to show him the book itself. No one else is so well able to correct any mistake, nor can he do this favor at all unless he reads through what I have written.[9]

This is a literary "effect of reality" obtained by the book's real author writing to one of his real friends so that this latter will contact one of the fictional characters of the book; this character purports to be the real author, the former claiming to be simply his transcriber.

Ironic Parentheses

But More inscribes this effect of reality within an ironic event that indirectly puts it into play—causes it to vibrate, so to speak:

> Nevertheless, to tell the truth, I myself have not yet made up my mind whether I shall publish it at all. So varied are the tastes of mortals, so peevish the characters of some, so ungrateful their dispositions, so wrong-headed their judgments, that *those persons who pleasantly and blithely indulge their inclinations seem to be very much better off than those who torment themselves with anxiety in order to publish something that may bring profit or pleasure to others*, who nevertheless receive it with disdain or ingratitude. Very many men are ignorant of learning; many despise it...very many admire only their own work. *This fellow is so grim that he will not hear of a joke; that fellow is so insipid that he cannot endure wit, some are so dull-minded that they fear all satire as much as a man bitten by a mad dog fears water.*[10]

It is not that description is really a trick, that the picture should serve an illusory function so as to be taken for an image or a geographic space in the other world; it really is a series of words, a language chain. With the book we have forever entered into words and signs, never to emerge again. But for this language picture, for this poetic and rhetorical, hypotypotic figure a substitute of a scene is given where the figure could be "represented" outside of space and within words, the substitute for spatial play that is text and only text. Here it is a question of a scene that forms the absent space of a map or the world by multiple voices. From theatrical performance it keeps the complementary play of words that are acts, polar forces of mythic contradiction that have become language in representation, played out in the luminous visibility of the stage. In short, the scenic space that visibly shows mythic antagonism within the discourse of tragedy is utopically figured by the various poles of speech and by their spacing. A space opens up in the words (dialogue), and the textual tissue is stretched in its very contiguousness so that the larger descriptive picture of Book Two can emerge: Utopia. But utopia is being constructed from the very beginning, as early as the preface, when More writes to Peter Giles to send him his book asking that Raphael, one of its characters, check and verify it. The text is being constructed there as a space of discourse without place, a multivoiced text, a stage for figure.

Dialogic Structure: Raphael's Two Voices

The importance of dialogue can never be stressed enough in either evident or disguised utopias. Its function is essential because it creates a text where space has been inscribed, where the utopic picture has been offered up to representation: More, Peter Giles, Hythlodaeus; Mentor, Telemachus, Idomenea; Cyrano, the Spanish philosopher; Elia, Socrates' demon...a detailed examination of the voices in More's utopia would verify this.[11] *Utopia* is forged out of the intervention and intertwining of two voices. Each occupies two positions, or levels, in the text. "I" is Raphael reciting the descriptive discourse of Book Two. This voice is double, invisible and all-seeing, omnipresent to the whole and to each detail, a cartographic eye, a viewpoint outside any point of view whose discourse can seem to be an image. But "I" is also Raphael, character presented in the discourse and actor seen and memorized by the storyteller. It is a viewpoint *within* the picture, a major element of the deconstruction of its figure in the narrative and in history. Indeed, notice that Raphael's second discursive position produces in *Utopia* the anecdotes and narrative illustrations that as previously shown, constituted the latent reversed history within real history. Raphael is thus the teller of the fragmentary narrative, the intervention of which in the picture is simultaneously the seeming commentary and profound critique. This critique reveals the formal process of production and the system of its content.

The double internal text of the picture that produces it as such (by producing its production in the text) is thus the resulting space of the interference, not of two discourses, but of two positions of speech. A sort of *discursive inclusion* results, and these two viewpoints seem to come from reverse positions in the discourse. The voice of Raphael, who utters the discourse of the describable figure, sees all but remains invisible. It is a discourse without a viewpoint; it finds its origin in the white textual space separating Book One from Book Two: "As for him, when he saw us intent and eager to listen, after sitting in silent thought for a time, he began his tale as follows: The island of the Utopians extends in the center..."[12] The space that separates the narrative from the representation, the frame of the painting, is impossible to locate. But the other voice through which the representation is reflected in the adjacent fragments of narrative is the voice of Raphael; it is produced on another level of speech. In order to create these narratives there must be empty surfaces within the picture. These absences or hidden elements must be discovered and successively be "invented" by the actoı as the narrative continues. The narrative is imbedded in the picture because the actor does not see the unity immediately. At the same time, however, it is precisely because the actor does not see everything that he becomes invisible, that he appears in the descriptive phrase as its producer and locus of enunciation. Thus the figure, as a product and process of production, comes into play, to vibrate, in the separation between Raphael's two voices and within the interference of their spheres of influence.

More's Two Voices

The other voice is Raphael's protagonist, More. "I" then becomes, in *Utopia*, the voice of a character of the dialogue, though it is also the voice of the writer-author of the text. More reveals his name as a signature at the end of the work: "The end of the afternoon discourse of Raphael Hythlodaeus on the laws and customs of the island of Utopia, hitherto known but to few, as reported by the most distinguished and most learned man, Mr. Thomas More, Citizen and Sheriff of London."[13] In its turn More's discourse englobes Raphael's double discourse in a dialogue slightly shifted with relation to itself. It relates this double discourse to another discursive system, that of historical narrative, and also, by means of the beginning of Book One, to an objective transcendent chronology: historical time, which is also the temporality of our act of reading. If, as we have seen, utopia is linked to real history by means of this articulation, and thereby acquires a density and presence that representation alone would not have had, then, conve-sely, real history as it would be tied to utopic fiction begins to take on imaginary aspects: the reader begins his trip to the blessed island.

In a certain way More's two voices occupy positions of speech homologous to Raphael's two voices. Thus, in Book Two we meet Raphael the builder of figure, who, seeing all, remains invisible and omnipresent to appear at the very end of the description addressing a universal audience through his present audience in the garden at Antwerp: "I have described to you, as exactly as I could, the structure of that commonwealth which I judge not merely the best but the only one which can rightly claim the name of a commonwealth."[14] In a similar position the author of the treatise on the ***Best State of a Commonwealth, or Utopia*** is an anonymous voice that never appears in the "body of the text," except in the letter-preface to Peter Giles and in the last sentence as a simple signature.

The Book's Exit

We thus meet Raphael, a figure in the picture and the actor in a certain number of stories. He is the one discovering a moral trait here, an accident of history there, while he sojourns for five years on the island. He is visible and curious, moving from surprise to surprise. We also meet Thomas More, ambassador to the Flanders of Henry, the eighth of that name, the most invincible King of England, interlocutor, in Antwerp, of Peter Giles and Raphael Hythlodaeus. At the beginning of Book One More occupies an essential place for interpreting *Utopia*; he also reappears at the end of Book Two to initiate an ambiguous transition toward the author of the book, *to exit the book.*

> When Raphael had finished his story, many things came to *my* mind which seemed very absurdly established in the customs and laws of the people described—not only in their method of waging war, their ceremonies and religion...but most of all in that feature which is *the principal foundation of their whole structure. I mean their common life and subsistence—without any exchange of money.* This latter alone utterly overthrows all the nobility, magnificence, splendor, and majesty which are in the estimation of the common people, the true glories and ornaments of the commonwealth.[15]

Thus begins a movement to exit the book, as is best, with the well-known phrase: "I readily admit that there are many features in the Utopian commonwealth which *it is easier for me to wish for in our countries than to have any hope of seeing realized.*"[16] This has been a movement interrupted in the preceding paragraph by coming easily and naturally back to More, the character and interlocutor of the dialogue.

> I knew, however, that he was wearied with his tale, and I was not quite certain that he could brook any opposition to his views, particularly when I recalled his censure of others on account of their fear that they might not appear to be wise enough, unless they found some fault to criticize in other men's discoveries. I therefore praised their way of life and his speech and, taking him by the hand, led him into supper.[17]

In other words, More's voice, interlocutor of the dialogue and *historical figure* (the special envoy to Flanders of Henry VIII), is enveloped not by a voice but by the discourse written by an author absent from the text he composed: a voice in the present, coming to its presence not in that space, but outside of space, in the book. This is the final fiction which is the only materially remaining form, the volume we open up and read today.

The Utopic Stage

This is how the spaces are constructed and locked each within the other. Their play against each other constitutes the utopic stage; it permits time and space to be interlocked in utopia and in history, in the figure and in the book. The island Utopia (as an image) and the work *Utopia* constitute these two non-spaces as limits where the exchange between the narrative of real history and its reverse image, utopic history, takes place. The spaces of the book and figure open up the space of a stage where a double scene is portrayed. There the readers discover how history reveals a narrative mirror image that lets them decode and become aware of it. By labeling our voices, we can diagram the constitution of the utopic text as the last utopia. Raphael I is the narrator of the representation of Utopia; Raphael II is the living figure of this image. More I is the author of the book *Utopia*, More II is the historic figure and Raphael's interlocutor (see Figure 9).

	Time	*Space*	
Raphael II	Utopia	image	Raphael I
More II	History	book	More I

Figure 9. Structure of voices in *Utopia*

There is a surprising consequence: the book *Utopia*, considered as a utopia in its general form, confirms not only the split within the authorial voice but also his disappearance. Of course an author split in two is also a disappearing author. By pointing at himself as a character in his book and, even better, as a *historically* existing figure, as a real representation, More erased himself as the text's author. He witnessed his own appearance and development. This is a procedure (both artificial and profoundly necessary) we will encounter often in the utopias to follow. It is as if utopia came to the author from the outside, as if it had no author or if, amounting to the same thing, the author were an "other." This formal device, "as if," the form that transforms into otherness, is the dialogue constitutive of the book's textuality, the various speech positions that open up the stage on which the utopic figure can be mounted and played.

The Myth of Staged History

Recall our second inquiry concerning utopic discourse: in this play of utopic representation is a myth or its equivalent constituted as true knowledge? Now we can answer this question; our previous analyses, in particular the discovery of the homologous positions of More and Raphael as characters, will come to our aid. It is remarkable, in fact, to note that each, separately—one in the dialogue, the other in the figure—plays the role of history. In the one case it is real history, where action and events have truly taken place. These are *past* events, of course, but they actually have taken place, and the text is a trace of their disappeared passage and place. It is a question here of an absent reality, but nonetheless a reality. In the other case we are involved in fictitious history: there are actions and events that our fictitious character Raphael has witnessed while he traveled through the fiction. These are missing actions or events, but the text of *Utopia* is the present inscription and constitutes its true reality. If the positions of the narrator of the figure and the writer of the book define the two poles of the utopic stage, it is legitimate to wonder if the visible result is not the representation of history—that is, the mythic narrative of history as a possible object of knowledge, as the possible place for *just understanding and action.*

The myth of history? What does this mean? That history is a fiction, but also that fiction can be historical. The reversibility of the proposition is demonstrated through the various stretches sketched out by More's and Raphael's voices presenting the figure of Utopia and the book that presents and exposes it. Within the weaves of this network the chief problem that utopia will hold up to Western scruples concerns ideology and practice. *History is fiction*: such could be a definition of ideology according to the road on the "left." *Fiction is historical*: such would be the practice of creating and transforming reality on the "right." Every utopia would attempt to go from one to the other, and such would be the object of representation, representation presented on the stage of the book, within the props of the figure. And such would be the myth of history coming to recognition, to the possibility of knowledge and awareness.

Satire and Utopia

One way of approaching this difficult problem can be glimpsed through the relation established between satire and utopia. A typology of literary genres and a differential description of their characteristics has been made.[18] Such a direction for research highlights the mythic ritual as the founding relationship between subversive violence—the ritual overthrow of family, social, political, and religious laws—and the periodic return of the norm and of institutions. Saturnalia, Fools' Days, and carnivals are the expressions of the same transgression in different cultural contexts. This transgression ensures the law even more solidly, whether it be the law of Zeus or of the Church. The essential literary forms of the carnival and satire have also been studied.[19] The celebration of violent repetition and its containment through laws and institutions are evident in the dialogic structure, in the mythic ritual, and in its discursive forms—poetry, theater, and literature. Here is performed the celebration of the founding of social institutions, of their norms and rules. Ritual—in this case myth translated into ceremony or the narrative thereby produced—in providing itself with speech is not a simple "safety valve" to release pressure periodically in order to ensure "social repression" by breaking the severe laws for a limited period of time. Without these laws social cohesion would normally not be guaranteed. The ritual does not constitute a therapeutics of legal authority and social discipline. It is the beginning and foundation of the law through repetition of the former disorder and chaos. But transgression is simultaneously liberating and constitutive. Every institution is repressive; the mythic ceremony performs its overthrow, but the social community exists only through it. The ritual of overthrow is also the ritual of foundation of the overthrown, of the reenactment of the law and of justice, of the norm, and of ritual order of subversion—subversion that existed before order and is again present in the ceremony. But the ritual is also submission of desire into the framework of the institution, in both its symbolic and periodic accomplishment. Thus subversion is also rite, and overthrow is also the institution of overthrow—affirmation of the law by challenging it.

The relation between the ritual of overthrow and satire, between satire and utopia, leads us to the ambiguity contained in every social critique. It simultaneously defines a norm and unfolds the discourse that would deny it. It cannot articulate a discourse without accepting as a presupposition the law that it questions. Adjacent to the critique of the institution is the institution as an idea; alongside real society is one that is ideal. Saturnalian anarchy is the negative, ritualistic critique of the institution in mythic narrative; the norm is this negation, its ideality, and also the positivity where it is accomplished, as the regulation of current constraints makes up the bliss of the Golden Age.

The Law of Transgression

It is clear that utopic dialogue has a critical function. The representation of the ideal city, of its mores, institutions, and laws—precisely because it is picture and representation—conjures up, as a negative referent, real society; it thus encourages a critical consciousness of this society. As one critic among a number of others writes, the entire work implies an *a fortiori* reasoning: "if peoples who have not had the privilege of the Revelation can acquire such virtues, Christ's teachings can inspire even higher ones."[20] If the non-Christian Utopians constitute the "sole republic which merits to be called one," what can be said of the Christian states of the Old World? What can be said of Western governments? Here utopia performs the role of a positively charged norm; with it as a reference the critique of real society will take place. There is a fundamental difference, however, between utopia and the simple critical or satirical discourse. Utopia established transgressions as norm. Subversion becomes figurative representation of the law. In other words, in utopia transgression is not related to the law; it has become the law.

Thomas More is very clear here. Recall the passage where we recognize the exit from Utopia, the beginning of the end of the book.

> Many things came to my mind which seemed very absurdly established in the customs and laws of the people described...most of all in that feature which is the principal foundation of their whole structure. I mean their common life and subsistence—without any exchange of money. This latter alone utterly overthrows all the nobility, magnificence, splendor, and majesty which are, in the estimation of the common people, the true glories and ornaments of the commonwealth.[21]

The fundamental defining law in Utopia is the transgression of private property. This law has been established by Raphael's interlocutor, the ambiguous author of the book *Utopia*: the dialogic structure of the text forces us to accept the position of transgression as law, of subversion as institution, because it allows for transgression of the law as transgression, but in textual form only. Reread similarly the transgression of the father-son relationship in the Utopia of Cyrano de Bergerac. The transgression has become a moral and social law in the Lunar Estates.[22] From this vantage point utopia is not a critique, or at least it can very easily not be one. It is at this precise moment when utopic discourse ceases, when the figurative picture is completed and a critical practice ensues, *outside the book, at the end of discourse.* Utopic discourse is thus constructed in such a way that its end marks the beginning of its meaning, its closure the true inauguration of its signification. It is a discourse that, through its very structure, indicates that critical practice is neither practice nor critical unless it is differentiated from all discursivity. It notes this negatively, in the margins, by an unsaid textual indication. More's political practice and very existence would attest to this fact.

The Political Ceremony and Irony

The revolutionary political ceremony as enactment and accomplishment outside of representation would constitute the passage to nondiscursivity. Nonfounding transgression (to be distinguished from saturnalia and rituals of the overthrow of social institutions) is excess, the gratuitous spending with total loss, completely excessive consumption that destroys limits, equilibrium, and compensatory exchanges (the first of these being substitution of discourse for the "language of real life"). It is in this way that the Münzerian utopia will emerge into history, some ten years following the composition of *Utopia.*[23] Actually, More's utopic discourse contains the equivalent or substitute of this completely gratuitous loss: irony, the *serio ludere.* Irony can be seen as the completely gratuitous loss of meaning; it annihilates meaning, every meaning, for its opposite. Utopic dialogue is the serious play by which discourse's signification is put into circulation to be immediately removed from it: its stable meaning is erased. The text offers to the reader the consumption of signifieds of completely freed signs. The signifiers, which up to that point seemed to have coherent meaning, are emptied of it. An example to which I shall return concerns the operation where the proper names in Utopia lose their meaning because of indetermination of the signified referent carried along by their signifier. This is so when the island's river is called Anydrus, "No-water," or when our storyteller's name is Hythlodaeus, "Non-sense." Similarly, Cyrano institutes a number of Lunar Estates' laws by creating a metaphoric expression out of ordinary language: song-cents or aroma-food, etc.[24] Irony, the *spoudogeloion*, or comic seriousness, constitutes several of the utopic ceremony's discursive manipulations. It is transgression of the law of meaning, one that becomes the possibility of a revolutionary practice of language. This is so because language is also a practice among others and not only a regulated order of signs, the legal system of discourse.

With utopia we discover absolute transgression. It is a transgression that has become law and therefore overthrows itself to become its opposite, to crush its own power. At least it *would* have done so if it had not been produced within a figure, a representation, a fiction. Compared to an institution in real society utopia is not another law inherent to an unknown people discovered by some traveling ethnographer possessing objective potential for establishing a blessed island, the *Perfect City* of *simple difference* next to the historical island of England or the real city of London. Utopic law is not another law; it is the "other" to the law. It is constitutionally the very reverse, the very negative, of the law. For the Western traveler America's Topinambu or Patagon are the living transgressions of European Spain or Portugal, because they follow certain laws and customs that are different from, and contrary to, theirs. For these idolatrous and ungoldy savages, these immodest creatures of hell, one solitary gesture suffices for reducing all difference, for bringing them into the order and stability of the Christian, European, adult, reasonable norm. The transgression is thus recognized, named, and reduced into a difference with respect to the law.

Utopic transgression is not the same. It is absolute; it is the law as is its other. It is the negativity of reality realized, or rather figured and represented, in fiction, the sole means of representing it in discourse. Utopia is the figure in discourse, created from discourse. It also represents its end, the real practice of transforming reality, of contesting the institution, of transgressing the law; it is the figure of historical negativity. Utopia is indeed a fiction and obeys the unobserved commands of the historically situated ideology from which it emerges. It could not be otherwise. But in this way it informs us that history is a fiction, that it, too, belongs to the discourses that men utter about history in order to give it meaning. It is not irrelevant, from this point of view, to note that More, the historical character from *Utopia*, is an essential element in a commercial venture to improve the economic positions of these English merchants and fabric workshops against whom a part of *Utopia* was written. Here we find a fiction of history through which is expressed an ideology. But Utopia is also the picture of a transgression that is historically determined; it is a transgression that has become the law of figure within figure. It is the figure of the negative of real society and of its laws; it represents transforming practice, historical negativity itself. Its inclusion in discourse can only mean its disappearance in a scientific theory of history. In this way the fiction is historical; it is the becoming negative of history in representation, and only this, because the fiction is but text and discourse. Its termination will mark the closure of the text, the end of the discourse, and the beginning of revolutionary practice. Its abandonment is signaled by the return to real society and to the general ideology it produces.

Notes

Chapter 3:

[1] See A. Green, *Un oeil en trop* (Paris: Minuit, 1969).

[2] With reference to this, see the work of W. J. Ong, especially his book on *Ramus: Method and the Decay of Dialogue* (Cambridge: Harvard University Press, 1958).

[3] J.-P. Vernant and P. Vidal-Naquet, *Mythe et tragédie en Grèce* (Paris: Maspero, 1972).

[4] Vernant, p. 14.

[5] Vernant, pp. 14, 27.

[6] Vernant, pp. 23–24. See also J. H. Finley, *Pindarus and Aeschylus* (Cambridge: Harvard University Press, 1955).

[7] Vernant, p. 15.

[8] More, p. 57.

[9] More, p. 6.

[10] More, p. 7 (my emphasis).

[11] David M. Bevington deals with this subject in "Dialogue in Utopia: Two Sides of the Question," *Studies in Philology*, 58 (July, 1961).

[12] More, pp. 57–59.

[13] More, p. 152.

[14] More, p. 146.

[15] More, p. 151 (my emphasis).

[16] More, p. 152 (my emphasis).

[17] More, pp. 151–152.

[18] Robert E. Elliott's work is essential: *The Shape of Utopia* (Chicago: Chicago University Press, 1970). See also his previous book *The Power of Satire: Magic Ritual, Art* (Princeton: Princeton University Press, 1960).

[19] Mikhail Bakhtine, *Problems of Dostoevski's Poetics* (Ann Arbor: Ardis, 1973).

[20] R. W. Chambers, *Thomas More* (New York: Harcourt, Brace, 1935). See also Marie Delcourt's introduction to her French translation of Utopia (Brussels, 1952).

[21] More, p. 151.

[22] Cyrano de Bergerac, *L'Autre Monde ou les Etats et Empires de la Lune*, Introduction by M. Langaa (Paris: Garnier-Flammarion, 1970), pp. 94–95.

[23] See Ernst Bloch, *Thomas Münzer als Theologe der Revolution* (Suhrkamp Verlag, 1964), Gesamtansgabe, Bd. 3.

[24] Cyrano de Bergerac, pp. 62–64.

CHAPTER FOUR

Of Proper Names in Utopia

More's text may be similar to a number of utopic texts; in general they perhaps all lack a reference, or more accurately, they create it as a textual or literary object. They would then be similar in function to the performative mode or to magical and religious enunciation, which during their utterance bring things into existence.

This first feature is not specific enough of the utopic text itself: we would need to define it as this place of discourse where the text's reference disappears into its other, this other being the text. Utopia, in its text, is the mark of the other coming into the text. Such as the hypothesis that I would like to show—though only partially—by examining proper names in Utopia.

No-place

U-topia, *ou-topia*, no-place: by its very composition the proper name that has given its title to the work begins the movement toward the boundaries of the text and world. More's own subtle awareness of this movement can be shown by looking very simply at the text of the letter Peter Giles, his friend, addresses to Busleyden. Giles answers a few questions concerning the island of Utopia. He talks of how moving Raphael's discourse was; he is a man "*haud vulgari praeditus eloquentia*,"[1] to such a point that, as More's book relates the description, the reader believes he is *seeing* the island "*sic depictam sic oculis subjectam*,"[2] that Giles himself, who had been present during the discussion between More and Raphael, believed to be hearing this latter's "own words sounding in my ears." He concludes:

> As to More's difficulty about the geographical position of the island, Raphael did not fail to mention even that, but in very few words and as it were in passing, as if reserving the topic for another place. But, somewhere or other, an unlucky accident caused us both to fail to catch what he said. While Raphael was speaking on the topic, one of More's servants had come

> up to him to whisper something or other in his ear. I was therefore listening all the more intently when one of our company who had, I suppose, caught cold on shipboard coughed so loudly that I lost some phrases of what Raphael said. I shall not rest, however, till I have full information on this point so that I shall be able to tell you exactly not only the location of the island but even the longitude and latitude—provided that our friend Hythlodaeus be alive and safe.[3]

The island, then, and its position—its longitude and latitude defined with reference to its spatial coordinates—all vanish in fiction because of a whisper and a cough, two vocal sounds, one quiet, the other violent. If the island's space is erased by the passage of air, it is perhaps because it had no other reality than breath itself, the resonance of Raphael's words, a resonance such that it is caught and stabilized in a text that, in turn, presents and brings it to light. Such is the trajectory of this slippage from geographic space to that of the text, and within the text to that of the figure: this is the displacement and work performed by voice on itself, erasing the world in its "telling" to emerge as a simulacrum in the fiction of writing. During this passage something has been lost, irretrievably: the island's very place in the world; it is found again but displaced to another space, as a figure in the text.

Of Truth and Falsehood

The proper names, first and foremost "Utopia," are the indications of this trajectory. They are the road signs that point out the reversal of the text's reference into its other. This "overthrow" belongs to the sophist's art; it is not surprising that we should find elements of it here in More's "limited" fiction. It is exactly this criticism to which More responds when he writes to Peter Giles; this letter should be carefully analyzed so as to find the mechanisms of fiction, *poiesis.* He speaks of a dilemma, one of truth and of falsehood: *si res ut vera prodita est, video ibi quaedam subabsurda* (says the censor). *Sive ficta tum in non multis exactum illud Mori judicium requiro.*"[4] The censor speaks in a black-and-white logic, one in which true and false exist. This would allow for a clear classification into the absurd or insufficient. More's answers remain in an intermediate zone where falsehood is but the shadow of truth that supports it and frames it. Together a reality of speech emerges that exists independently, simultaneously true and false: fiction-simulacrum.[5]

In this attempt designating the river, city and even the island itself by strange, meaningless names is extremely important, because More justifies their truth precisely because of their absurdity. If it were simply a matter of disguising truth under the veil of fiction, it would have sufficed to leave a small trace of the disguise: the wisest of readers would have caught on. We could have trusted More to rely on methods other than the most obvious proper names: each of them could have contained a symbolic and allegoric meaning; they could have referred to some beautiful and profound idea that would have been both concealed and revealed by them.[6] Here there is none of that: "Unless the faithfulness of an historian had been binding on me, I am not so stupid as to have preferred to use those barbarous and meaningless names, Utopia, Anydrus, Amaurotum, and Ademus."[7] Their absurdity guarantees their truth because absurdity cannot be invented. Raphael Hythlodaeus actually did tell him this story. Because he was trustworthy, More believed him. That is why More tells the story in turn, in writing; and More, of course, does not lie. Using utopic discourse, he is able to elude the censors: synthesis of truth and falsehood, belonging to neither white nor black. He goes beyond and accomplishes truth within falsehood. This truth then becomes the transparent veil behind which there is nothing: representation, if you will, but in the sense of *Darstellung*, a fiction that achieves its meaning solely by its own means. Thus, as More provides the explanatory etymologies of *Utopia*, *Anydrus*, *Amaurotum*, or *Ademus*, he disavows etymology as a source of designation. He refuses to admit that these names were constructed from scratch artificially to signify mystically a meaning from behind the veil. On the contrary, he maintains that they have no meaning and that this is their truth and proof. Their absurdity is the proof of their fictional reality: the etymology does not signify artifice or disguise; it signifies something else, something other.

The Negative Proper Name

Utopic proper names contain their own negation. U-topia, An-ydrus, A-demus, etc. What is this effect? They by no means signify that the island does not exist, that the utopic river has no water, that its government has no one to govern, that its capital is a mirage. These names do not mean that the island, river, prince, and capital exist only in More's imagination. This would be an incorrect interpretation, one that More had warned us against. It would be based upon naive etymology, and the proper name would fall into allegory. That means that the reality of island, capital, and prince is designated by a name that itself effaces its own naming ability. The negation does not affect the name's referent but does affect the name itself, which designates an "other" referent. It is this other referent that More affirms within the proper noun's play of internal negation: it says simultaneously that it is a faithful and trustworthy transcriber of Raphael's narrative. It tells the truth.

Now grasping how the whole problem of utopic discourse comes to depend on the proper name is easy: all of its real meaning is affected by it. The proper noun is in fact a specific case of the code's circularity: it signifies a being named by this name. The code thus refers to itself in this particular area because Smith designates whomever is named Smith. With the proper noun the code no longer functions as a tool but as an object of reference. The logical relation between the proper noun and an index or diectic can also be easily seen. Because the proper noun designates whomever carries this name and only he or she, it must be situated on the borderline of meaningful language, beyond which there is only a gesture, a finger pointing toward this being present in front of me. The proper name thus has a prelingual, gesturing function, but it performs it in language. It performs mime in the milieu of linguistic signification. It represents on this stage the original production of meaning that reproduces the appropriation of the object through its grasp, disassociated from its natural space. Is this not the same violent separation that Utopus brought about when he took the island from the continent and made Utopia exist as "Non-Abraxa"? With the proper name language creates the illusion of rediscovering the original gesture: a unique naming reserved for the presence of a unique being, signifier of its signified being discernible from every other being, even if there are a thousand with the name of Smith. "In each system, proper nouns represent *quanta of signification.* Beyond these, all that remains is to point."[8] A reciprocal appropriation whereby name and being, each acting on the other, melt into a mutual unit: with this we enter into the circle of representation.

There is another double structure with another type of internal overlapping in language. This involves a message referring to the message. Quotation is a prime example. Here the code does not function as an object of reference but as the message itself. Notice that More's discourse does not describe an object in the world. That is not its referent. More's discourse repeats Raphael's discourse. Utopia is actually a long quotation: Book Two of More's text. The caesura marking it is the space separating "*hunc in modum exorsus est*" from "*Utopiensium Insula in media sui parte.*" Bloomfield calls this a relayed, or displaced, utterance. These words must be carefully weighed, especially since the enunciating subject, with his message within a message, is removed from his enunciative function by his proper name: *Hythlodaeus-ûthlos-daïos*, "knowing in nonsense." As we go deeper into More's discourse, we find a series of subtle reversals that eat and chip away at *Utopia*. They destroy the "normal," meaningful function in discourse that consists in saying something about something. As this discourse slowly unfolds, what it speaks about or what it has just said is nullified and destroyed by a certain play in language negatively circling itself.

Indication

The proper noun thus negates its very nature. The naming function referring to the presence of a determined, individual nature is affected by the corrosion of the negation it carries along with it. Apply this to the Syphogrants–*sophogerontes*. The risk, and even error, in this type of interpretation would be symbolically to designate the contrary of what the proper meaning, the etymology, would suggest: transforming the negative proper nouns into metaphors of a reality that could be obtained through reverse transformation. Never, then, will the city be more urban, the river more overflowing, the magistrate wise, and Hythlodaeus logical when called "non-city," "without-water," "stupid," "nonsense." The proper nouns in Utopia would not reverse the content of what they designate by their internal negation, and in so doing come across an ideal reality in a sort of Neoplatonic symbolism. They do not designate and they do not name. Utopia is this nonplace where names do not properly or "correctly" designate; there is nothing proper in the name. They designate the "other" of proper. There is disappropriation in their naming function, an absence in their power to indicate presence. There is metaphor within the proper; this is the deconstructive power that utopic proper names realize. As they are uttered, they create the other of place, of the river, city, wisemen, or meaning. It is their dispossession and denunciation at the very moment language would take hold.

In his letter to Peter Giles More explained that the proper nouns in Utopia had no meaning (*nihil significantia*) and thus, having no meaning, affirmed their "historical" reality. They performed an effect of reality. But at the same time More gave their etymology and, in so doing, their meaning: is this a simple ironic game? Or does this playful irony here have another meaning, one beyond etymology and the nonsense of reality clearly indicated to us, as More implied to his friend? To say that a proper noun has no meaning actually posits it as a pure proper noun. That gesture forbids translating or substitution; it cannot be transformed so that an equivalence is established between this name and another group of names, an equivalence that would dissolve the former into generality or integrate it into a symbolic system of exchange between names as parts of a system. If this substitution is not possible, if a name has no signification, cannot receive definition at any level whatsoever, then this name is nothing but a sonorous expiration, a noise, or yet possibly the indication of a unique thing or being, present in front of the figure pointed at it. The name then would be the verbal transport for it, its metaphor. This transference from "gesture" to "name," however, would indeed constitute a translation and a primitive substitution installing the proper name within a system of exchange, this time not intrasemiotic, but intersemiotic, and its general nature is transposition and transmutation.

Is the "gesture" of indication itself as simple and immediate as I have claimed? Indication involves tracing a direction toward something. Is it not a possible, ideal line in the space in front of me toward the object, a possible ideality that is the mark of unconquered distance between me and the object and that is also as this mark of distance, the tracing of the seizing, possessing, and appropriating gesture? It is potential, but does it even involve a gesture? Is it signifying or symbolic behavior? It seems not: thus the chimpanzee taking his master's hand and placing it on the desired morsel of food. This is a presymbolic appropriation in the *contact* of a human hand, the master's, and an animal paw on the food. The indicating gesture that is the first to signify thus seems to be the second signifier of a nonsignifier that precedes it. It is within this gap that distance is produced, and with distance, the constitutive displacement of the symbolic.

When More declares in this same paragraph of his letter that the proper nouns of Utopia signify nothing (and thereby that they belong to the reality the historian describes and that their etymology is the most clear and authentic [*etymon*] mark of fiction), he describes a process very similar to the one we just outlined. Pure proper nouns *indicate* the real, but because their meaning also exists, they become part of a system of classificatory names. They have generic signification. It is in this way that they designate their fictional quality. These proper nouns—crossed out, if you will, in their very being as proper noun—in the final and last definition of the "properness" of the name, mean (here is perhaps More's "serious play") that fiction is reality. They signify that there exists a being of simulacrum that is pure emergence, referring to nothing other than itself: *poïesis.*

Eutopia

More also used the proper nouns of *Utopia* in a different way. This second way parallels but reverses the negative type that deconstructs them from the inside. He uses them in a positive fashion. In fact, More hinted at this himself: Utopia is *oú-topos*, no-place, but it is also *eú-topos*, place of happiness. It is true that the person who signals this transformation from the negative to the positive is Anemolius, poet laureat and nephew of Hythlodaeus (he who is knowing in nonsense) by his sister. *Anemolius*, he who is light and empty as wind; *Anemolius*, vain and useless. This etymological play continues, and the Syphogrant, from stupid, becomes wise, and the Anydrus will swell to the rhythm of the tides, similar to a new Thames. Henceforth the Utopian proper noun will designate simultaneously the same and the other. Or, more precisely, the "same," the positive shading, will only be designated by changing one letter of the "negative" name. This literal play of the name's graphic inscription merits investigation. It differs from equivocal or ambiguous meaning or signification because ambiguity applies to a univocal name; it carries two meanings. But with "Utopia-Eutopia" the very name is written double. *Utopia* is simultaneously *oú-topos* and *eú-topos*, the negative of the positive and the positive of the negative in the spelling of the signifier, one in the other, as if it were a monogram where both must be read, one, then the other, in the same literal figure immediately given. This double reading, simultaneously *and* successively, of happiness in indetermination is suggested in Anemolius' poem:

> *Utopia priscis dicta ob infrequentiam*
> *Nunc Civitatis aemula Platonicae,*
> *Fortasse victrix (nam quod illa literis*
> *Deliniavit, hoc ego una praestiti,*
> *Viris et opibus, optimisque legibus)*
> *Eutopia merito sum vocanda nomine.*[9]

From the Republic to England

Plato's *Republic* is only "sketched out" in letters. It has but a literary existence in the Platonic text, whereas in the text, in Eutopia, it is shown in its reality. Notice that Anemolius (or More) never "translates" *Utopia* or *Eutopia* in his poem. *Infrequentia* is used for a deserted *place*, little populated and rarely frequented; it is used for a *little-used* word, one that is rare. This desert isolates itself in its own vacuum, the text in the rare quality of its reading. As for Eutopia, the only near "translation" is found in the fifth line: men, wealth (resources), and excellent laws. One might contest that only the allusion to Plato's *Republic* provides the reading of *Eutopia* in *Utopia* and of reality in the text: *Eutopia* is a sort of nickname for *Utopia* read through its invisible surface. It is a pseudo-homonym and quasi-antonym, a poetic play of words because here the opposition between the paradigmatic and syntagmatic is violated; so is that between reality and text. *Eutopia* is the realization of the Platonic *Republic*, this latter having no existence other than literary. That is why *Eutopia* is the right nickname for *Utopia*, as great numbers of men, resources, and excellent laws can be used for a seldom-frequented, deserted place. These are the surprises in store for us in the monogram; it joins together in one (literal) structure four terms: "reality : text : : abundance (presence) : scarcity (absence)." *Eutopia* acts simultaneously in the text and in reality as the signifier of presence (Happy Land) and the signified of abundance; Plato's *Republic* in the text only as the signifier of presence, *Utopia* as the signifier of absence.

The three superposed names in the monogram—*Eutopia*, *Utopia*, and *Republic* (the final one constituting the written guide for the two others)—leaves empty the fourth quarter in a diagram we could construct. There is one area of the structure that is not named. It is where reality and scarcity meet. In a certain way it is the exact opposite of Plato's ideal Republic because its nature is scarcity and reality. Is not this empty area, neither shown nor designated, historical reality itself? Is it not the England of the beginning of the sixteenth century where More will become lord chancellor? The rare text is *Utopia*; the reality of this rare text is its nicknamed antonym and homonym, *Eutopia*, obtained by transformation of this "abundant" text, Plato's *Republic*, which would define the ideal. The starting point for the transformation would be *Utopia*, signifier of scarcity that names the same in the other, the being of the other, "eutopic" fiction, by opposing and transforming the ideal. This latter offers the presence of the signified in the text only, while *Eutopia* actually refers to this signified, which is absent in the text's very reality, and which is its real scarcity shown as absence in its fictive abundance: historical England.

Model

We find in the structural diagram in Figure 10 the slippage from reality to text and from text to reality we have already seen. A more formidable, more specific characteristic has been added, however: evidence of a blank space "emerges" in the text's play of names and discourses. There is a "blind" spot, but yet visible: historical reality. This texture of names and of utopic discourse, of their literality, creates as their absent signified the appearance of the reality of which Utopia is the "poiesis."

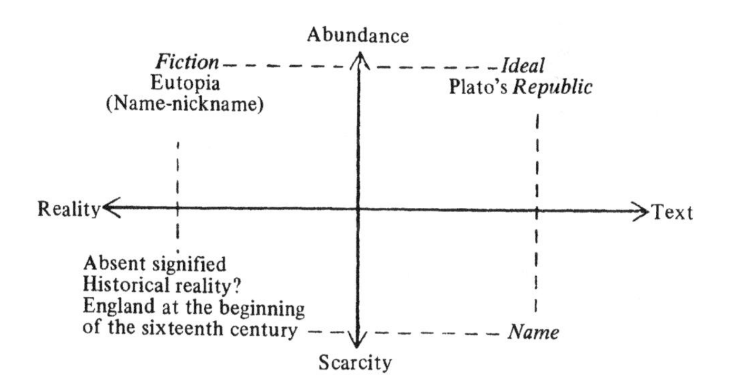

Figure 10. Theory of proper names: structural diagram of the "monogram"

To start the signifying machine we might add that the base of this analysis assumes a short poem written by a Utopian named "Wind-Insignificant"; the maternal uncle is the great traveler named "knowing in nonsense," Hythlodaeus. The play between name and nickname (*Utopia-Eutopia*) continues between the poem and its author. Doesn't the name of the subject of enunciation nullify what is enunciated, just as *Utopia*, the Desert, could be read in *Eutopia*, the Abundant? And doesn't the system of names continue here the system of lineage? Remember, also, so that fiction here can reach its maximum of dizzying heights, the small poem is not part of the actual text of *Utopia*. It is written on the back of the second leaf of the volume as a sort of "authentic" document. It is a preamble situated next to the Utopian alphabet and four lines of verse in the Utopian language. The Latin translation reveals that the island of Utopia, which originally was not an island, is the only truly philosophical City on earth without philosophy:

> *"Utopus me dux ex non insula fecit insulam,*
> *Una ego terrarum omnium absque philosophia*
> *Civitatem philosophicam expressi mortalibus,*
> *Libenter impartio mea, non gravatim accipio meliora."*[10]

"True ethics does not concern itself with ethics, and true philosophy does not care about philosophy," Pascal will say a century and a half later. He is affected by the same infinite flight of meaning through its signifiers, a flight to be accompanied progressively by a self-denying discourse surrounded by two chasms it crosses by deepening them as it continues.[11]

Prophetic Speech and Utopic Negation

A comparison will help us understand the nature of the utopic discourse as it is plotted out by proper names. There is a well-known text from the Old Testament book of the prophet Hosea. The Lord has sent his prophet into the land of Israel: "'Go, take unto thee a wife of harlotry and children of harlotry; for the land doth commit great harlotry, departing from the Lord.'...And she conceived again, and bore a daughter. And He said unto him, 'Call her name Not-Loved; for I will no more love the house of Israel...' Now when she had weaned Lo-ruhamah, she conceived, and bore a son. And He said, 'Call his name Lo-ammi; for ye are Not-My-People, and I am Not-God for you.'"[12] Since the formula for the Covenant between God and Israel is the positive and reciprocal affirmation, "You are my people," and "You are my God," Hosea's children in their birth and *filiation* and in their *naming* (the latter continuing the former) bring about a rupture in the Covenant. Better yet, there is instead a sort of blank space, an interruption of relations between Israel and God, that is of a different order than simply broken promises. The internal negation of the name negates the very naming, the very act of possessing the individual being by him who names. The daughter and son of Hosea and of Gomer, the harlot, are indeed named by God, and he takes possession of them by this act. He creates a link with them through the name, but this possession, this subjection of the subject by his name, as a subject of the Covenant, is dispossession because of the internal negation of the proper name. It is denunciation; the Covenant is broken within the Covenant and through the act of designation itself.

The Covenant is not abolished. The history of God's people is not denied. But within this history and Covenant a sort of vacuum has erupted. A presence of absence has emerged, which belongs to another order, the order of the other side of this nistory. God's negative affirmations ("Call her name Not-Loved; Call his name Not-My-People; I am Not-God for you") do not dialecticize the history of the elected people through a work of negativity, pushing it forward progressively.[13]

There is a sort of negative fringe in the affirmation as such which is its other side, its shadow, through which comes the affirmation of the same and the other, through this other of the same. Henceforth the same is affirmed.

The act of possession takes place in the proper name but through the expulsion and rejection of what the proper name possesses in its articulation. Neither denial nor negativity, negation's true face is "the presentation of what is, of what I am, but in the form of not being."[14] Others define it as "the procedure whereby the subject, while formulating one of his wishes, thoughts or feelings, which has been repressed hitherto, contrives, by disowning it, to continue to defend himself against it."[15] The wish, thought, or desire is continually repressed and thwarted, but the representation or representative content is nonetheless admitted into consciousness: "intellectual admission of the repressed," writes Freud. "Through the symbol of negation, thought is freed from the limitations of repression."[16] It is its *Aufhebung*, its supersession, but denying and conserving what it suppresses. The Lord does not say, "You will not call her 'Loved One' or 'My People,'" but rather, "You will call her 'Not-Loved,' 'Not-My-People.'" There is indeed affirmation of the denied that remains denied. More does not write that Utopia is not in the reality of geographic and historical space. He writes, while naming the island "Utopia," that it is Not-Space, the No-Place. This Not-Space is very precisely utopic space. Not-Loved, Not-My-People are actually Loved and My People in the affirmation of the broken Covenant; Utopia, the place in the affirmation of the poetic object.

In both prophetic and utopic discourses there exist a background and base of "reality" that is simultaneously kept and rejected, conserved and suppressed, in the same gesture and at the same time. The "symbols" of negation that these proper names carry with them indicate the rejection of this real positivity in the very act by which this positivity is designated, in the very way it is gathered up and accepted in speech. But in this act of possession surrounded by nothingness reality itself undergoes a profound change, worked on as it is by these symbols. Reality springs back, not to be perceived truly or felt in its fullness, but to haunt subliminally the words and phrases that utter it. In the margins of discourse and in the intervals that are sculpted in the proper names themselves—"Not-My-People," "No-Place," "Nonsense," etc.—reality returns to be the other side of what it is: fullness, thickness, obstacle, and presence.

In other words, reality, rejected and expelled, returns as the reality of the text within the articulations of what we also call the "poietic object." Thus the utopic and prophetic texts are not purely and simply ideal or imaginary representations of reality, the likes of which we would decide by means of the law of contraries, one of the rules for the construction of allegory. Historical reality (or human reality in its holy relation to God for prophetic speech) does not constitute a reference point for discourse the code for which this latter would construct in a more or less complex way. Historical reality has always already been rejected and expelled; it never could be the referent for discourse. This is clear from More's letters already quoted and because of the particular mark of rejection constituting the negation that affects the proper name. This does not complete the procedure for the constitution of the utopic or the prophetic. Rejected reality, as referent, returns to this very same discourse to make up the reality of its text. We have the markings of this operation as well, the same markings that informed us of the movement of rejection, but they are articulated in a different way. The nonsignification of the proper name is a mark of its nature as proper name, for example. But this nonsignification signified the rejection of its reference into the imaginary. This accounts for the sense of "presence" of the utopic or prophetic text—but presence that is different from real presence. It acquires from this its powerful impression of force; the writer seems removed from it and, even though he wrote it, overwhelmed by it. The text functions as real because expulsed reality has returned to its points of articulation. We once again see how proper names as indices (whether scientifically founded or ideologically projected) hold the function of privileged reality, how they constitute the very special field of study that certain "discursive beings" aim at: poems, prophecies, and utopias.

In conclusion, the play of language brought about by proper names should be mentioned. Discursive irony is the serious play whose meaning is consumed in the text's play. The maxim *serio ludere* in Renaissance philosophy and mysticism has been widely studied. There exists the example of Nicholas of Cusa looking for an unusual object wrought with contradictory attributes so that the soul will be inspired by play and distraction to think about God's incomprehensible nature.[17] Play is initiation; it incites the spirit (see any number of More's contemporaries, such as Ficino, Pico, or Bocchi) to the contemplation of nature's or God's secrets inaccessible but through the use of figures, images, or narratives, which seem to negate them because they disguise as well as present them. Here is the text reemerging through its own play: "the art of weaving divine secrets with fables so that those who read them [he is referring to the Orphic hymns here] will think that they contain only wild fables or simple stories."[18] Emblem of myth: the truth or fantasy of desire is figured and lost in its figures, unless its play frees it from its shackles to allow it to develop and to shape reality as it will. This is satisfaction that the text, in its play, will grant.

From this analysis proper names become the fantasmatic signs of this play where reality and desire attempt to create presence and absence, signs that raise the text to a state of play so that desire, fusing with and disengaging from the text, can thereby stimulate action.

Notes

Chapter 4

[1] Thomas More, Complete Works (New Haven, London: Yale University Press, 1965), Vol. IV, p. 20. This comes from a letter from Peter Giles to Jerome Busleyden: "a man endowed with no ordinary power of expression..."

[2] More, p. 20: "So well described..."

[3] More, p. 23.

[4] More, p. 250. In his letter to Peter Giles More quotes his critic's words: "If the facts are reported as true, I see some rather absurd elements in them, but if as fictitious, then I find More's finished judgment wanting in some matters."

[5] See M. Détienne, *Les Maîtres de vérité*, pp. 75-77.

[6] For Renaissance literature and painting, see E. Wind, *Pagan Mysteries in Renaissance Art* (New York: Norton Library), pp. 1-16, 218-236, etc.

[7] More, p. 251.

[8] Lévi-Strauss, *La Pensée sauvage* (Paris: Plon, 1962), pp. 285-286.

[9] More, pp. 20-21: "The ancients called me Utopia or Nowhere because of my isolation. At present, however, I am a rival of Plato's republic, perhaps even a victor over it. The reason is that what he had delineated in words I alone have exhibited in men and resources and laws of

surpassing excellence. Deservedly ought I to be called by the name of Eutopia or Happy-land."

[10]More, pp. 18–19: "Utopus, my ruler, converted men, formerly not an island, into an island. Alone of all lands, without the aid of abstract philosophy, I have represented for mortals the philosophical city. Ungrudgingly do I share my benefits with others; undemurringly do I adopt whatever is better from others."

[11]See L. Marin, *Etudes sémiologiques* (Paris: Klincksieck, 1971).

[12]Old Testament, Hosea, I, 2, 6, 9.

[13]This is perhaps the danger of Andre Neher's analysis in *L'Essence du prophétisme* (Paris, P.U.F.).

[14]See Hyppolite, "Sur la dénégation, commentaire parlé sur la Verneinung de Freud." *La Psychanalyse* (Paris: P.U.F., 1955), pp. 31 ff.

[15]Laplanche and Pontalis, *Vocabulary of Psychoanalysis* (New York: W. W. Norton, 1973), "Negation," p. 261.

[16]S. Freud, "Die Verneinung," 1925; *Gesammelte Werke*, XIV, 12–13 (London: Imago, 1940, 1952).

[17]See the treatises of Nicholas of Cusa, *De ludo globi* or *De Beryllo Philosophische – theologische Schriften* (Vienna: Herdern, 1964), Bd. II.

[18]Quoted by E. Wind.

CHAPTER FIVE

About the Creation of the Island of Utopia

Book Two of Thomas More's *Utopia* is nothing other than a long first-person discourse given by Raphael Hythlodaeus. It opens with a description and a narrative, the description of the island of Utopia and the narrative of its creation as an island. These two modes of discourse find their origin in two very different literary forms; their opposition seems significant to me here in More's *Utopia* and in the utopic discourse in general. In the description the island is offered to us from a point of view where one can surmise it from every angle. This description proceeds as if we were seeing a painting in the simultaneity of its various parts, of a figure that the descriptive text offers for viewing. But our reading of the painting is given in the necessary succession of our reading with an emphasis on the spatial and the whole. The narrative, however, is immediately categorized as history as the relating of former events: "*Caeterum uti fertur*..."[1] The events will be related as the text unfolds—indeed, in its very becoming—and its mode will contain unexpected surprises. The time of the narrative creates events and human actions. This is why narrative is read and is not seen. But in our text it should be noted that in the apparent succession of unexpected events that the narrative relates (or will relate) they are also inscribed within the painting of the island brought forth by description. "*Caeterum uti fertur, utique ipsa loci facies prae se fert.*"[2] The exterior form and general appearance of the place carries with it the trace of the events that Raphael will narrate. Within the visibility of the narrative we find inscriptions of what we will read. The visible of what is described is at bottom nothing but the writing of what is narrated. We could never have imagined as much when we opened More's book at the beginning of Raphael's discourse: the island of Utopia was not an island in the beginning; a "veritable" incision—a real inscription—was needed in order for it to become one. If there is a visible aspect to description, it is because there is a narrative to be composed—in such a way that its description retains and presents only its trace.

Narrative Fragments and Narratives of Foundation

I would like to undertake the analysis of this opening description and of the narrative that follows it. We perceive that the narrative is the foundation for the description even though it follows it. Thus the narrative, coming later in the space of the text, allows for the description that precedes it and that comes to dominate the entire book. The narrative provides it with an object to describe. Let me then propose this general hypothesis: there is evidence to suggest that this No-Place (Utopia–*oú-topia*) is none other than the very place of the text, than traces of writing, because Utopia is itself the result of a written foundation, an incision in continuous space: narrative of foundation.

It is also interesting to note that there exists in *Utopia* a small number of very short narratives that seem to appear at the surface of the text to illustrate Raphael's generalized description. These are exemplary narratives that lead the description of Utopia into didactic fiction. I reversed the preceding statement–in the name of the paradigm that the first two or three pages constitute–and wondered if this descriptive cloth, ripped here and there by narrative in twelve or thirteen places, does not reveal a narrative chain that would tell the history (the myth) of the passage between nature and culture, the profane and the sacred, Europe and the New World. In short, I wanted to see if in this space of "new geography" there existed a deeper history of the rupture of modern times. The initial principles of our analysis, of course, sufficiently show us that the description in *Utopia* and its narrative traces are not at all the pure and simple metaphor of "real history," even with imaginary or dream displacements. More's utopic discourse is its own referent. It presents itself as a "figurative text"; as a textual object it transforms itself into real history. In short, *Utopia* belongs to this particular class of literary objects that make up their own reality; they thus have a certain power over, and poetic effect on, reality. I would thus propose as my reading strategy a double narrative and descriptive continuity in the weave of the text; it contains a double "discourse" that breaks apart into fragments varying in size. It is a text that has emerged from a narrative chain and from a descriptive texture whose reciprocal references constitute the poetic textual reality of *Utopia.*

Book Two includes only two narratives where the founding hero, Utopus, appears. The two narratives, as we saw, frame the space of the text; one opens it, the other closes it. Their function is important as founding narratives (the founding hero is present in them) because they also found the text, outside its linear temporality, as would a frame or a limit. At the same time these narratives define the text itself as a space of visibility in which the elements are given all at once, like a space of description. But, as I indicated earlier, this space of description is constituted only by the narrative that provides its limits and, in so doing, conditions it.

Textual Narrative

Here the literary form and the content of this form must be joined in a meaningful circularity. The initial founding narrative is the narrative by which a trace —an incision—closes off a space, that of culture, within a wandering nature defined as earth or barbarism. The ending narrative, belonging to the same founding gesture, includes an opening of space—but a space of religion, not culture. The narrative that opens the space of the text is a narrative of the closure of Utopian space as a space of profane culture; the narrative that closes it is a narrative of the opening of this same space as sacred and religious. Thus the text itself, and in its very makeup, moves from the profane to the sacred, from the closed to the open, as the founding narrative (in which the hero appears twice) of Utopia is repeated. In the "in-between" of this identical and double (displaced) narrative the narratives of positive and negative contact are developed, of "acculturation," expansion and assimilation of the unknown.

In one of these narrative types the Utopians open up to the outside, here represented by Western European, Greek, Latin, and Christian elements. The representatives of this culture are Raphael and his companions. They become "other" as a result. But this procedure is recuperated in advance by Book One, because the Utopians have learned science and art from the shipwrecked Romans and Egyptians, originally Greek.[3] Thus Utopian acculturation is really a return to the source, anamnesis toward the archaic founding of the Utopian nation.

In other narratives the Utopians come into contact with fictitious peoples who belong to the same space as does Utopia. These contacts are always negative; they are hostile, warlike, and defensive. They are of a "colonial" nature or else suggest ironic indifference or rejection. But here again Book One had already subtly prepared for this eventuality, this departure into fiction. It had slowly cast off all ties with the mapped world, with the world of geography and history. Recall that the Polylerites, Achorians, and Macarians mark our way into the text's eccentric center, "outside this world," Utopia. But once in this Utopian-utopic center, the contacts Utopia will have with these peoples "outside this world" will always be negative. Utopia's logic dictates that only a negative contact with itself can exist where the other is neutralized. Utopic practice produces the neutral itself. This logic as such, with its neutralizing power, constitutes the complex, positive values in the text of *Utopia.* However, when the other (other of the text and of utopia in general) appears, when the real in the form of the West or its representatives erupts into the text, Utopia welcomes it without difficulty or resistance. This other soon turns out to be the same, and Utopia is soon discovered to be already the Christian West. This is the power of utopic neutralization, converting everything it meets into its contrary. Perhaps this is the final reversal we need to understand. Is the whole West pushed into Utopia first by Constantine, then later during the Renaissance? Does it not disappear between the lines of More's text and of Raphael's discourse?

The Figure of the Island

Utopia, in fact, never admits anything exterior to itself; Utopia is for itself its own reality. The descriptive mode, seeing all in its gaze, demands that narrative unfold temporality, only to bring it back into a kind of circular movement. If the textual forundation is both at the beginning and at the end of the text, and if the intermediate narratives interrupt the visible descriptive surface only to sketch out or suggest this circular movement of a neutralization that affirms negation and denies the negative, then we can understand how the narrative founds or at least conditions description. Previously the narrative seemed to work against it by clawing at its surface. This complex structure articulates a number of elements: form and content, narrative and description, deep diachronic and surface-level synchronic structures, *dis-cursus* and *facies.* In this poetic object called *Utopia* all these elements are announced from the first lines on by the opposition set up between the island's description and the narrative that follows and conditions it, because we are there to witness it.

Circles

Utopia is not only an island, but a circular island, even if Raphael describes it in a strange way: "The island extends in the center...for two hundred miles... out toward both ends it begins gradually to taper."[4] This description seems even more strange since we learned in the previous phrase that the broadest part of the island is in the center. But the circularity is not complete because the island is shaped like a crescent moon – in fact, a waxing moon. "The horns...are divided by straits about eleven miles across." There is thus a sort of indentation hollowing out its edge, if not its center. It creates a large gulf filled by the sea, surrounded by terraced hillsides, and forms a "bay which is like a huge lake, smooth rather than rough, and thus converts almost the whole center of the country into a harbor which lets ships cross in every direction..."[5] More explains that it is very dangerous to enter into the gulf. A Utopian pilot must accompany all who attempt it. And even he must carefully follow the signals from a number of landmarks erected on shore. "If these were removed to other positions, they could easily lure an enemy's fleet, however numerous, to destruction."[6] There are a number of other ports around the coast of the island, but the "landing is so well defended by nature or by engineering that a few defenders can prevent strong forces from coming ashore."[7]

This is the first and fundamental description (quoted almost entirely); the narrative of foundation will follow it. Utopia is a circular island, but it is both closed and open. It is closed off to the outside, and engineering, *arte*, and nature have fortified the coast to such an extent that any invasion is impossible. It is open to the inside from this gulf, both lake and port, which is difficult to navigate (closed) but open to anyone once the hidden obstacles are overcome. The outside is simultaneously warmly received on the inside and rejected on the outside. The image, as we can see, is carefully prepared here in the description. It is also already a complex image bringing together closure and opening depending on whether the surrounding sea allows or refuses entry. More underlines the island's closed quality by giving it its circular form. It is a line closed off to itself; a centered circle (all the more so because the capital is situated there) gives strong connotations of geometry, astronomy, and magic. It makes up a topographical paradigm whose structure would include an "ethnographic" code of inclusion and exclusion, acceptance and rejection, and where the various narratives' rules of articulation for the text in general would be found. In addition the center, the geometric and imaginary correlative of the circumference, contributes to the closure of the whole; it provides a pivot or anchor. The very terms we are using to delineate the signifying correlation of this "figure" of the center and of the circle only inspire other diverse imaginary images.

Matrix

This circular line is not closed, however; or, rather, it is not totally closed. It is hollowed out internally; before coming full circle, it creates another circle. It opens up its closure in its very center. Thus the part that comes closest to the center is not full and stable; it is empty and aquatic. Read More's Latin text: "*Cuius cornua fretum, interfluens millibus passum plus minus undecim dirimit, ac per ingens inane diffusum, circum iectu undique terrae prohibitis ventis, vasti in morem lacus stagnans magis quam saeviens omnem prope ejus terrae alvum pro portu facit.*"[8] This empty open space of the island in its center is an *alvus*—bowels, womb, or stomach. And this pivot (the root and central density) that before had made its correlative circularity an enclosure is a hollow, empty space. It is no place, a "no-place," a *u-topos*. The central empty circle, stomach and womb, is the "other" of the full circle surrounding it—the moon, the island—as if it were the negation of it.

It is an ambiguous negation, however. The womb's function includes receiving the seed; the stomach should fill with food. But this empty womb in the island is in fact a huge port: "*magnoque hominum usu naves quaqua versus transmittit.*"[9] Through the empty presence of the central womb in a lunar form we achieve a fantasm of pure exteriority. The outside—the positively charged outside—is inside as an empty space being filled, as an always-absent presence. The negatively charged outside is rejected outside "*fauces hinc vadis, inde saxis formidolosae,*"[10] "*Fauces,*" the mouth of the interior harbor (but also the throat, the narrow crater), is a source of fear and terror. How does one enter into the port? How to get to the womb? How do we fill the stomach?

Behind the description of the island figure several vague semantic dimensions provide a guideline that relates to food and fertility in the image of a waxing moon, "*in lunae speciem renascentis.*"[11] It is quite remarkable, in fact, that this empty space to be filled appears in the image as a form of rebirth, as a moon will become round, as a woman, and as the earth. It is also amazing that this fictional geography, exact in its contradictions—in its signifying ability—puts the capital Amaurotum in the island's exact center, in its stomach's navel "*ea urbs quod tanquam in umbilico terrae sita maxime jacet omnium partium legatis opportuna.*"[12] The center is empty and full, interior and exterior, place and space, just as the island circle was enclosed by an opening, welcoming but hostile. The same circular utopic practice that affirms negation and refuses the negative is at work here on the level of textual content, similar to what we saw on the level of the overall structure of the text.

As I said before, in its structure the utopic text is a cloth woven with narrative and description, with the readable and visible, with time and space. We can put it better: in its very textuality the text is the reciprocal determination of discourse and figure, the figure of discourse, the discourse of figure. The utopic text allows the narrative weave only as inscription within the descriptive chain; it folds the time of the narrative over onto the space of description. Thus time becomes the wake of an already past narrative left in the places described; it is the wake, a trace, and a "no-place." What has been indicated in the form of the contents is also marked out in its substance. The rejection of the negatively charged outside and the inclusion of the positive outside on the inside act like an empty fullness. They sketch out a time other than one that is linear and marching onward. It is a time where events accumulate, which is the opposite of an irreversible time. In Utopia exists a time that is rhythm, alternation, and periodic dance. The "waxing" moon, figure of the Utopian island, is also the map of its temporality, different from repetition, the same and the other simultaneously in the moon's phases. However, the text as it is presented cannot bring about the return of the same (and thus obey a nonutopic logic). It is in the space of description and visibility that the other is drawn from the same, where fullness is vacuum, and vice versa. The maritime matrix, the womb, is the navel of this soil. Such is the mysterious rhythm of time in the space of visibility, the affirmation of the same and of the other, of the other and of the same—difference. From here we can move to a questioning about the relationship and opposition between the fabled, mythic space of Plato's Atlantis and the utopic, representative space of More's island.[13]

Birth of the Island

Here the narrative begins: "*Caeterum uti fertur utique ipsa loci facies prae se fert, ea tellus olim non ambietur mari.*"[14] Before, the name of this land was Abraxa, and it was connected to the continent. Utopus seized it and gave it its name. Once victorious, Utopus had a 15,000-foot isthmus cut to separate Abraxa from the continent. Undertaken both by his army's soldiers and by the local population, this enormous project was completed so quickly that those neighboring peoples who had at first derided him changed their attitude to one of admiration, astonishment, and terror. The backward, savage people who lived in Abraxa became a population far surpassing all other civilizations.[15]

Nature-Culture

Such is the narrative of foundation of the description that precedes the narrative. These are the events that brought about Utopia. The narrative axis is obviously the passage from the state of nature, "*rudis atque agrestis turba*,"[16] to the state of culture, "*cultus et humanitas*" and to the state of true humanity. As always in utopic discourse the "meaning" of the narrative is given before the narrative itself. Its presentation is so obvious that it is only a superficial conceptualization that does not completely fill the narrative signifying field. The "meaning" of the narrative is a conceptual and didactic capsule, a "condensation," no less meaningful than what is found in the dream. It is not a summary nor simply a disguise; it is the true presentation, but "implied," of what the narrative explains on another level. This passage from nature to culture—the founding of Utopia—is a radical passage, a pure act of creation, because the continent becomes an *island* and *Abraxa*, *Utopia.* The change in the figure is at the same time a change in the name. The continent is thus written in another way because it is written by Utopus as *Utopia*, island. This fundamental act, properly speaking, is a double act for the hero: he cuts the isthmus and he names (the island with his name). This act cuts out land and a name. It is a caesura and a cutting of the naturally given, the strip of land 15,000 feet long that attaches Abraxa to the continent; it made Abraxa a part of the continent. The island, then, is artificial, a creation of "culture." However, it is remarkable that this creation does not bring about being; it constructs nothing. The work of the army and the local population is really a deconstruction of nature, a destruction or even a ripping apart or separation. This act supplies an interval where before there was the continuous. It separates one from the other discrete, discontinuous elements and articulates a name. This act designates in language the power of the neutral (following utopic logic): the name used for the naming is here a negative name, *Utopus*, *oú-topos*, the "no-place." I will come back to this and its signification. Utopus' act is a violent act of repression against nature because it cuts the isthmus joining the future *Utopia* to land. This is a symbolic act of negation and of censorship; we will look further into its polysemic ramifications.

Naming: Moon and Sun

Utopus creates the island and names it; he does so by articulating a continuum of land, the other side and figure of its verbal designation. It is a sort of writing on the surface of nature. But by cutting apart earthly nature, here this stretch of land, Utopus does not create a new "earth." He creates an island in the form of a celestial body, a "lunar" island. This new field of meaning is rendered by the island's name; *Utopia* is Not-Earth. It could be seen as an earth in the sky. From what seems to be free association initiated by the utopic text, we can surmise the signification of Abraxa, the name of the continent Utopus had separated by his island. The name can be deciphered by giving a numerical value to each of the Greek letters. The total is 365, and according to the Heresiarc Basilides Abraxas is a combination of celestial spheres, godly presence, ultimate power, and the highest element of the celestial hierarchy. The name *Abraxas* is all this: the most noble and the most complete, the solar year, and the generating force of the gods.[17]

By cutting the isthmus, Utopus not only separates the earth from itself; he also distances heaven and time, the solar time from ultimate power, and finds instead the lunar temporality of rhythm and repetition in the waxing and waning of the moon. This has enormous mythic significance: the moon represents the law of universal becoming within the unending periodicity of its phases. The moon is born from its own being. It destroys time in a cyclical becoming. It is death in life. Thus the island created by Utopus is a figurative "not-space" that simulates a "not-time" in its fictional spatialization as a star that is forever reborn.

In fact, this code for mythic fictional spatialization and temporality is even more complex. It is especially clear near the end of Book Two, when Raphael mentions the Utopians' religions and holidays. This solar power that the first narrative had separated and censored will return in the form of the father and as Mythra. The rules and demands of authority and of the institution also come back with him. From one end to the other of utopic discourse a lunar-solar bipolarity appears: profane space limits religious space. The first narrative of foundation emphasizes their separation and opposition; the final discourses in the text underline their conjunction. The first narrative is emblematic of a kind of disappearance of time as power and history. It is transformed into a fictional spatialization where periods and circularity reign. The latter discourse traces the return of time as a calendar of holidays and of work; it becomes a repetitive—and institutional—framework for activities and organization.

Birth, Rape

I mentioned in the island's description preceding the narrative of foundation the latent value and archaic meanings and connotation of a certain number of terms used by More. The interior gulf is described as bowels, womb, or stomach, for example. The island's center, where the capital is placed, becomes this "stomach's" navel. My methods have organized these elements around the "semic categories" of vacuum and fullness, the closed and the open, inside and outside. I claimed that the stomach-womb-bowels, or the navel, of the island seemed to bring opposites together. Spatial (and spatialized) difference inscribed by the hero in this continent begs for another "offshoot" of meaning.

In this inaugural story it seems that we are witness to both a rape and a birth: rape of the earth, which has been opened up by the hero and his army, birth by cutting the umbilical cord. Witness: "...*primo protinus appulsu victoria potitus, passuum milia quindecim, qua parte tellus continenti adhaesit, exscindendum curavit, ac mare circum terram duxit.*"[18] The images—or fantasms—pile up one on the other, and far from contradicting themselves, they come to play with the text's margins, and in the description, to create an affective level of meaning with its own internal echoes. They, in turn, set off other reverberations, forms producing forms: imagination without barriers. The island of Utopia, womblike matrix and mother, originates in a violent gesture aimed at the earth itself; its birth is work of no less violence. The narrative produces a new tension or ambivalence as a result. On the one hand is offered to us the image of a welcoming enclosed space, tranquilly situated about a center that is to be both vacuum and fullness. On the other hand we see war and violent aggression opening up space. It detaches and separates. Utopus is the male, the father; Utopia is the lunar island, enclosed and warm, the mother. This is desire wrapped in contrary figures. It traverses them successively, as if proof of itself.

But this initial violence with respect to nature is accompanied by another violence with respect to mankind: the indigenous peoples (this "*rudis atque agresti turba*" Raphael talks about) are forced to create this rupture, this distancing of their own earth from the earth. The configuration involves a reflecting of violence back on itself. Violence is "channeled"; the result will be culture on the inside, terror and astonishment on the outside. The forced labor (creating distance) serves a double function in the narrative. First it channels the conqueror's violence toward the vanquished. It must not be forgotten, all the same, that these vanquished peoples are still a part of nature, "a wild, natural society." This enterprise has all the trappings of a fundamental metaphor: that of murder in the work of the slave. The slave's travail is a deferred murder that has been displaced onto mother earth.

But by working with their conquerors the vanquished peoples channel their resentment into a violence aimed at the earth; they become a civilized—and "civil"—people. This second displacement alters the meaning of the first metaphor. Thomas More, of course, does not explicitly make the connection between the two statements, but he insists too heavily upon the channeling of forced labor into willful labor so as to not underscore this second, less psychological meaning. This signification, more sociological or metaphysical, seems evident: culture comes about through a mystification of violence, through a misplaced metaphor of murder. What would normally have been seen as an essential humiliation is altered because the conqueror works alongside the vanquished, the master with the slave. But this mystification is in itself denounced because work is carried out on the home soil of those defeated, which will, through their own labors, be severed apart by them. They are conquered twice: by the forced labor resulting from their defeat and by the fact that this forced labor is directed upon their own soil. The culture that the conqueror gives to "this rude and rustic people" cannot be separated from its narcissistic and masochistic background: those defeated defeat themselves through work on their own soil and come upon their humanity in this self-reflexive violence.

From the very first the "utopic" narrative eliminates Hegel's master-slave dialectic through the fantastic interiorization of the master in the slave (in the space of the island and text). That is what this amalgam Utopus, in his wisdom, realized. There is no dialectic in utopic discourse. It does not move through the "slow, patient and painful" mediation of the work of the negative. There is no mediation in this discourse because negation performs a totally different function. It is present from the first in the fiction of the text, and it is from this fiction in its incessant repetition that Utopia, this textual object, acquires its active poetic force. This is its neutralizing function; the narrative of foundation contains its figurative marking in the inaugural gesture of Utopus.

Writing Utopia

To come back to the letter of our text, and to conclude, four levels of meaning emerge in the creation of the island of Utopia: (1) the creation of the "lunar" island by cutting off the omnipotent sun; (2) the creation of a harmonious civilized and "civil" society by reflecting violence on itself in the form of work; (3) the creation of a world of fictional Utopians by cutting off and separating them from land; (4) the creation of a circular, repetitive, and periodic time by cutting off linear, progressive, historic time. But cutting through the isthmus of Abraxa, a series of narrative and descriptive "semes" are either joined together or separated into categories of nature and culture, earth and sky, the real and fictional, time and space. These very general categories are true pockets of meaning and permit various representations of complex polysemic groups to invest in them.

Allow me to underline only one of these groups. As we have seen, the savages of Abraxa become wise Utopians. Perfect humanization arises through the reflection of violence on itself by joining the infrahuman to the superhuman, the animal to the hero. The two join to work together against nature. This is how a perfect mankind is created. The foundation unifies Utopus' *warrior* heroes and the agrarian, earthly savages of Abraxa. Warring violence is definitively absorbed in working against the land to such an extent that the Utopians avoid direct confrontation and violence *at any price* (here, the money of betrayal). In order not to fight, they pay the Zapolets, specialized warriors who are always excluded from the island. If it were absolutely necessary, the Utopians would, of course, fight, but in that case all of them would fight, women and priests. Thus we see that there are no warriors in Utopia, and violence has been forever banned from the island. It has been banned because the island owes its creation to violence. By maintaining its expulsion, Utopia represses and buries its origin, now imperceptible and impossible to locate except in this gesture of inscribing the caesura and difference accomplished by Utopus, and whose name is metaphor itself—"No-place." More reaccomplishes the gesture by writing *Utopia* and by carefully hiding its origin. He would have us believe that his work is representation and not fiction.

Notes

Chapter 5

[1] "As the report goes..."

[2] "As the report goes and as the appearance of the ground shows..."

[3] More, *Utopia*, pp. 56 and 104.

[4] More, p. 59.

[5] More, p. 59.

[6] More, p. 60.

[7] More, p. 60.

[8]More, p. 59: "The ends form a circle five hundred miles in circumference and so make the island look like a new moon, the horns of which are divided by straits about eleven miles across. The straits then unfold into a wide expanse. As the winds are kept off by the land which everywhere surrounds it, the bay is like a huge lake, smooth rather than rough, and thus converts almost the whole center of the country into a harbor..."

[9]More, p. 59: "...which lets ships cross in every direction to the great convenience of the inhabitants."

[10]More, p. 59: "The mouth of this bay is rendered perilous here by shallows and there by reefs."

[11]More, p. 59: "The island looks like a new moon."

[12]More, p. 61: "For this city being in the very center of the country, is situated most conveniently for the representatives of all sections."

[13]Plato, *Critias*, 113b ff.

[14]More, p. 60: "As the report goes and as the appearance of the ground shows, the island once was not surrounded by sea."

[15]More, p. 60.

[16]More, p. 60: "...rude and rustic people..."

[17]More, pp. 5, 60.

[18]More, p. 60: "he...gained a victory at his first landing. He then ordered the excavation of fifteen miles on the side where the land was connected with the continent and caused the sea to flow around the land."

CHAPTER SIX

The City: Space of Text and Space in Text

In this chapter I will again deal with space and language, with places and discourses, but more specifically as interrelated in the text. Language and discourse are presented as a sort of architecture; various levels and maps are created that set up among them a complex system of relations with diverse overlappings and conjunctions. In this discourse I will also deal with spaces, in particular the hierarchical relations between different levels and maps, whose "weave" constitutes human dwellings: cities and homes. What sorts of secondary relations—secondary because we are talking about relations of relations—exist in *Utopia* between the space of the text and space in the text? Remember that the space of the text is constitutive in many ways of the utopic figure in discourse. The discourse refers to the space in the text and speaks of it in the figure utopic fiction creates. I will attempt to deal with these problems, which emerge in a few of the passages I have chosen. This questioning has a contemporary ring, also. If architecture is the art of constructing buildings and/or organizing space in order to create a space where humans can live, what is its relationship to the text? If this act involves manipulating and arranging space into a system of spaces through an architectonics of "living space," what can be said of the connection between architecture and writing and drawing, discourse and blueprint, with signs arranged on a visible surface and constantly grouped and regrouped, torn apart and rearticulated into new groups? It is not absolutely sure that a dwelling or a city is a discourse translating a blueprint into language, or a written surface transposing words and ideas (i.e., desires) into sketched figures.

Topography-Topic

Because a utopia in general is a discursive organization of space that is constituted into a specific text, it is also perhaps the best framework in which to conduct such a study. *Place* has two meanings: *topic*—rhetorical and poetic thoughts and formulae—and *topographic*—a fragment of space possessing its own unity and (often) its own name. *Utopia* is considered here as the "original" utopia, if only because of the proper name given it for this type of place and discourse. It will be the particular laboratory for my experimental analysis.

I make three remarks, first, to summarize the problem.

Narrative-Space

Scholars know that Book Two of *Utopia* was written before Book One. This means that the immediate order of reading the work, from Book One to Book Two, contrasts with another textual order that produces a remarkable effect of meaning. It is this "retroactive" reading effect that produces *Utopia* as text. From this it follows that an order is evident in the text's production. This order contradicts the syntagmatic organization of the narrative-descriptive discourse, that is, the discursive *line* of the work temporalized in an ordered and irreversible chronology of incidents and events. All this is for the benefit of a textual space: a-chronological, reversible, and structured by a system of relations and correlations through which "meaning" is produced. It is possible, in fact, to construct the political and historical discourses, the micro-utopic narratives and descriptions of Book One, based on the narrative-descriptive discourse written in Book Two. If this is true, Book Two would be syntagmatically composed of paradigmatic strata ready for our inspection. Far from constituting a number of series in absentia, they would physically form Book One in its length and breadth. As such, *Utopia* would be similar to a "poetic object," because the reader witnesses a projection of the principle of equivalency from the axis of selection onto the axis of combination. This is especially true on the level of large constitutive discursive unities. But *Utopia* also is similar to an "iconic object," because its whole function as a text, as production of meaning, consists in the effects of spatializing temporality, succession, and chronology.

Space-in-the-Text

The second comment I will make about the description and the analysis of space in *Utopia* concerns space in the text. Analysis generally develops on the surface of a text's readability. A story is told to us. A description is offered to us. We ask: What does this story tell us? What is the object offered to us in description? We immediately convert these questions into others, however: How is the story told? How is the object described? We realize that the way to tell the story constitutes the story. The story tells only the way it manages to tell it. Its object is the "narrativization" of a procedure for producing meaning. Such is the *operation* analyzing the space spoken about by the discourse. We need to transform this space, this referent, which is fictional (but do not novels and history equally partake of this fictional quality?) and is the space of a text. This is not simply a meaningful metaphor of the word "space," because this space is one of the operations, relations, and correlations that are a-chronological. Through them a narrative-descriptive discourse *speaking of space* becomes a text and produces meaning that is within, as well as way beyond, the boundaries of this apparent referent.

Space-of-Text

Finally a third note about the utopic referent, a problem that the book indirectly raises. "Where is the island of Utopia to be found?" asks More's correspondent. As we know, More explains through a third person that Raphael had been asked this question. He also answered it, but his answer was obliterated by a servant's unfortunate fit of coughing. They forgot to ask again.[1] The question concerning place had been brought up, but a "noise" interrupted the transmission of the message. This noise caused the shift in referent from being that about which the discourse speaks to being that in which the discourse speaks about. Finally the discourse is what produces it. This noise performs the closure of the discourse on itself. It makes it its own object. Perhaps it creates the utopic object as a text (space-text) by separating it from real or imaginary travel narrative.

In other words, the question about the utopic place is the very question of the text. It is a discourse organized in an intransitive way, as the discourse of its own constitution. The textual question is the result of a distraction and a detour: a sort of channeling away from the question of place. More does not want to give away the place because the place is nothing but a name. And the name is all that can be said about the place. The name is a "no-place," i.e., the very place of the text: ***Utopia is not a topography but a topic.*** It is often said that it is an imaginary place. Rather, it is an indetermined place. Better yet, it is the very indetermination of place. Actually, the narrative-descriptive discourse is going to describe and recite very precisely the place of *Utopia.* It will only be discourse, however. This is what we mean by distraction and detour: the question of the place has been channeled into the discourse where place is discussed. The discourse will speak the place; the place is nothing but the place as told, recited. Nonetheless, this distraction goes along with another detour of place into discourse. This latter development is brought about through work on the discourse itself precisely because it is a matter of place and space. The discourse works in the guise of text because it speaks of space. Space, in turn, when it is *said*, necessarily creates effects in discourse. The text is constituted by these effects; a *space of text* is created.

From the Island to the City

The organization of urban space seems to be inseparable from the description of the island's space. A topography of this space in the form of a rough sketch with its guidelines is only fitting. There we would find a structure made up of oppositional relations between the opposites that urban space produces. This second level should facilitate, if not thoroughly transform, our conception of that space. The articulation of the island's space described by the narrative functions as the paradigm of spatial organization in general that will be manipulated by this discourse. It will be repetitious at every level. The same oppositional forms will be repeated from the whole down to its constitutive elements. But while returning to every level of this description of space, the contrary oppositions cannot come to rest. We are, as it were, flying over the space of description; we are not brought along by a narrative's development. Therefore, these groups of oppositions abide by procedures of displacement, erasure, and overextension, but they do so outside the space the narrator's discourse speaks about. This other discourse, an "other" discourse (alongside the first), opens up the work of the text: space as text. I propose to study these operations.

Geography

And we thus come to the first major topographic opposition of the island *Utopia*. It is circular, but within this large circle of land a second and smaller maritime circle is inscribed. The discursive description does not tell us if the center of this circle (presenting the island) is over land or sea. Perhaps it should be considered as over both land and sea. Then it would occupy the same position on the geographic map as the complex term occupies in the structural space of its semantic substance. Read analytically, the descriptive discourse creates a notion of contrariness. It is not a completely logical notion, however. It is the contrariness between the mapped, geographic vision of the narrator and the production of figures within this vision while it is recited and while discourse takes responsibility for it. Raphael recites less than what he describes in a sort of "simultaneous succession"; this is textually given as an image or synopsis. Of course, this discourse's aim is the production of a map of the island. Or rather, this discourse aims at producing an island that would have the reality of a geographic map. It would be a limited space where nothing would be beyond its frame. More says it this way: everything "under the eyes of all."[2] No area is left hidden from the *gaze which is not included anywhere, but which views the whole as a surface.* Description can produce this map as a synoptic image only through discourse. Here the successive "prints" in discourse would constitute its map in a sort of serialization.[3] These prints do not mechanically reproduce the map of the island or one of its parts; they produce it through differential play, through variations that seem to reconcile the contraries when superposed and displaced one onto the other. These versions of the map are *figures* that are *differentially* superimposable. Their differences mark out the displacement of the spatial image within the discourse during its various successive moments.

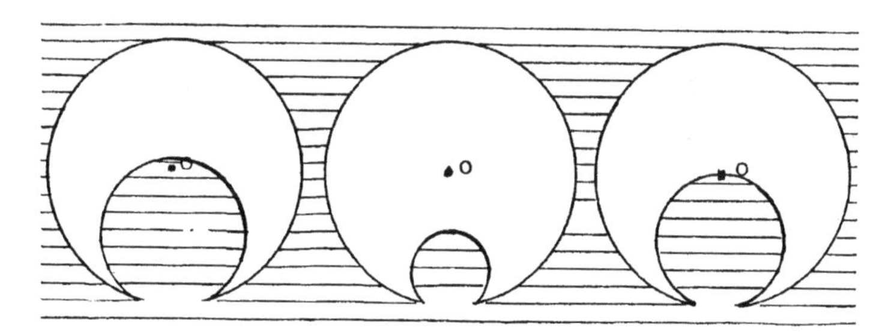

Figure 11. Possible versions of the map of Utopia

"The island contains fifty-four city-states, all spacious and magnificent, identical in language, traditions, customs, and laws. They are similar in layout and everywhere...similar even in appearance.... Amaurotum...being the very center of the country...is considered...as the capital city."[4] Here is the second topographic opposition in which the first opposition is repeated but modified: a *complex* center (land and sea) and the space it centers, as in:

$$\frac{\text{encompassing land = island}}{\text{encompassed sea = gulf}} \quad \text{and} \quad \frac{\text{encompassed land = island}}{\text{encompassing sea = ocean}}$$

The problem as it is set up here consists in the regular distribution of identical elements. The cities are all equidistant (twenty-four miles apart) in a circular space where the capital city is also the only one named, Amaurotum. In other words, because of the island's form its geography is a heterogeneous space in which the homogeneous elements that constitute it are opposed to the center. This latter element regulates and constitutes their homogeneity, however.

$$\frac{\text{multiplicity (= cities)}}{\text{uniqueness (= capital city)}} \simeq \frac{\text{identity (= spatial elements)}}{\text{difference (= the center)}}$$

$$\simeq \frac{\text{homogeneity (land // sea)}}{\text{complexity (land} \cup \text{sea)}}$$

Politics

But the articulations of this geographic and topographic space are displaced, reworked, and obscured by the articulations of the political space. Indeed, the rules of representation will insert the notion of power (or difference) into the identical and equal. The representation we speak of will be political, within the discourse of the institution. It no longer concerns a geographic or topographic representation in descriptive discourse. Every year each city elects three delegates to fulfill the representative function. They meet only in a central place. If political representation duplicates the identical quality of each geographic point (city), and if it causes geometric difference to be known (presents the circle's center), then it also becomes the metaphor for the opposition between the homogeneity of geographic space and the functional heterogeneity of circular space within this other opposition between equality among all and the privilege of a few. This latter opposition, of course, comprises the representative delegation for this totality, the group of 162 older men who meet in a city, creating a capital out of it. Here we have the political metaphor of two divergent spatial "diagrams." One involves a homogeneous stretch; it is neutral, isotropic, infinite, and continuous. The other involves a topologic figure possessing order and hierarchy (a regulatory value). This latter is defined both by its closed-in and central nature. This is true in the *equality* of all the Utopian citizens, which the representative gesture affirms in no uncertain terms, and in the *power* delegated to a few older men. In other words, the center is different, and its difference is power.

Economy

There is one last topographic remark to make before going on to analyze the city. It concerns the discovery of a socioeconomic stratum articulated by the opposition between city and countryside, urban and natural space. Keeping in mind the displaced oppositions of which the center is the complex unifying term, this new opposition reveals their meanings. It shows us simultaneously in what direction the displacement affects them and the aim that provides them with their signification. It also outlines the opposition's general form and the characteristic movement of opposites within their complex unity. The center is earthly umbilicus and maritime womb, land and sea, capital and city, place of power for older men and simple undifferentiated space for all other Utopians. This elementary conflict between land and sea, displaced, is brought to a resolution socially, politically, and economically in *Utopia.* This is done so through enormous colonialist and commercial projects. The maritime center is a port. From it are exported all surplus goods (cereals, honey, wool, wood, etc.). The land center is the city through which all precious metals pass. The city is both maritime and land-related when it comes to the contrary flow of merchandise and money. As a center, it is the very place of flux and reflux (not of the tide, but of the tide and river). As flux, the earthly river becomes sea; as reflux, the ocean becomes river. This is a periodic movement, a shrinking and swelling movement repeated as a sort of primitive rhythm. It recurs in the very opposition between city and country. The city (demographically and economically) is a highly concentrated countryside; the country, a city expanded.

Such is the general form of the movement of these elements: rhythm, periodicity, repetition, repetition of difference in identity. The utopic discourse is nothing but the different displacement of this repetition in the text. The fact that Utopian space is a space of rhythm has profound effects on the discourse that utters it. Rhythm, while affirming that all is identical, authorizes at the same time a constant descriptive metonymy. When the narrator describes a point, he describes all points; a city, all cities; a house, all houses. This identity is not just a simple identity, however. On the contrary, it is an opposition between center and space, capital and city, land and sea, etc. This opposition, however, is a periodic difference. It is a difference whose contrary elements are exchanged in their very difference. Their opposition is constantly neutralized in its affirmation. Simply put, it is *identity that is the movement of difference.* The solution of Utopian–and utopic–antinomies is perhaps in their periodic repetition. Compare this repetition with the repetition the narrative produces. This latter is the supplement that narrative dynamics introduces; it signals transformations and change. *Utopia* is not a narrative. Utopic discourse is the textual trace of the rhythm and space of which it speaks. The repetition (and not the reproduction or reiteration) of spatial oppositions, a repetition that is displaced all along the discourse, produces it as text, transforms it into a space of text. This transformation is very different from narrative transformation. It does not concern itself with content; it adds nothing to content. It is nonetheless transformation, because this immobile passage (displaced inscription of periodic traces) of space within discourse into the space of the text allows for the appearance of the empty play of exchange in the analytic discourse that studies. This is the true theoretical neutrality from which the utopic text derives all its productivity.

The City in Its Periodic Capital: Amaurotum

"The person who knows one of the cities will know them all, since they are exactly alike...I shall therefore picture one or other (nor does it matter which), but which should I describe rather than Amaurotum?"[5] Amaurotum is the seat of two privileges: it is the place of power and the place of the narrator. It is in Amaurotum that the discourse of the Senate is signaled. The Senate, recall, obtains its power by representing the whole. It is in Amaurotum, also, that the discursive enunciating subject is signaled. The descriptive discourse opens with a metonymic movement: "I shall picture one or other (nor does it matter which)..." The metonymy ends with a twofold metaphoric position. One is a spatial structure in the discourse, the other is the position of discursive production where the city is discussed. "First, none is worthier, the rest deferring to it as the meeting place of the national senate; and secondly, none is better known to me, as being one in which I had lived for five whole years."[6] The discourse describing the city is itself the metaphor of representative power that privileges this city above all the others. The representation of political power distinguishing it from all the others, this city also represents the production of the discourse about the city. In other words, the enunciating subject, because he is a delegate (Raphael with respect to More himself), is somehow related to the representation of power through the delegation of elders in the same city. This involves a movement of closure by which the discursive "imaginary" referent becomes itself the discourse, posing as its own referent.

In addition, choosing Amaurotum seems completely fortuitous. Raphael happened to spend five years in this city. Therefore, by chance, it will become the paradigm for all identical cities. This "choice" is made because of the most absolute of differences, one having neither regulation nor law. Therefore, the initial reason for the choice (the presence in Amaurotum of regulation and law, the power deciding these matters) is compromised, even erased, by Raphael's presence—having no reason or "law"—a pure event. This event (of the narrator or of the enunciating subject in the discourse he produces) removes any structural necessity for the object of his narration, for the enunciated content. A double operation of displacement and erasure comes into view: Amaurotum as a place of government in the discourse displaces/erases the position of the enunciating subject (delegate) of the discourse about the city. The object of discourse, the city, becomes involved in the movement where at its end the city is the subject of discourse. This is a reversible movement as well. It is because the city is first the subject of discourse (the city is Raphael's discursive position) that we can forget it as the object of discourse (the city is the capital, center of decision). Put in another way, utopic discourse must erase its *ideological* "origin" (among identical cities there is one that is the capital, the *head*) and its *metalinguistic* position (it is itself its own object; it has only a discourse for referent). It cannot, however, do this simultaneously. It must periodically erase one and the other pole of difference. This is the movement of difference in whose play the text is produced in its own particular space.

Central Square

"Amaurotum is situated on the gentle slope of a hill and is almost four-square in outline."[7] Built neither on a hilltop nor on the plain, Amaurotum is neither castle nor open city. The capital is first and foremost a square, a square inscribed in the center of a circle. And if the island, as circle, circumscribes a circle, the sea matrix, then the point joining them (the one in its center, the other at its circumference) is a square. The play between the limit and the center is constituted through an *other* form. It is true that the other fifty-three cities in Utopia are also square. But because there is a square in the center and on the circumference at the same time (circumscribed-inscribed circles), this square is singled out as the capital. It owes its singularity as a square to circles.

The square is the configuration that most clearly signifies the homogeneous quality of space; it entails a repetitive geometric quality, mechanical and redundant. It has no dominant part or privileged direction. But the square is here in this exceptional spot. It occupies the privileged central point that joins together the farthest inland point with the most extreme outward maritime point. Exceptional by its position, but because it is conversely ***at the center and at the edge***, it is the negation of the heterotopy and of the circumference's center with respect to the space that the circumference encircles from the center.

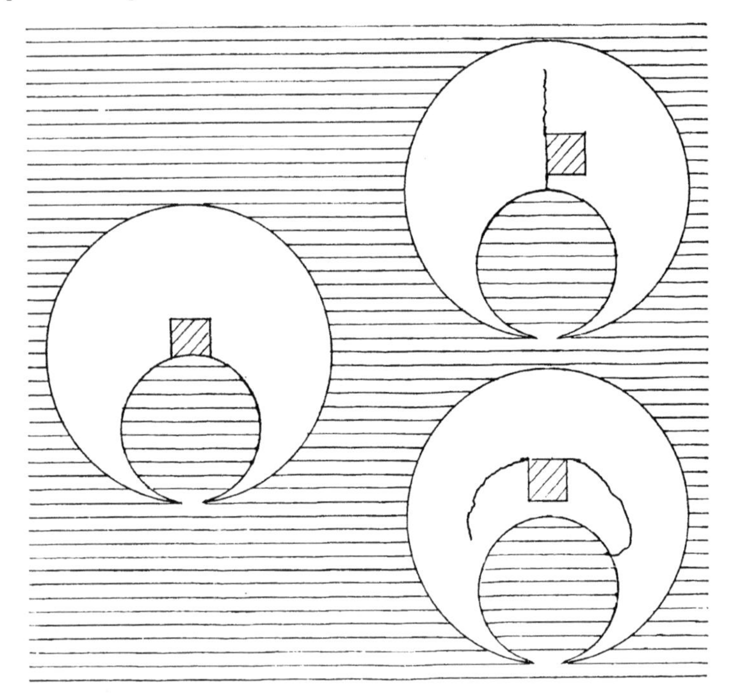

Figure 12. The central square and Utopia's circles

Figure 13. Two possible maps of Utopia[8]

As a result, displacing the first periodical rhythm we find another. The fact that the square is a city may bring about a double negation of the city as different from its surrounding space and as differentiated space. The spatial homogeneity the square carries with it compromises the square city as an articulated urban space. There is a possible twofold solution involving a quantitative limit, on the one hand, and noncongruent qualitative networks, on the other. Let's look at the first solution. The square city is surrounded by walls, but the description says nothing about the existence of gates. The walls rigorously inscribe the difference between the city space and the natural space of the countryside. There exists also an internal "closure," a demographic "ceiling" and "floor"–

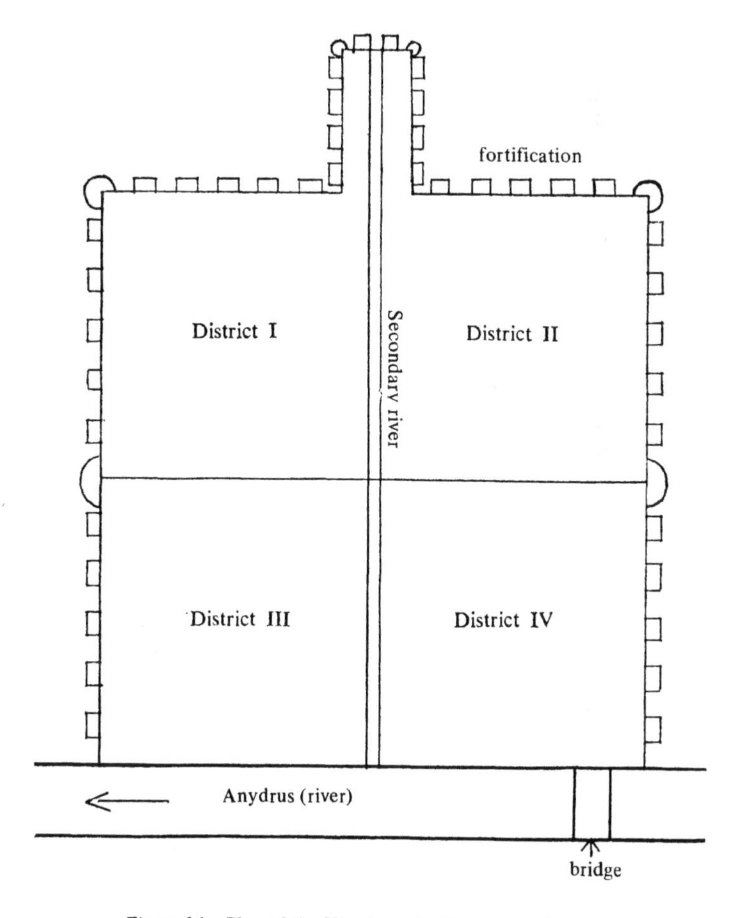

Figure 14. Plan of the Utopian city (Amaurotum)

6,000 families of not less than ten and not more than fifteen adult members. Two spatial logics are opposed here. Two topologies are expressed, each in its own "topic," simultaneously geographic, social, and political. There is the topology of the homogeneous, on the one hand, which is indicated in various ways: equality, identity, reproduction, characteristics important for a particular topic. On the other hand, a topology of difference exists; it inscribes the preceding topic into an anisotropic horizon: oriented, hierarchized, etc., whose topic is of places and not of parts, of the ordinal and not of the cardinal, of integration and composition and not of juxtaposition and exteriority.

Very different from narrative or from the dynamic logic of narrative discourse, utopic discourse does not transform one topic into another by applying a certain number of operatory rules having to do with narrative models. There is an example of this type of transformation at the beginning of Book Two. There the conqueror of Abraxa, Utopus, brings about the transformation of the continental, open, and as yet formless space into one that is circular, closed in, and insular. But from then on, with the description, we are involved in an iconic quasi-space within a discourse where the spaces it speaks about are constantly covered over by it. The topics of the same and of the other, of identity and of difference, come into play alternately. The latter is inscribed in the former as a necessary articulation. The former is the latter's necessary "material" condition for support. The figures of the one and of the other occur in the *fictitious model* of Utopia recited by the descriptive discourse. They occur at various levels in the discourse. But the model is neither discourse nor narrative. *Utopia* is not a true iconic space, and it does not tell a story. It "tells a description," a discourse where discursive figures are at play. It is a textual space which is the substitute for a transforming story, of a practice or praxis whose narrative is the outward manifestation.

The Networks of Urban Space

Three superimposable but not totally congruous networks of the urban space can be constructed. These three networks are not all equally inscribable topographically. The incongruity of articulation in the same space, and inequality in treating its various units, will reveal the traces of transformational play specific to utopic practice.

The Quarter, Street and District

The unit of the first network—the social space of the city—is the hippodamian *insula*, the quarter (*vicus*) of social space. It is a square formation of houses surrounding an open common area. There a garden is cultivated with grapes, fruits, vegetables, and flowers. The quarter (or element) of the city reproduces the city in its form. But it also closes off a space reserved for "countryside," for cultivated nature. The periodic operation affirming and doing away with the difference between city and country by exchanging twenty city-dwellers and twenty people from the countryside is here *traced* in the space spoken about in the discourse. It is done so in a complex reverse structure. The simple and reciprocal exchange of city-dwellers and country people (and vice versa), introducing only a difference of places and of local positions, is metaphorized in the stable, irreversible inscription of these places. In their structure, however, they will have to *repeat* the diachronic periodic nature of the population exchange. It is in this way that the *city, as the sum of entirely identical quarters, closes itself off to the countryside that surrounds it by means of gateless city walls. But each quarter, as a part of the city, encloses a "countryside" internal to it by means of houses having permanently open doors.* The quarter, as *part* of the city, repeats the opposition between city and country by reversing it and by reducing the scale—gearing it down, as it were, since we are dealing with space and not time, even though it may be periodic.

The unit of the second network of urban space is the street. Here it is a unit of political space. "The streets are well laid out for traffic and for protection against the winds,"[9] but it is a unit of articulation only because a "syphogrant," or "phylarch," resides there. Recall that each group of thirty families elects a magistrate once a year. "Every thirty families choose annually an official whom in their ancient language they call a syphogrant but in their newer a phylarch."[10] The thirty families are divided into groups and live on one side of the street in the phylarch's dwelling, where the communal meals are eaten in his presence. In other words, the political network based on representative delegation of power is characterized by a juxtaposition of syphogrants, just as the social network was characterized by a juxtaposition of quarters. But one syphogrant belongs to two quarters. That means that *political space breaks up the quarter centered on the community garden. It is articulated on the two sides of the street. The street is then less a means of circulation and exchange than a unit of representation* that *repeats*, in turn, the representative structure that made Amaurotum, city among many, a capital, *the* place of power on the island, through a representative delegation of the fifty-four cities of Utopia, Amaurotum included. The same can be said of the "street." The syphogrant's lodging, one dwelling among others (all identical), is the place of power on the street through representative delegation, thirty families in a phylarch.

The unit of the third urban network is the district (or economic space). "Every city is divided into four equal districts. In the middle of each quarter is a market... [where] any head of a household seeks what he and his require."[11] The district, like the city and quarter, is square. Similar to the quarter but different from the city in that it encloses something, it nonetheless encloses something that is completely open. This open area is not exactly topological (as are the house doors, which open with a slight shove); rather, it is economic. "Without money or any kind of compensation, [the head of the household] carries off what he seeks."..."No compensation except that to designated market buildings the products of every family are conveyed. Each kind of goods is arranged separately in storehouses."[12] *The center of the district is the topographic inscription of an operation of exchange, just as the center of the quarter was the topographic inscription of an operation of production. The units here are not the same spatial "level" because the district, enclosing twenty-five quarters, concentrates* the products in a central market. Then it *distributes* them among the families of these twenty-five quarters. The relationship of enclosure for the district and quarter (the same for exchange and production), in the repetition of topographic articulations at various spatial levels, is the opposite of the relationship of displacement of the street relative to the quarter, in the difference of topographic articulation, but on the same spatial level.

However, for the political realm it is clear that the district is rearticulated to the street according to the reduced system of representation, because each district proposes a candidate for the magistrature, the *principatus* (a candidate supposedly elected by members of the district). But the 200 syphogrants elect the governor by secret ballot from the list of four names specified by the people.[13] After this the three networks—social (quarter), political (street), and economic (district)—are paired up in the following way: the quarter and the street, the district and the quarter. These two pairs have only a topographic relation, whether it be one of displacement or enclosure. The street and the district have a connection simply within the political realm, but the inscription of this is impossible to find within the space the discourse speaks about.

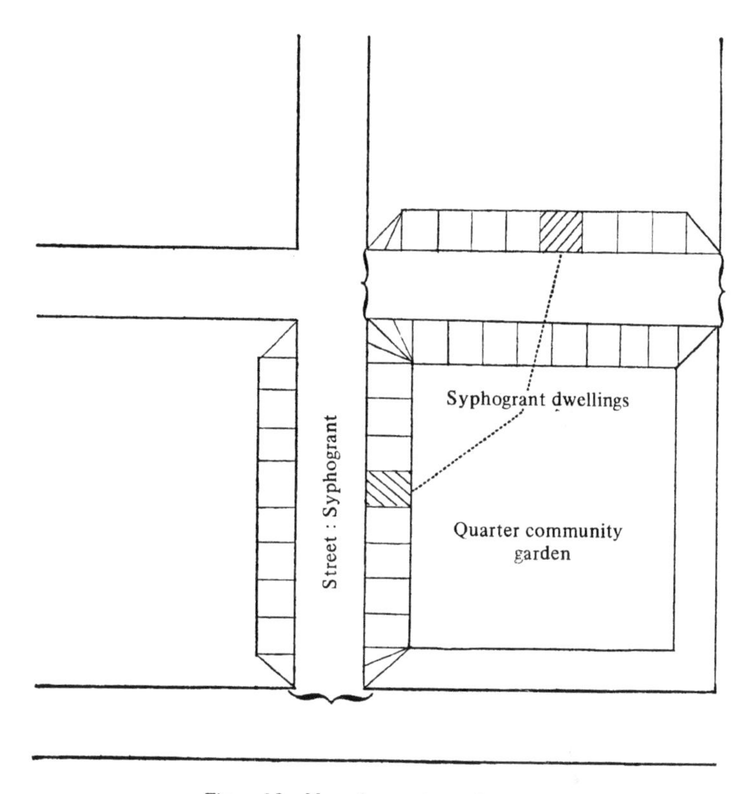

Figure 15. Map of a quarter and street.

I do not want to give the impression that it is possible to inscribe the district's central marketplace in iconic space or in the image of the map of which the utopic discourse is offered as the descriptive commentary. If the district is made up of twenty-five quarters, and if it is in the form of a square, it is very difficult to find the empty space in the center of the map where products are brought together and distributed. Doing this and keeping the form of a square and the number of districts to twenty-five are near impossible. Recall that we said a square has no center. Now we have geometric proof. But if the economic space of exchange cannot be inscribed on the map, given its rules of construction provided by descriptive discourse, it is, on the other hand, clearly inscribed in the space the discourse speaks about, in its fictitious referent. For this reason we should consider it in our analysis. Just as a square city has no center, neither can

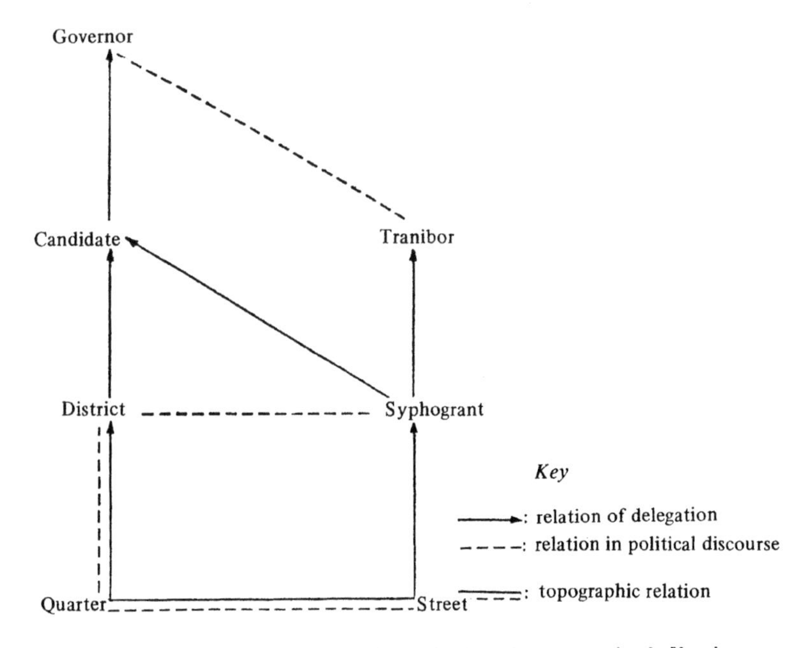

Figure 16. Diagram of the political organization of representation in Utopia

any of the "four-square" districts themselves have one. But this is for different reasons, and the utopic discourse carries marks of this difference. ***The discourse will not talk about the city's center, but it will inscribe the centers (not iconically representable) of economic exchange, while decentering other places of exchange, outside the city, and this due to still other reasons.***

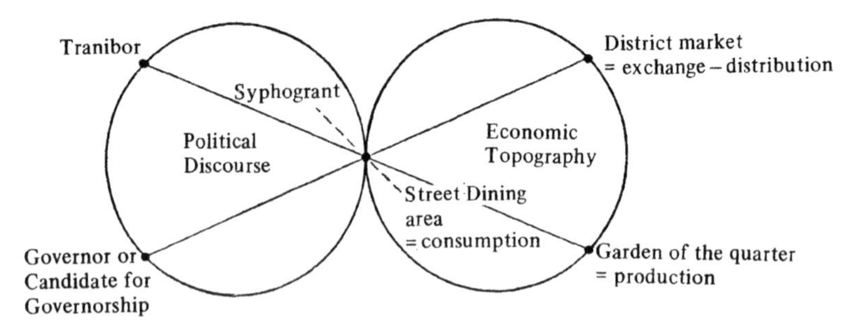

Figure 17. Articulation of topographic and discursive systems in Utopia

Incongruity

I would like to make three remarks concerning these three topographically inscribed networks in order to define the general topic of spaces they articulate, each in its order and according to its function.

The three networks are superimposed without coinciding. But each link of each network has its spatial (or topographic) center and signifier (or topic). Thus the quarter has at its center the garden. Its function is to produce consumable goods, both material (food) and aesthetic (flowers). Thus the street has at its center the syphogrant's dwelling. In this place the community dining hall serves the "function" of consumption. Finally, the quarter has at its center the market. Its function is exchange: to concentrate and distribute consumable goods. Note, however, that these different places are not centered in the same way. The marketplace cannot be inscribed on the map, even though it is in the space the discourse speaks about. This is very different from the garden, which is inscribed in the discourse and inscribable on the map. The dining hall, on the other hand, is a center in the middle of one of the sides of the street. It is not surrounded or enclosed, as is the marketplace, by quarters, gardens, or houses. It is a determined spot in a row or line facing another row or line. This fact is directly related to the position of political and economic discourse in *Utopia.*

Each center (in the broad sense) is independent of all political activity. The quarter is the unit of the social network. For the street and the district, however, things are more unusual. Each is inscribed in the space the discourse speaks about, but there they do not signify as political units (of the syphogrant) or, at the local level, in the election of the governor. Their space does not include signs. There are indices of the political function inscribed in the discourse that speaks about them. This political function, however, is essential because it differentiates a homogeneous and amorphous space by the geared-down play of representations and delegations of power.

The political function is related to both of the other networks but is inscribed in neither: it remains free, simultaneously abstract and precise, above the spaces it represents without ever giving itself away, just as institutional discourse has a certain relationship to the space the discourse talks about but does not come from. If the district's center is inscribed in the space referred to by the discourse, the Parliament's meetings are only "told," as the delegate assembly of fifty-four cities. The same holds true for meetings of the syphogrant and for this imaginary parliamentary building supposedly sheltering the deliberations of the governor and tranibors. In other words, the administrative and political centers and discursive chambers have been erased and hidden by the play of the city's spatial networks. These are, of course, superimposable, but they do not coincide. In fact, they cause the discursive structures of the political institution to vacillate. If the operations of representation and delegation for the street and district come together in the person of the governor, is he only the governor of Amaurotum, or governor of Utopia because he is Amaurotum's governor? If the latter is true, isn't his situation ambivalent, just as might seem the position of the Bishop of Rome, who is also the Pope?

Split in the Utopic Object

In any case representative democracy and gerontocratic oligarchy are reconciled in the "vibrating" position of the governor in More's political *discourse.* The Ademus are the "Not-people": the name of this people indicates the separation between the elected magistrate of the city and the island's king. "Not-people," a people nowhere—not in the city, not in the capital, not on the island: U-topic. The political function (the articulations of the political institution) in the discourse traverses this discourse in its entirety. The executive utopia represents and sums up (nowhere) representative ubiquity (everywhere). The governor is nowhere; election by the people is everywhere. It is perhaps nowhere because it is everywhere. Let it suffice here to say that this chain of delegations by which the Utopian people express their power cannot be inscribed in the space referred to by discourse. However, it is unfolded and revealed in Utopia's constitutional discourse, the discourse constitutive of Utopia itself.

Conversely, the number of centers inscribed in the city's space indicate, as if indices or signs, three moments in the economic process: production, exchange, consumption. There exist areas of production, the *quarters*, which are different from the units involving consumption, the *streets.* There an exchange is necessary to bring about their displacement and dismemberment, to be brought back into a structural ensemble that would include both of them and articulate them on each other: the *districts.*

Thus we note the split in the utopic object in the city: the space *in* discourse carries along with it indices or signs of the multicentered economic process that is connected among its various networks, circuits, and units. The space *of* discourse clarifies and *presents the meaning(s)* of the political institution while keeping absent from the capital city in its topographic inscription. Present as u-topic in the textual space, the political realm designates within this very space its other, reality, about which it speaks while speaking about the political. This is the construction of economic processes.

The utopic discourse's very minutely detailed description (in a meta-linguistic position) of the city's space and its discursive networks all reveal blind spots and empty spaces in it. These are the political places that have been erased from the map, the space the discourse speaks about. These political spaces have been considered as the institution's places of discourse. On the other hand, the various political units shown to be the places of the institution's discourse can be found only outside the political realm: in the dining hall or at the marketplace, namely in the *inscription* of two phases—one intermediary, the other final—of the economic process. Exchange and consumption are a result of the productive activity of the quarter and garden, a nonpolitical social unit.

The political is present in discourse but absent from the map, the space of reference by discourse. Because of this absence it designates the economic process. In turn, the economic process is *indicated* on the map in referential space, supporting the "meaning" of political organization while being developed independently of it in utopic discourse. This is a switch between topography and discourse, between the political and economic. Through the play, or application, of the networks that constitute space in the discourse, the space of the text is promoted as its nascent truth. This space must allow the text to signify from the very place we utter the present discourse.

Chiasmus of Space and Discourse

The problem created by the social and political articulation of the economic process must consequently be reexamined. This problem is raised by the chiasmus of space and discourse in the utopic text.

It is clearly the shift between the networks in the social and political spaces—the quarter and the street—that causes exchange to occur. The unit of consumption, the street, does not coincide with the unit of production, the quarter. In addition, the community of the quarter (communally exploiting the garden and engaging in a purely aesthetic competition with the other quarters) cannot consume what it produces because it is split up between four syphogrants. The unit of consumption must resort to another kind of unity of distribution in order to work. Therefore the central marketplace of the district exists. It is inscribed in the referred space of the discourse, but it is not on the map. The quarters constitute the economic network, which here is simply one of exchange. Currency does not exist in Utopia; the operations of exchange involve simple operations of redistribution with an aim toward the communication between the quarter that does not eat what it produces and the street that does not produce what it eats.

Marketplace and Dining Hall

The districts' marketplace thus seems to be the semantic juncture between the enclosed "plenitude" of the quarter and the open "vacuum" of the street. In fact, the central market is both reserve and expenditure. This may be the fundamental reason why it is impossible to inscribe the market on the map. The market is an expenditure in the exact proportion that it is a reserve. This is precisely the dictionary's definition of an *economy*: savings in expenditure and, conversely, expenditure in savings. The marketplace is the reserve generated by the garden's production; it is the place of juncture for the "full"—the social community and profuse production—and the "empty"—representation, delegation, and consumption. Both full and empty, the marketplace is exchange not only in terms of the economy described in the utopic discourse, but also in semantic terms, the various city spaces. It is the means of communication of the two, the first and the last, of the urban networks. Because of this it appears inscribed in the space referred to by discourse as to ensure its coherence. It makes the different parts communicate, allowing for the exchange of meaning that is constitutive of the text.

Metonymy and the Political and Economic

The political institution is not inscribed in the urban topography. Its indication is absent except in one spot: the place of consumption, in the middle of one of the two sides of the basic units of political representation. The thirty families electing the syphogrant constitute the two sides of the street. In the middle is the dining hall, where the elected official presides. It is in this spot, at this point, that the institutional space of discourse is articulated with the space utopic discourse speaks about, with urban topography. Notice that this central place of the political network's unit is not a political unit. It is, rather, the place of consumption for the group, which is defined politically. But it is also in this twofold spot that the utopic institution causes the initial distortion in the economic process. The producer does not eat what he produces (in the quarter's garden) while in the syphogrant dining hall. But the initial distortion is followed by the solution—the district's central marketplace inscribed in the space the descriptive discourse (of the city) speaks about. As a result the political institution's discourse is able to flourish completely in the topography, or topic, of the economic process. It can do so both through a metonymy due to a twofold tangent between the space referred to by discourse and the space of discourse itself, and through a hidden metaphor, one I will attempt to clarify using the functional differentiation of the various realms.

The metonymic displacement of the political discourse into the economic process necessarily brings about the supersession of the self-sufficient stage of the closed domestic economy. There, producer (P) and consumer (C) are identified with one another. It also overthrows the stage of simple exchange or barter, where the producer of a product (P_1) gives it to a consumer (C_2), himself a producer of a product (P_2), which he gives to consumer (C_1), the producer of a product (P_1). The barter circuit is mediated by the market (M). Political discourse (with the shift we saw in the specific political network) demands this form of economic process.

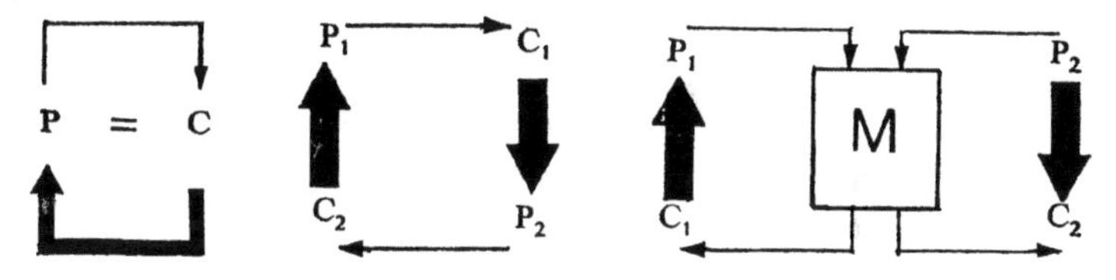

Figure 18. The processes of exchange

Money

We are thus witness to the confrontation between space-in-discourse and space-of-discourse, between the networks inscribed in the space referred to by discourse and those of this written discourse. Resulting from this is the transformation of product into commodity. The market is the center of the district; it inscribes the following *thesis* in urban space: the incongruity of the social and political networks resolves into an economy of exchange in the market. The producer does not consume the products of his own labor; he consumes the product of someone else's labor. But he does not simply barter with this other producer, *because he is in the place of exchange*, the market. When the product of labor comes into the place of exchange, it becomes commodity; when it comes out, it is again a product, but of consumption. In short, in these centralized places (in the squares of the districts which are the unrepresentable substitutes for the centers of the city's squares) products are bought and sold. The market is generalized and presented as the rational stockpile of all products. It is the taxonomic system in which all the particular products of labor for each family are multiply classed and sorted. The market is a place *of places*, within the space of the city, where products become generalities, "exchangeables," concepts and/or commodities.

The central marketplace of the district, in short, inscribes *money* into the referred space of discourse. Money is the present and irrepresentable "place," the *topos*, the universal and abstract equivalent of all products. It is the figure of an "abstract reality." The market as the district's center is money: the money so carefully rejected from the utopic city. It is the metaphoric figure of gold, which had been rejected from Utopia's social, political, and economic relations. More precisely, the market is the metaphoric figure, in space and as space, of the process of separating the product's exchange and use values. Recall that the shift between the social and political networks had signified the same thing in the city's space that was talked about by the utopic discourse.

But the district is *also* a group of 1,500 families who choose candidates for the highest political function: governor. The district's unrepresentable center is the market, place of commodity and figure for money. This analogy reveals the metaphor that is constitutive of space in the text, because designating a candidate for governor is in the *political institution's discourse*; this agrees with the constitution of an abstract universal equivalency in the "*course*" *of economic value*, both concealed and unthinkable, but present in the market as *the place of inscription in space the text talks about*, even if (and especially if) it is unrepresentable on the map. It is a plural space, for there are four of them, into which this *other* place bursts: *no where* inscribed on the map, *nowhere* written in discourse, the place of places for the city, the place of the governor. The marketplace is substituted for it or represents it; it displaces his place or explains it in space as that place where the city communicates with itself in the exchange of commodities.

There is an interesting textual mark of this operation. Recall that this operation involves the displacement and condensation of political discourse revealed by its own space (designating a candidate for the function of governor) in the district's market. It appears in the space utopic discourse speaks about, but the "course" of economic value is concealed by it in this very space (the split between use value and exchange value in the monetary sign of this separation). We can sketch the textual mark of this operation: there is no *money* inside the city, but there are markets there. There is much money *outside the island*, and there are markets *outside the city*.

In effect there are two types of markets connected with the city: the first, which we just examined, involves the exchange of products made by each family. There are, on the other hand, outside markets, "storehouses, where are brought not only different kinds of vegetables, fruit and bread, but also fish.... Outside the city are designated places where all gore and offal may be washed away in running water." These markets share this mark of exteriority (with respect to the city) with the hospitals (there are four, also outside the city walls). In other words, *exteriority connotes refuse, rot, and sickness.*

Outside Commerce

In addition, another noteworthy characteristic is brought out by comparing the island's internal exchange system with its external commerce. This first system is one of compensation between abundance and scarcity, due to the centralization of economic data and to the decisions taken by Amaurotum's senate. Recall that this organism has its "centrality" nowhere inscribed within the capital city.

> [The government] at once fills up the scarcity of one place by the surplus of another. This service they perform without payment, receiving nothing in return from those to whom they give. Those who have given out of their stock to any particular city without requiring any return from it receive what they lack from another to which they have given nothing. Raphael-More continues, Thus the whole island is like a single family.[14]

This means that the system of a closed domestic economy expands to include the whole island. The shift between the social and political networks had ensured going beyond the city to a commercial system inscribed in the district's market. There is thus in the process a circularity that repeats, in compensation and periodicity, the inscribed-circumscribed circularity of the island and gulf. As for the process on the level of the entire society, it compensates and cancels out its distortion, even though distortion is necessary (but to what extent?) on the level of these smaller, partial societies the cities make up.

Political Discourse and Economic Topography

Outside commerce allows for the flow of surplus commodities and for the importation of needed products: "The only thing lacking is iron." But this involves a whole *commerce* that brings many things to the island: "a great quantity of silver and gold, this exchange has gone on day by day so long that now they have everywhere an abundance of these metals, more than would be believed."[15] But gold and silver are used in two ways, as *currency* and as metal, as sign and material substance. They are a sign of currency for relations outside the island; gold and silver will pay the mercenary troops who defend the island against external enemies, or the metals could even be used to "pay off" these enemies, or to provoke disorder and betrayal in their ranks, or to encourage civil war. Inside the island gold and silver will be used to make slaves' chains and citizens' chamber pots. Gold and silver thus also are related, somehow, to crime and to refuse. A chain of equivalent semantic dimensions can be set up to summarize these first ideas:

[interurban market : extraurban market] : : [internal exchange : external commerce] : :

[simple distribution by exchange : distribution mediated by signs] : : [beauty goodness : refuse disease crime] : : [island : external world]

The fundamental operator of the topography of places, as it is for the topic of discourses, is the topological semantic category interior//exterior, which allows for the valorization of the paradigmatic contents "markets," "relations of exchange," "economic processes," in their negative and positive relations. The equivalencies put forth above include an even more general correlation: that between the utopic discourse and the political, or historical, discourse. This correlation is shown in *Utopia* in the way Book Two is related to Book One; the first is truly utopic, the second is political and historical, containing a few utopic pockets. Look in particular at the entire discussion between More and Raphael concerning monetary problems. It moves through successive allusions to historical events (the financial policies of Henry VIII, the monetary activities of Edward IV, Henry VII, Henry VIII, and Edward VI, the fiscal policies of Henry VII, Edward IV, et al.) and to the micro-utopia of the Macarians, Utopia's neighbors. These people in their micro-utopia function as the antithetical corollary to historical and political discourse. A last equivalency must be appended, Utopia : history. This completes the entire span of *Utopia*'s content through a relational series, positions of internal homologies. Form cannot be disengaged from content; utopia is but an instrument working on reality in a very specific way.

We return to the correlative elements of the political discourse. Ademus, the governor, is "Not-people," "nowhere." He is situated neither within the space of the map nor in the space referred to in utopic discourse. This governor represents and reverses the ubiquitous nature of the political, itself unsituated in this same space. Is not this function articulated by the institution's discursive places? Starting with the political discourse's shift into the economic process, we can try to construct a utopic *textual space* in a diagram. The unbroken lines correspond to the manifest portion of it, whereas the dotted lines represent the hidden or latent relations. The right side of the diagram symbolizes the *discursive* political system; the left side, the *topographic* economic system. It is clear that here, in this diagram summarizing our preceding analyses, *money* occupies the position of the governor on the left, but as a *"blank" spot in discourse*, corresponding to the *"blank" of the spot of the governor* when we reverse it. Money, the pivot in the "commercial" formulation of the early capitalist economy (C - M - C), is erased from discourse, just as the governor's palace is erased from the urban space (uttered in the discourse): The *u-topic governor* is the positive *logographic figure* of a *u-logic reality; money* is only shown metaphorically and symbolically in its *negative topographic figure, refuse.*

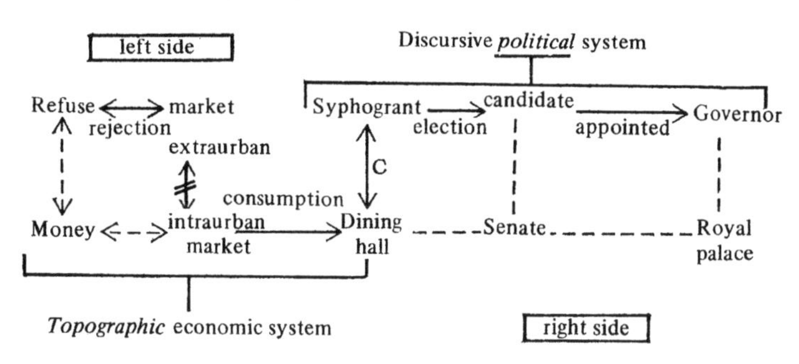

Figure 19. Diagram of the internal process of exchange in Utopia

As for the external economy of Utopia, its outside "commerce" can be explained by another diagram (Figure 20) that just transposes our previous analyses and the relations in the preceding diagram:

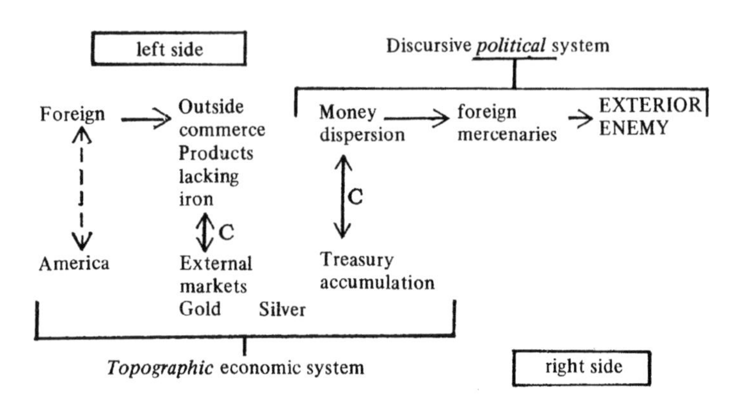

Figure 20. Diagram of the external process of exchange in Utopia

The central portion of Figure 20 should be explained, however, as should the left side, America. Recall the importance of the treasure accumulated in Utopia after the commercial exchanges with the outside have taken place. This "vast treasure," More shows a few lines later, is gathered together, "but not as a treasure. They keep it in a way which I am really quite ashamed to reveal for fear that my words will not be believed." This method of *accumulating* a gold treasury consists not in *conserving* it, but in dispersing it *everywhere:* "from gold and silver, they make chamber pots and all the humblest vessels for use everywhere...They employ the same metals to make the chains and solid fetters which they put on their slaves. They make gold and silver a mark of ill fame."[16] Money is everywhere, and its accumulation is a dispersion in Utopia; it is the container for refuse, crime, and infamy. Money, just as we saw for the political function, is nowhere because it is everywhere, negatively. "If in Utopia these metals were kept locked up in a tower, it might be suspected that the governor and the senate...were deceiving the people by the scheme and they themselves were deriving some benefit therefrom."[17] It is the recipient of no topographic inscription and will become a monetary sign only in the discourse of foreign policy, where it is one of the instruments.

There is an exterior geographic place, however, in which this ambivalent figure—gold and silver, as sign and metal—comes to be really inscribed. This place is outside the island, exterior to utopic discourse, because the island has no place other than its name's utterance: it involves America. Why America? Because the New World hovers on the horizon of the utopic discourse, far off from the island Utopia, *terra* still *incognita*, a place different from the historical and political land that is Henry VIII's England. In the space that More-Raphael's discourse talks about, U-topia inscribes the separation and difference between historical time and geographic space. It inscribes the limit not only of the known and unknown world, but also between historical time and geographic space. This "place" is neither one nor the other; it is the neutral term impossible to inscribe on a map, impossible to record in history. Wasn't Raphael one of Amerigo Vespucci's companions, and wasn't the island to Utopia described in Raphael's discourse somewhere over toward America?

Our second diagram can thus be put into language. *Pan-Utopic money* is the *negative logo-graphic figure* of an *u-logic reality, America*, itself shown only metaphorically and symbolically in its *negative topographic figure:* the outside. As a general rule, on the island, *money* and *America* are the two realities hidden by the utopic discourse. Outside the island money is the abstract universal equivalent for exchange value; America is the concrete geographic place of the metal where this value finds meaning. These two realities are not dissimulated as such. They are dissimulated only in their concepts and in the theory where they exist as (1) the objectified form of social work and (2) the characteristic place of a form of precapitalist exploitation. Even though they are unthinkable as theoretical concepts, utopic discourse nonetheless sporadically marks their empty positions in its play. Utopic discourse, as enunciation, is produced by a historically situated narrator and is caught in particular historical, economic, and social contexts. As such, and with reference to this context, it sets up a signifying praxis whose utopic discourse is the "playful" manifestation of topographics and topics created by this discourse.

Tentative Propositions

Social theory, in its scientific essence (or in its theoretical concept), consists in—

1. seizing the real in a reverse logical statement, and
2. constructing this statement independently from its apparent relations.

Utopic signifying praxis, as opposed to scientific theory, consists in:

1. A shift *outside* a historically determined place (an indefinite place). But this shift will allow for a *figure.* With theory we arrive instead at a concept (for example, money or exploitation) through the manipulation of surface social structures;

2. Anticipating, but blindly. The *present* for More (or his delegate in language, Raphael) does not have the objective possibility of constructing its theory's concepts. Here we encounter the notion of an epistemological break. The utopic figure presents this possibility, not in its theoretical power but in a poetic and representative form. Utopia does not construct the concept or the theory. It builds a stage; it makes a space of representation that, in a certain way, is the schema corresponding to the construction of the concept, but blindly.

Utopia constructs a space (the *space-in-the-text*) made up of articulated spaces. They are places about which the discourse speaks. This constructed space-in-the-text allows for the analysis of "white zones," *terrae incognitae* that do not show up semantically in the utopic discourse, in the *space-of-the-text*, unless displaced or condensed in a figurative form. These white spaces on the utopic *map*, signified blindly by utopic discourse, are the places for unthinkable theoretical concepts in forms to be thought about. Therefore the comparative analysis of the differences that control utopic space, in the text and of the text, leads to the development of the historical conditions of possibility for theory.

Additional Note

The same type of analysis could be used to look at the ultimate spatial unit of the city: the house receiving the thirty families of a syphogrant during a community meal. The dining hall and disposition of the members repeats the noncoincidental superimposition of the various networks I noted on the larger level of the city. Each table performs the articulations between age and sex. The women are seated on one side of the table, the men on the other. Along with this segregation according to sex, on each side of the table an older person alternates with a younger person. The syphogrant and his wife sit across from each other in the center, the position of surveillance and command. This center has no political value, however; it only has a familial or paternal signification. There is a repetition of sex and age differences in the sameness of a single oppositional structure. Refer to Figure 21, and note that each table is made up of a series of four-person units: two men, two women, two young people, two older persons.

On the level of both the home and the city there are phenomena of rejection that can be noted. Gathered outside the city walls (without gates) we find

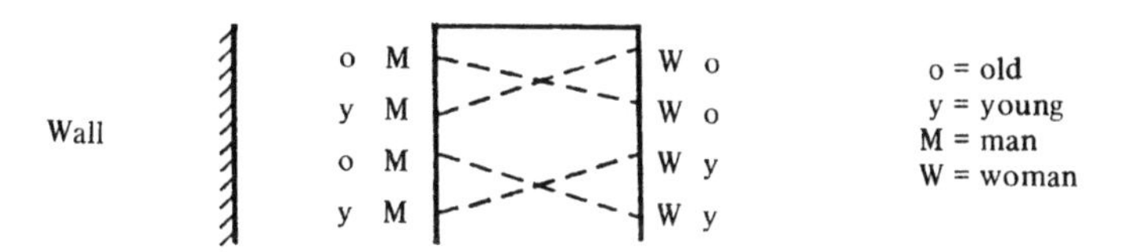

Figure 21. Diagram of the table seating in Utopia

hospitals, slaughter houses, and butchers, all expulsed from the city. Separated from the dining hall, similarly, we find young children and their nurses (the women who take turns caring for the children). The sick and the butchers find no place within the city walls. The one dirties the city by his condition, the other by his function. The child is also excluded from the family's gathering-place during meals. Thomas More rationally justifies this rejection in all three cases. But is there more? These are symptoms, but of what? What are the risks? Would the city's equilibrium and harmony be threatened? The sick person and the butcher both are connected with death: the one awaits it, the other gives it. No one is forced to go to the hospital, yet no one prefers treatment at home rather than the hospital. Conversely, it is against the law for citizens to become butchers: slaves take care of slaughter. It is feared that people would slowly grow accustomed to it and that humanitarian feelings, the most noble in the hearts of mankind, would disappear. Both butchers and the sick are related in that refuse, animal matter, the butcher's garbage rot, spread illness. There is thus the expulsion of illness, of violent death, and of the disorderly spontaneity of life at its beginnings. Anything threatening the rhythms and orderly variation in the repetition of difference in identity must be rejected from the enclosed and harmonious totality of the city or of the dining hall. There differences are but the internal vibration of the whole. Just as the Zapolets, the warriors, had been carefully kept outside the island, so also the butchers and the sick are forbidden to enter the city, and young children the dining hall. In every case violence is rejected, whether it be the violence of death or life, given or received. And this because violence is the absolute beginning, the pure starting point, the decisive rupture.[18] As we have seen, this violence must be rejected from Utopia because it was there at its origin. It was like the founder Utopus-More's act of writing. It must forever be hidden, denied, and rejected from the utopic object, but it nonetheless remains in its textual self-referentiality as a pure fiction, and founds and creates it.

Notes

Chapter 6

[1] See Peter Giles' letter to Jerome Busleyden already quoted.

[2] More, p. 83.

[3] See Brian R. Godey's article in the *Geographical Review*, (January, 1970), pp. 15-30, "Mapping Utopia, A Comment on the Geography of Sir Thomas More."

[4] More, p. 61.

[5] More, p. 63.

[6] More, p. 63.

[7] More, p. 64.

[8] These two maps are schematic reconstructions. The first is a result of two engravings accompanying the first editions of *Utopia.* The other is constructed from the island's description in the text. Both are possible. The first one gives the predominance of the circular structure. The other shows the circular structure articulated by the diametric structure.

[9] More, p. 65.

[10] More, p. 67.

[11] More, p. 77.

[12] More, p. 77.

[13] More, p. 67.

[14] More, p. 83.

[15] More, p. 84.

[16] More, pp. 84–86.

[17] More, p. 85.

[18] The system of rules and laws governing Utopian travel within the island may also be a part of this rejection. Traveling means breaking the ritualized rhythmic changes between rest and work in a specific spot. It introduces the unforeseen. In fact, it means creating new pathways in time and in space. Thus, here again, travel is a form of rupture and violence regarding totalities, whether they be habitual, ritual, or spatial.

CHAPTER SEVEN

Criminal and Proletariat

There is another kind of spatial play that is characteristic of utopic praxis. This play is perhaps more difficult to grasp than that which simultaneously regulates and disturbs the island and city in order to get at the empty places, the *terrae incognitae*, in *Utopia*'s text, revealed by the incongruity of their successive mappings. Later the concepts of social theory will bring them together in the text of history. This spatial play is not so easily glimpsed because the space it orders is neither geography (even if imaginary) nor geometry (even if non-Euclidean). It is the result of a former construction, itself the result of a careful and precise analytic reading. At each step of its discourse and movement what it has achieved is brought into this imaginary space raised to a second order. This space performs for the human sciences of today the function utopia performed for social reflection in the past: the space of a model.

We should have read, rather than immediately rewritten, the descriptive discourse in its mapped figures. Then we could have used them in a second discourse to judge the shifts among them. Here we reverse the process. The "epistemological" figures will be secondary; they will explain what the first discourse dissimulated in the dialogue which seemed to move too easily. In the meantime, from one study to another one reading has become retroactive: it sent up, rather than down, the flow of writing. It went through the book backward. It traversed the volume "involutively," though maintaining its order of creation, the hierarchy of its own history, and the time of its author. In the meantime we went from imaginary geography to real history, from a synoptic description to an analytic and exploratory narrative, from Utopia to Henry VIII's England, from Book Two to Book One of the text.

This backward movement in no way excludes literary fiction; one of the most lucid analyses of an economic and historic situation ever written is the staged banquet scene, performed around a table and involving a dialogue between Cardinal Morton, Raphael Hythlodaeus, and guests. Here a Machiavellian and a

Utopian, a historical hero and a fantasmatic herald, confront each other.[1] Through a strange reversal the strictest historical truth will creep into the side of imaginary speech. This comes about, in addition, because of a clever trick, and More, Machiavelli, and the other guests are all ignorant of it. Simply placing Amerigo Vespucci's companion and the cartographer of *Utopia* together at the table of this "fifteenth-century Talleyrand"[2] would not be sufficient to recognize the major traits of utopia within the scene of this fictional dialogue (satire is common in these passages, which authorize and promote the most persuasive critiques of current mores). In addition, we note a first textual fissure. The text is separated from itself, and it is here where utopia enters into the discourse. This fact, here, during the most "historic," sociological (or economical) moment in the text, is not bereft of meaning. Utopic practice cannot enter into the text without intruding vertically, without interrupting it in order to give it another dimension, a discourse within discourse: can it also be something else? Utopic practice does not continue the discourse of history, sociology, or economy in order to complete or perfect it in an asymptotic truth. Rather, it distracts and deters it, deters it from itself to utter, in a figure outside this discourse the truth it was powerless to formulate.

> "What," I asked, "were you ever in our country?" "Yes," he answered, "I spent several months there, not long after the disastrous insurrection of western Englishmen against their King, which was put down with their pitiful slaughter. During that time I was much indebted to the Right Reverend Father, John Cardinal Morton, Archbishop of Canterbury, and then also Lord Chancellor of England..." "It happened one day that I was at his table when a layman, learned in the laws of your country, was present..."[3]

It is in this way that More, author of *Utopia*, diminishes the marvels of fiction to affirm very exactly the time of the meeting—a de facto necessity of historical past—and the elements of chance. "It happened one day that I was at his table..." just as Raphael happened to be in Amaurotum for five years. Utopic practice cannot become part of historical discourse without the absurdity of an isolated event, completely out of character, for no other reason than the necessity of its own intervention.

Theft: Theology and Sociology

The topic here at this meal is theft and its legal repression. [It should be noted that this crime is not any general crime.] It involves specifically theft, its merciless punishment, and the paradox of this punishment. "The layman, learned in the laws of England...began to speak punctiliously of the strict justice which was then dealt out to thieves. They were everywhere executed, he reported, as many as twenty at a time being hanged on the gallows, and added that he wondered all the more, though so few escaped execution, by what bad luck the whole country was still infested with them."[4] The thesis that Raphael so "freely" defended in front of the Cardinal is twofold, de facto and de jure. De jure: the death penalty is too severe for the crime of theft. "Theft alone is not a grave offense that ought to be punished with death." De facto: "No penalty that can be devised is sufficient to restrain from acts of robbery those who have no other means of getting a livelihood."[5] For him this point is essential, and examining it bolsters his argument. The lawyer knows the law, but only the law. At this moment in history, seeking the objective causes for England's criminality is more important than theologically affirming the unequal nature between human life and money. More precisely: this ethical and theological affirmation has become separated in form and in content from the examination of causes. The distinction between de facto and de jure continues, forcing a fissure between the historical and the theological, between the sociological and the moral.

This fissure may be related directly to the creation of the utopic figure. Theological discourse of and by itself is unable to articulate causes and the basis for them. This is perhaps because this basis is not to be found on a moral or theological level. It is perhaps this fissure, then, or its lack, that allows for the irruption of the utopic figure in More's discourse. Here we find an indication (this time totally negative) of utopic practice on the level of the text's content. It would be similar to the slight shift I tried to explain betwen the "isotopic" systems of mythic narrative, but here in the didactic discourse of political and historical order. This discourse has two levels, because the ontological legitimation—moral or theological—is absent from it. The two levels are juxtaposed and hierarchically related, but in a heterogeneous way. Human life cannot equal a sum of money. Therefore, thieves cannot be sentenced to the gallows. How this de jure argument (theologically well founded—one commentator has mentioned Exodus XXII[6]) can in turn provide a basis for the objective analysis of the problem of theft, then move on to the logical policies that emerge from them (here, the seizure of enclosures), is certainly a problem. The utopic intervention will emerge in this hiatus by covering objective truth with a fundamental theological proposition. Utopic practice will imply that the equivalency between human life and money is somehow related to extending the grazing land for sheep. The manifest discourse was unable to do that because it moves by concepts and by subsuming experience under distinct categories of thought. Utopic practice, on the other hand, moves by figures and symbols, by fiction and simulacra of experiences.

Reversal

A reversal of the ethical or theological basis of the de jure proposition would have been necessary: "I think it altogether unjust that a man should suffer the loss of his life for the loss of someone's money. In my opinion, not all the goods that fortune can bestow on us can be set in the scale against a man's life." Because "God has said, 'Thou shalft not kill,'...God has withdrawn from man the right to take not only another's life but his own. Now, men by mutual consent agree on definite cases where they may take the life of one another."[7] Reversing this statement shows that, far from there being an ethical or theological basis, we only perceive one that is economic. It is not God; it is the sheep. It is not a question of international law dictated on Mount Sinai, but rather the imminent consequences of a productive process. The statement of law is reversed and becomes its contrary; it is explained and justified by it. Human life equals a finite sum of money or possessions. Raphael's affirmation of nature's heterogeneity ("Not all the goods that fortune can bestow on us can be set in the scale against a man's life.") is but an illusion, hiding a quantitative equation: human life = money. But for the illusion to appear as such, human life must somehow be reduced or related to a quantitative element. It is this reduction (and how strangely unconscious it is) that, symbolically, will be created in the utopic figure. It is also strange to see that it will be this figure that justifies what it would have hoped to denounce. It was to demonstrate, de jure, gross injustice and, de facto, the inefficient nature of the English penal system. Yet, on the contrary, it will justify it.

The Political and Social Discourse

What, then, is Raphael's exemplary analysis of the causes of theft in England? It has a twofold development, and Raphael's proposed social and economic solution emerges from them both.

Causalities

The first cause of the increase of crime and theft is the breaking up of the feudal manor. The lord is surrounded by vassals and men of arms who do not work. They live in the luxury and abundance of their master, and when he dies (as often happened during the War of the Roses), these dependents are jobless and penniless. They are rejected by other noblemen, peasants, and workers.[8] There is thus formed an army of potential, then real, thieves. They make up a sort of *Lumpenproletariat*; creating a professional army would make use of them neither in wartime nor, a fortiori, in times of peace.

The second cause of theft comes from the establishment of a precapitalist competitive-market structure.[9] Large landowners convert their farmland into grazing areas for sheep. They enclose communal and unused pastureland by joining it to their own domain, then become wealthy by selling the wool. This economic mutation triggers a rural exodus to the cities. There the peasants are unemployed because they only know how to work the land. They are thus reduced to theft and vagrancy.

In both of these cases, but for different reasons and according to a reverse social motivation, a social group has been sent away from a structure of which it was a part. It is now estranged from the newly constituted structure, and adopts a corresponding social behavior. It is marginal and behaves in a way society forbids. But in the first case the rejected group is residual; it is made up from the pieces broken off from the feudal community, which had been based on individual relationships. In the second case a true social class has been separated from the means of production by a radical change in the productive processes and by the emergence of new forces and forms of production. Raphael and More do not seem to connect the two causes: the rising movement of the second is the "positive" side of the degenerating movement of the first. "Yet this is not the only situation that makes thieving necessary, there is another which, as I believe, is more special to you Englishmen."[10]

If we combine these analyses and reduce them to their essential elements, we can construct a model in which different social groups are arranged in a schematic diagram. A comparison between conformities and nonconformities can then take place. This would comprise an articulated sociological or epistemological space that refers to a geographic, cultural, and social space. It then could translate certain chosen relations for us. This space is once removed from our original one, because it is an analytic mediation of geography, demography, and history. It would be capable of "play," however, just as the schematic spaces of the utopic island and city have been. The space of the model constructed by reducing the analysis of a social and economic historical juncture is on the same level as utopic space, offered by an imaginary description. The only difference between them is that one is made by the reductive analysis of a real contemporary situation, whereas the other is provided by a figurative synopsis. Being on the same level authorizes the use of transformational operations and manipulations that are similar in nature. Here utopic practice meets historical discourse. Both constitute a homogeneous material for an analysis that seeks out the traces of transforming forces in the structures they inscribe in the form of texts and figures.

The two diagrams in Figure 22 translate the twofold causal process analyzed by Raphael. The arrows indicate a relation of opposition, or contrariety, between the two elements of the diagram. The continuity of similar processes is highlighted by building the two diagrams. Actually Raphael-More juxtaposes only the essential points. By inscribing in phase 2 of diagram 1 the shared element of property, "sheep," between noblemen and peasants, we obtain the first phase of diagram 2. The main problem brought forth the structure in phase 2 of diagram 2. Raphael's discourse of economic and social policy intervenes for this reason, and the utopic figure's transformational work will center on it.

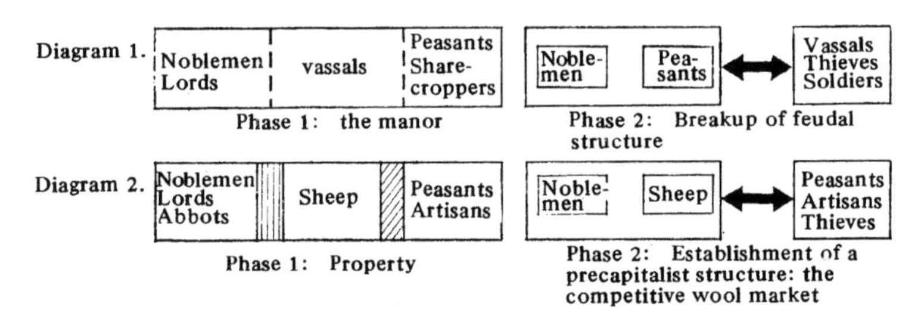

Figure 22. Diagrams of the causal processes analyzed by Raphael

Plans

What is Raphael's "solution"? "Rebuild...restore...restrict...resume farming..." Raphael's political discourse is a return to a former situation, though it integrates the excluded group into a structure of production related to the most current agricultural methods, albeit on a small scale: "Let cloth-working be restored once more that there may be honest jobs to employ usefully that idle throng, whether those whom hitherto pauperism has made thieves or those who, now being vagrants or lazy servants, in either case are likely to turn out thieves."[11] Whether it be controlling monopolies, fighting against the hoarding of raw materials, restoring diversified agriculture, or developing complementary local wool industries, all of Raphael's measures aim at rebuilding a former situation which has been renewed because of the crisis. He aims at stamping out vagrancy and idleness (and thus crime).

The reformer's political discourse and More's plans for general change (in reality, the plans of Henry VII and Henry VIII) attempt to relocate a feudal structure. They do, but by accommodating it to certain new elements. Thus the lord's vassals and men of arms become woolen goods manufacturers integrated into peasant groups; they become farmers "honestly working the cloth-industry."[12] He wants to go back to phase 1 of diagram 1 but sheep will replace the lord's vassals. Sheep are the raw material of the complementary industry allowing for the reintegration of the domain for the peasants. They will live better. Removing the arrows of opposition in phase 2 of diagram 2, we encounter a new type of manor. There all the vices of unemployment and underemployment as well as of wealth and aristocratic leisure will be excluded.

It is this economic and political discourse, closely related to the analysis of the objective causes of theft, that is interrupted by Cardinal Morton. He returns to the problem of the system of penal repression: wouldn't abandoning the death penalty be seen as a reward to crime, an invitation to do evil? This detour of the reformer's discourse into the juridical and ethical level invites theological and moral observations concerning life and money, God's commandments and human law. It seems as if the uncertain nature of this political project could be wiped away or forgotten by a discourse with an ontological and axiomatic basis. But what if this detour were not accidental? Raphael's "solution" is a complex one, both archaic and modern. Without actually appearing to be so, this plan is contradictory in a very real, if not logical, sense. It follows real presuppositions analyzed from the objective situation in contemporary England.

This economic and social political discourse of Raphael unfolds in the same *topos* as did the real causes for the criminality in England. The only difference between their exposition amounts to the change from an assertive proposition to one that is imperative. The first is statement of the situation whose causes are analyzed; the second presents new causes that are to produce new effects. And this actually happened. Henry VII had tried to check the transformation from cultured fields into pasture, thus gaining popularity with the peasants. In 1514 a law from Henry VIII forbade any more conversion.[13] A certain policy's success can be measured by the influence of these causal grafts and by the force of their transforming power. Political discourse is a linear, flat discourse. It picks up on cause-effect relations; political practice is the true expression of it and is what is inserted into the tissue of historical, textual events. This is how this discourse, no matter what it pretends to bring about, is totally absorbed by the referential level. It is completely reduced to what it talks about, to the real situation currently perceived by political beings. The proposal is inserted into the situation as perceived in order to modify it because it is inserted.

Presupposition

Raphael's discourse thus accomplishes historical analysis in a political proposal. He moves from the real to the possible by articulating the possible with the real in a seamless continuity. Meanwhile he cannot get away from either social experience as it is lived in the complex system of surface relations or the categorical model allowing them to be contemplated partially. It is quite amazing that this proposal puts forth, as did Henry VII and Henry VIII, a feudal conception of the productive system. Its historic failure points out a contradiction between this feudal conception and the explosive development of productive forces. A true contradiction can never function as a political proposal. The solution cannot be a complex "semantic" term that limits itself to joining opposing elements. For example, the wool industry as it developed is viewed as a craft *complementary* to diversified agriculture, both part of a system guaranteeing work for all. The English kings will be incapable of arresting the capitalist evolution of cloth manufacturers, even though this proposal resembles Raphael's. They could not remove the wool market from the basic system of supply and demand in order to go back to a medieval system of "just," imposed prices. Why? Because they depended on those whose interests were directly opposed to these policies: landed gentry, yeomen, merchants.

In a sense it is precisely because Raphael is capable of lucidly and precisely analyzing the causes for the growth of crime and theft in England that his political proposal remains caught in its own terms, especially in the referential framework of the real situation needed for this analysis without questioning this framework. It is an essentially ethical and religious framework of economic and social life. For this reason, and far from being a detour from Raphael's discourse as we were led to surmise, the Machiavellian Morton's question relating to the death penalty for theft is directly related to our reformer's proposal. It illuminates the proposal's normative background, a context that is no longer able to provide a coherent basis for an objective analysis of the real situation's causes and for the complex political proposal Raphael draws from it. Raphael's moral and theological thesis concerning the death penalty for theft implicitly refers to a value system that authorizes only one part of his proposal for reform. In addition, the proposal itself is not without ambiguity. It combines the old with the new, the modern with the archaic, and the precapitalist forms of a free market with a feudal structure of socially connected relations of production.

From this, and because it is based on an ethical-religious thesis, the economic and social proposal can no longer be theoretically conceptualized to its fullest. If the thief robs and violates the laws of private property, it is because he is forced to do so by the misery in which he is made to live. By solving the problem of poverty, the reformer solves not only the problem of theft, but he also protects social tranquility and private property. Workers from the fields fall into the clutches of vice because they stop working. They fall prey to laziness and poverty, then to crime, then to the gallows of the police state:

Field workers → the unemployed → the poor → thieves → those sentenced to death by the *law*

Our Cardinal's guest, the English lawyer, only retains the last two terms from this cause-and-effect chain of events. More, and Raphael, illuminate the first two terms through objective analysis. They reveal the passage from agricultural production to an unemployed state. This view is wider, but hardly more profound, than the first. Political discourse, whether it be historical analysis or a reformer's hypothesis, never for once leaves the surface of social experience. But the operation's justification can be seen in the two middle relations, moral and social: unemployment engenders poverty, poverty engenders theft and crime. Changing the economic conditions of existence for the poor is justified by reforming general customs and morals. It is not reduced by this, however. This reform is justified by it, and without any explanation using notions of sin or evil. Legitimation and justification are not explanations, and it is this distinction that develops a fissure between Raphael's two theses we talked about earlier. It also helps us to understand them. Side by side, More's moral reflection and historical analysis for the future become more and more incoherent:

> Alongside this wretched need and poverty you find ill-timed luxury. Not only the servants of noblemen but the craftsmen and almost the clod-hoppers themselves, in fact all classes alike, are given to much ostentatious sumptuousness of dress and to excessive indulgence at table. Do not dives, brothels, and those other places as base as brothels, to wit, wine shops and alehouses...all...soon drain the purses of their votaries and send them off to rob someone?"[14]

We thus witness arguments against the death penalty for theft and against its dissuasive effects. Raphael's argument is concluded because the program it entails has been completed. There has been an analysis of the problem's causes, a proposal for the reform of the social and economic conditions, and a position put forth underlining the moral and theological theses that censure the death penalty for theft and, in the final analysis (as it were, externally), justifying the project itself.

Utopic Discourse: Challenge and Neutralization

It is here that Raphael must rely on a type of argument that will appear later on in Hume: it discusses a priori proof of a necessary relation: an argument of challenge, "as to the repeated question about a more advisable form of punishment...."[15] This challenge concerns not so much the social and economic proposal as the penal system. After criticism of the death penalty for theft must come a proper punishment that is both dissuasive and legitimate, morally and logically justifiable and logically efficient. In other words, by opening up the debate, every political proposal must be accompanied not only by its positive goals but also by its means.

Let me briefly examine the implicit presuppositions of Raphael's challenge against himself. If the death penalty is illegal and inefficient, another penalty, both legal and efficient, morally and theologically justified, and socially and politically possible, must be proposed. First, what are the causes of theft? Unemployment generates laziness and, eventually, poverty. Work stamps out unemployment, which then would remedy laziness and poverty. The solution implies work, but inaugurating a system to encourage jobs contradicts the "request," because *instituting it coincides with the objective suppression of the crime it is supposed to do away with.* The penal system for the suppression of theft that Raphael's system suggests is nothing other than doing away with the penal system by doing away with its object. A sufficiently profound reform of society and its social connections renders null the question of reform within the English penal system. This reform had been sketched out in Raphael's economic and social project, but it took the form of the eventual contradiction that brought it about. We have seen how little chance political discourse has to be able to break free from a theological and ethical context. It cannot be presented independently from an axiomatic system of society or freed from a formulation of the problem in ethical and judicial terms for crimes, delinquency, vices, or for penalties and punishment. There seems to be absolutely no solution.

The complicated model of the political proposal gives way to a neutralization of the terms of opposition the model joined together. It is no longer a question of being archaic or modern, old or new. Put more precisely, it is no longer a question of feudal structures involving productive forces and their relationship with ethical and theological bases. This was the problem that the most proper punishment for theft raised. It is neither any longer a question involving pre-capitalist forms for market economies, the problem raised by the enclosure question. Nevertheless, this neutralization should clear the ground for the problem of the old and new; it should connect with the crisis England is experiencing. The crisis, of course, is the decline of feudalism and the emergence of the first forms of capitalism. The neutralization of the terms of historical contradiction allows for the displacement and transposition of this crisis and of this emergence. In short, the time for utopic practice has come. It will not reconcile contradictory terms or nullify the negation in a new position of dialectical synthesis. Instead, it will change their position. It will create the possibility for the appearance of a discourse being the blind carrier for processes and terms authorizing a true understanding of the historical contradiction in which this discourse is born.

Utopia always appears as a rupture within a discursive continuity: "I can find no better system in any country than that which, in the course of my travels, I observed in Persia among the people commonly called the Polylerites...."[16] After rejecting Rome as an example, Raphael becomes utopia's mouthpiece: "Why should we doubt that a good way of punishing crimes is the one which we know long found favor of old with the Romans, the greatest experts in managing the commonwealth? When men were convicted of atrocious crimes they condemned them for life to stone quarries and to hanging in metal mines, and kept them constantly in chains."[17] This is the utopic paradox within the argument and in the discourse: it cannot be used as an argument, and it cannot become one of the moments in the continuity of discourse, even as an illustration. The

Polylerites do not illustrate the political discourse about the English penal system, as the Romans might have done because they "were the greatest experts in managing the commonwealth." They did so for obvious reasons. How can an imaginary figure or a fantasized diagram become a link in a chain of reason purporting to be a discourse presenting proposals for reform? Unless here, through yet another detour, the proposal itself has ceased functioning coherently because of the utopic intervention. Or perhaps the utopic fantasm has begun to reveal the contradiction it represents, because this contradiction is produced in a space or moment hidden by discourse, between contrary elements. This would then be a new way to emphasize this rip in the text's surface, for both content and form, that utopic description and narrative cause; it is this textual surface that is a double for social experience and its relations.

Polylerites

The Polylerites have all the characteristics of utopia except one. We will see the role that this one exception plays in the "play" of epistemological spaces constructed from the elements of its social structure. Their government is important, well run, free, and autonomous. Enclosed by a mountain range, it is completely separated from the rest of the world. Few travelers go there, and very few Polylerites venture into the external world. There is one other reason for this closed geography: the Polylerites are "altogether satisfied with the products of their own land,"[18] so well that they have no need to enter into commerce with their neighbors. War with them, a specific type of commerce, is also unnecessary. An ancient tradition keeps them from expanding their borders, and "they easily protect what they have from all aggression by their mountains."[19] Their land is one of happiness in that it lacks being a land of glory. This is Utopia and Eu-topia, ignored and blissful, simultaneously a-historical and a stranger to the "natural" destiny of all human societies, one of scarcity and poverty. But could Raphael have chosen a more inappropriate example? The most important elements of his political argument consisted in showing that moral and economic poverty is one of the reasons for theft and that military glory brought a society to dissolution. Thus unemployment would exist for field workers and men of arms of the feudal aristocracy. The roots of theft are to be found in poverty: "no penalty that can be devised is sufficient to restrain from acts of robbery those who have no other means of getting a livelihood."[20] But if this is true, we see that the "example" of the Polylerites is certainly not appropriate. Its function is neither exemplary nor paradigmatic but, rather, productive: an element of the expository operation. What is produced remains to be seen.

The land of the Polylerites has all the characteristics of utopia except for one, I maintained. This one exception is fundamental. This exceptional country has nontheless not cut the apron-string of geography or history. Raphael traveled in Persia in order to visit the Polylerites. These people were to pay their annual tribute to the Persian king, who protected them from armed foreign intervention. On the space of the map, like that of their institutions, these happy people have a place. It is an autonomous Persian province, one of its states. This crevice in the otherwise perfectly smooth utopian surface has a meaning: it is the nearly imperceptible mark of displacement, of metaphor, in which the figural work consists. It is the trace of utopic production in the textual product where utopia is exposed and is described.

Utopic Thieves

But there is also another crevice in this otherwise perfect example: some Polylerites are thieves. How is this possible, since there is no poverty or unemployment? And shouldn't the best penal system be illustrated by an irreproachable example, one superior to the historical paradigm of Rome? I shall return to this. The Polylerites punish their thieves by sending them to work in camps organized by the state. Endless work is the most severe sentence prisoners can undergo; there are no others. Raphael goes into more detail and tells us that those punished wear uniforms. Having in this way become interchangeable, they are also immediately spotted as ones punished, but not as individuals. "One and all are dressed in clothes of the same color." All forms of exchange, communication, and commerce are absolutely forbidden them. "The gift of money is a capital offense, both for the donor and for the receiver... money would merely insure the detection of the crime.... [The slaves] are so little able to conspire together that they may not even meet and converse or greet one another." But the state and even private citizens provide for their keeping with a "fixed wage, a bit lower than what would have been paid for free labor."[21] They are in fact sufficiently nournished by the treasury and locked up in dormitories at night, after a roll call. There is no exchange between Polylerite slaves and free men in society, I said. There is one exception, however. Whether it be on a public or private level, immediately or mediated by a salary, an exchange between their labor and a fixed amount of food does exist.

The Utopic Model

Having clarified this, and realizing the aforementioned contradiction (thieves cannot exist in the Eu-topia of the Polylerites if thieves can only be the poorest of the poor), it is obvious that the repressive subsociety of the Polylerites is not an example for the best, most efficient, or most legitimate penal system possible. It is instead an example of the "solution" Raphael puts forth to come to terms with the social and economic crisis facing England at the beginning of the sixteenth century. Because it was a political proposal laid out according to the causes and effects of linear discourse, Raphael's plans could only be explained with reference to the opposition modern/archaic. It could only be expressed in the complex form of an "integration." It integrates historically new elements, which our protagonists are currently experiencing, into a former structure whose dissolution is analyzed but whose frame of reference is not questioned or challenged. By neutralizing the contrary elements and by residing in the crevice created by the actual historical contradiction (utopia can do so because, unlike historical discourse, it does not try to undo it), utopia allows for the description of a model of a penitentiary system that is none other than the projection of a true, but nonexistent situation. Political proposals cannot do this. The true but nonexistent system is the possible, new, and future situation of the English farmer and worker.

The institutional social space described by Raphael during his trip to Persia can be diagramed as in Figure 23. Persians are to the free Polylerites what these

Figure 23. Articulation of Polylerite social space

latter are to their slaves: protectors, guarantors, and masters. Doesn't the law strike in order to "discourage criminal actions and to save men so they will not be forced to repay with their whole life the crime they have committed"? Isn't this similar to the role of the Persians, who receive an annual tribute and guarantee the Polylerites from every possible threat? But the diagram in Figure 23 does not fit with the model of the English situation. This incongruity between the two organizations is necessary because of a twofold incoherence: utopia is

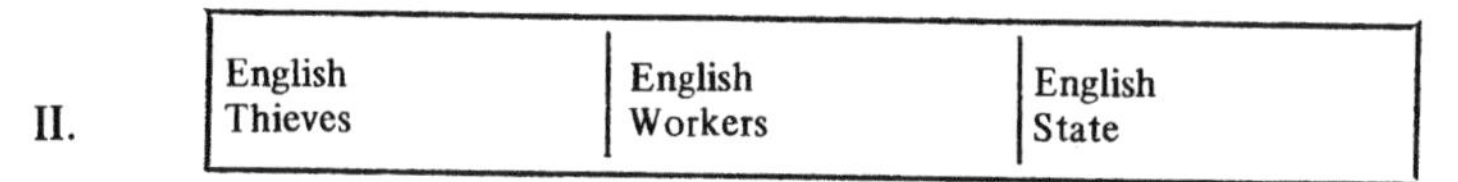

Figure 24. Articulation of English social space

the place where punished thieves cannot exist; historical society's reforms should lead to the disappearance of all penal systems. The complex diagram in Figure 25 is the result.

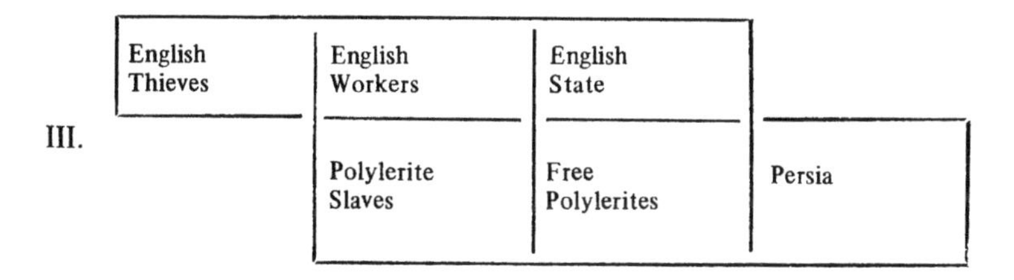

Figure 25. Articulation of the two spaces in the model

From Model to Theory

In other words, the utopic "example" that describes the system for controlling crimes of theft in a utopic society (crimes that cannot happen there) is the paradigm, not of the ideal system for controlling crime in a real historical situation, but rather of a possible social system, simultaneously real and to come. It would be the system of a social space whose articulation has not been historically produced.

The Transforming Operation and Its Critical Force

Figure 25 lets us see a double operation that the "incoherencies" in the very production of the Polylerite utopia indicate. Recall that these "incoherencies" include the presence of Persia as a protecting and hierarchically superior law and the existence of thieves in a society of abundance. The political discourse describes the processes of referential causality by which English workers become unemployed and then become thieves, by which a complete society becomes an oppressive and repressive state, "grossly unjust," because it "takes a man's life because he has taken money." These processes are displaced by utopic description, outside of narrative history, in the crevice of historical contradiction through the neutralization of its terms. What does this operation produce? What benefits do we reap from this displacement? Is it the pure and simple repetition of a real situation in a mirror's ideal image where the imperfections would be corrected? Not at all. The displacement produces a result: what utopic description reveals within this double relationship between public and private, from the entire society down to its "slaves," is a fundamental element that can appear only with reference to slaves, prisoners, or punished thieves. This element is the *exchange of the work force for a salary meant to ensure the upkeep and renewal of this force.*

This essential element is left out of both the political discourse and the utopic description. Recall that political discourse is a proposal for reform in a cause-and-effect linearity for a present historic society; utopic description presents an abundant society lacking in private property (and therefore lacking incoherency). Neither of these discourses reveals the exchange of the work force for a salary. A "model" that is distant from "historic reality" but anchored in its particular contradiction must be constructed. It must be a model that includes the possibility for this sole exchange process. This model society must contain not only the particular contradiction of the real, historical society, but also the *neutral possibility* for its transformation. *We posit this possibility, after the fact and affirmatively*, by talking about a society that allows that single form of exchange between the work force and the salary meant to ensure its upkeep and its renewal so that a certain quantity of force equals a certain sum of money. But isn't this actually the place where, *in complete justice*, money equals human life, once human life has been transformed into a certain quantity of productive labor? The utopia of the Polylerites (allowing slaves into their society by a significant incoherency) reveals that form of exchange to which slaves are exclusively forced to accept: they can only give their labor. But this is so because of the presence of *slaves*, not sentenced *thieves*.

The "Floating" Concept

The operations of utopic practice clearly reveal their critical force in the example of the Polylerite nation. Utopic practice's metaphorical force resides in this nation's historical distance from the present and in the geographic distance involved in crossing the mountains that normally forbid access to this land of abundance. Its metonymical force comes from its movements and changes of emphasis: the Polylerite slave slides from the signifier "thief" to the signifier "worker." The emphasis is displaced from one system to another. This means that the (English) thief has no Polylerite signifier, just as (historic, utopic) Persia has no English signified. Utopic practice thus produces a twofold absence by its double operation. It affects the signified by displacing it and the signifier by developing it. The critical force of utopia is not contained in utopia itself or in its narrative or descriptive discourse. Its effect is in the crevice (producing meaning) that this discourse creates with the discourse with which it is confronted. It keeps its distance from this second discourse, whether it be a discourse of praxis (political reform, as we have seen here) or simply "the discourse of reality."

Utopia's critical work becomes manifest in the noncoincidental relation between two articulations of social, historical, or utopic spaces. This displacement of relations with discursive, political, and utopic discursive topics reveals the critical force at work. Utopia is not a mirror of social reality, whether anamorphotic or through reverse images. Neither is it the simple discursive relation between political discourse and reality. Why does More's micro-utopia, developed afterward in Book One, refrain from informing us that there are no thieves in the Polylerite nation because there can be no thieves in this happy country, where all inhabitants work in peace because of Persia's protection? Isn't the answer contained in the fact that utopic practice is not simply the reverse ideal model of a painful and paradoxical reality of contradiction and twilight? Utopia is a discourse produced by a symbolic and signifying practice, itself very specific. It is the end of a long labor whose markings are carried with it. It is not the reverse representation in the camera obscura about which Marx speaks in the well-known text from *German Ideology*. It is, rather, the product of signifying and productive forces that are critical, figurative (not conceptual), schematic, and aesthetic (not categorical), according to the level of analysis we observe. This practice reveals a fundamental phenomenon that neither an ***analysis*** of a real, historical situation can bring to light nor an ***ideal representation*** can produce (being the simple reversal of this situation or of the model produced by objective analysis). This fundamental phenomenon is utopic practice's product. It is the operative space or crevice between the discourses of reality and fiction. It is the exchange of work force for a maintenance salary: work force as commodity.

However, utopia does not go so far as to conceptualize or categorize its product. If we take either the description of the Polylerite nation or the discursive confrontation Raphael uses to contrast it to contemporary England, we see that never is there mention of quantifying work or of selling it as a commodity in terms of a social contract. Work force as commodity, in the text and in the analysis, appears only in the form of a double absence "in play" between fiction and reality, between the two models of a political project and a utopic description, between two "epistemological" spaces. Their incongruity reveals a political signified lacking any utopic signifer on one end of the paradigmatic articulation, and on the other end a utopic signifier lacking any political signified. The shift between the two series of signifiers and signifieds, of the utopic and of the political, of the fictional and real, etc., forbids any stabilization of meaning. Meaning hovers, or "floats," between the two series.

Utopic practice indirectly denounces a situation of historical and textual crisis, where a study of residue and lack is set up, or the analysis of figures, metaphor, and metonymy, neglecting exact and rich representations. Utopic practice reveals to us an instability. Through a "displacement of parameters" and the play of "odd" remainders it shows us historical moments where meaning is not representable in isological signs or in allegories controlled by a system of manifest correspondences. Meaning must be sought outside of signs in symbols, in the symbolic workings where equivocal signifiers wait for univocal signifieds to replace them, and where, conversely, signifieds cease to emit meaning and begin to fossilize erratically in a field of archaeological digs. These are moments of "crisis," where structural analysis reveals the passage from one systematic organization to another. It achieves this by activating, shaking up, and displacing the differential relations. The question could be asked, actually, whether the historical movements of societies do not appear in texts as these rips and "crevices" in discursive continuity. These rips, however, are provoked by the effects of discourse itself. They are thus more thoroughly clarified, in order to reside in images without residue. Within the space they create within the texture of arguments these images from objective analyses and "realistic" proposals change into figures and smear the correspondences. They introduce signifying supplements that cannot be assigned to any one element and that cannot be positively qualified. Simultaneously, they remove from the other end of the chain signifiers that had aided our comprehension rather than clouded it.

The Recurrent Discourse

Assigning this supplementary signifier would thus belong to a recurrent discourse, one that emerges after the fact. It would speak *after the end of history* to qualify it through a rigorous conceptual determination. This is the essence of scientific theory in general, and of the scientific theory of society in particular. Recall for a moment a passage of *Utopia* that has the remarkable characteristic of presenting in the same split but unified text a strongly objective political and historical discourse and a utopic discourse that seems, but only seems, to be the imaginary schematization of it. If we can specify utopic practice in such a passage, what would the movement to scientific social theory be like? My own analysis has tried this: how would it work?

Two observations should be made here: (1) scientific theory will have to result in a critical reversal; (2) the play of discursive topics between historical policies and utopic fiction sketches, but negatively, the *topoi* of this reversal. It does not bring it about, however. Utopia is at one with ideology; utopic practice is its critique.

If we briefly diagram this critical reversal, we can see that our actant and semiological analyses show a syntactic reversal on the part of subject and object, of actor and him who is acted upon (Figure 26).

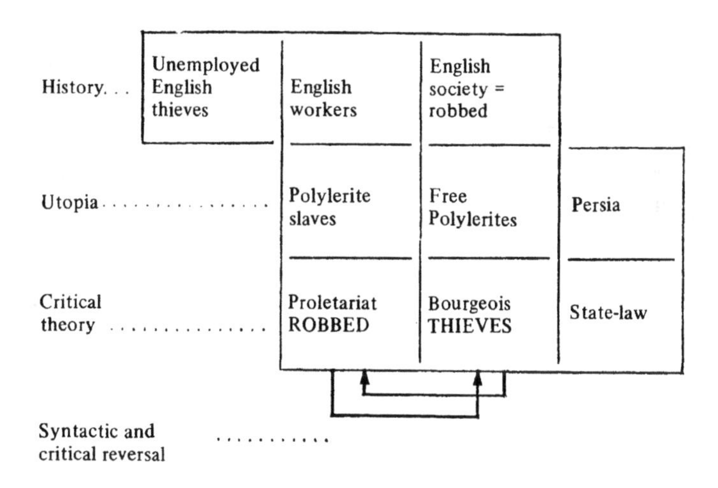

Figure 26. Model for the articulation of history, utopia, and critical theory.

Now we see that Polylerite slaves, coming from a faraway geography and a distant ethnology, are the proletarian workers of future history. We need only quote Raphael's description of the early factories and their organization:

> They neither are confined to prison, nor wear shackles about their feet but, without any bonds or restraints, are set to public works....If they do a good day's work, they need fear no insult or injury. The only check is that every night, after their names are called over, they are locked in their sleeping quarters. Except for constant toil, their life has no hardship. For example, as serviceable to the common weal, they are fed well at the public's expense, the mode varying from place to place...whenever a private person needs a hired laborer, he secures in the market place a convict's service for that day at a fixed wage....The result is that they are never out of work and that each one, *besides earning his own living*, brings in something every day to the public treasury.[22]

Free Polylerites (the rest of society) make up bourgeois capitalist society. Persia becomes the state apparatus, protecting and guaranteeing the dominant class's activities. But this one-to-one correspondence would be the simplest of allegories if our critical reversal did not intervene. It validates this correspondence and reveals the difference between the symbolic workings of utopic practice (metaphoric and metonymic) and the categorical and conceptual workings of critical theory. The critical syntactic reversal is critical discourse's essence: *the robbers have been robbed, and vice versa.* The formula unearths the idea of exploitation; Raphael almost formulates its corresponding notion: *surplus value.*

Theoretical Critical Reversal and Utopic Practice

Two movements make up social theory. The critical movement attempts to seize reality as the contrary to its logical structure. The theoretical movement, then, tries to construct the concept or structure that makes it intelligible to us. It does so independently from the apparent social relations and the surface of social experience. Seen in this light, Polylerite utopic fiction is not actually a return to reality or the construction of its structural logics. It has simply been shifted out of a historically determined place: there it erects as a "fiction" or a "figure" in a fictional context the place of punishment for theft. Theory, by reversal of the superficial social relations, did this on the level of the concept. Specifically, the work force as their sole possession can be exchanged by the worker for a salary, thus letting him continue to work. Capitalist exploitation (work force as commodity and surplus value) is the reversed capitalist expression for the punishment of theft in the Polylerite nation, just as theft had been the figurative expression, only displaced and metaphoric, for the agricultural and capitalist England of the future.

Utopic fiction is thus an anticipating, but blind, judgment. The objective analysis of the causes of theft in England at the beginning of the sixteenth century cannot create a theoretical construction. This is so because for Raphael and More their present, their society *hic et nunc*, does not include that possibility; it cannot articulate its own concepts. That will be the epistemological privilege of the emerging society, of which symptoms can be glimpsed in sixteenth-century England. That is the function of utopic practice: it is revealed by the play of "epistemological spaces" of the various discourses it activates. It renders these theoretical constructions present. It does not present them in all its *theoretical* power, however (it cannot: the utopian thinker is not a historical prophet); utopic discourse offers them as *poetic figures.* In other words, utopic practice does not construct a theoretical concept through the play of its discursive topics. Rather, it offers the setting, the space of representation. It provides the place of figurability, which is the imaginary schema and sensuous framework for it. In Kantian terminology utopic practice is the schematizing activity of political and social imagination not yet having found its concept. A blind activity, but one that would trace out the place, or the topic, of its concept for knowledge or action. It is a schema in search of a concept, a model without a structure. The figure that utopic practice produces is a sort of zero degree for the concept. It is the place of the transformational synthesis of contrary elements. The neutral space separating them opens up the poetic possibility.

The voices in *Utopia* produce the blindness: insofar as they are the voices of utopia, Raphael and More—but also to the extent that the political discourse is itself a part of fiction—Morton, the Machiavellian and the English lawyer all designate objects in the spatial and temporal field where political and historical discourses are uttered. But these voices are vulnerable and neglect to criticize their own discursive position. The critique of the objects under scrutiny, stamping out theft and crime in England at the beginning of the sixteenth century, is not itself criticized. The critique of this critique is the syntactic and actantial reversal of the model's poles, the robber being robbed, the victim the criminal. This noncritique is precisely the utopic projection far from this historically determined *hic et nunc*, far even from a past historical reference—Rome—into a present and a space that are neither scientific theory nor contemporary history. This present is neither a-chronic nor historical. It is an "other" space, utopic: the space of fiction. This fictional a-temporality is a freedom of play; it liberates a plural voice by playing multiple spaces of imaginary scenes one against the other.

It also opens up, but blindly, the theoretical field in which concepts and categories will be able to be elaborated historically.

Notes

Chapter 7

[1] More, pp. 19-20.

[2] This is Marie Delcourt's phrase from a note in her edition of *Utopia*, op. cit.

[3] More, pp. 19-20.

[4] More, p. 20.

[5] More, pp. 20-21.

[6] Marie Delcourt, op. cit.

[7] More, pp. 29-30.

[8] More, pp. 21 ff.

[9] More, pp. 24 ff. About his, see M. Beresford, *The Last Villages of England* (London: 1954).

[10] More, p. 24.

[11] More, p. 27.

[12] More, p. 27.

[13] See M. Beresford, op. cit., and Marie Delcourt's notes in her edition of *Utopia*, op. cit.

[14] More, p. 27.

[15] More, pp. 30-31.

[16] More, p. 31.

[17] More, p. 31.

[18] More, p. 31.

[19] More, p. 31.

[20] More, p. 20.

[21] More, pp. 32-33.

[22] More, p. 32 (my emphasis).

CHAPTER EIGHT

Utopian Culture: The Monkey and the Neophyte

The utopic scene Raphael composes for us presents stories and apparent illustrations of certain characteristics of the representation. They can be classed into two large groups, each having a similar structure. The first includes narratives of successful cultural contacts between Raphael, his fellow travelers, and the Utopians. These latter have easily assimilated the Old World's science, technological advances, and humanities. The second group is made up of stories with a negative character. Here Utopia has expanded into neighboring "utopic" societies, exploiting them commercially, waging imperialist wars against them, conducting a corrupt and deceitful diplomacy toward them. These are the "moments" when the Utopians have mixed with the "impure," blood and gold; they mastered this contact by rejection, be it political, geographic, or axiomatic. Gold is thus for outside use only, untouchable and untouched. It is a means of corruption in foreign places; it "contains" corruption at home. It is in this same way that blood is spilled only outside city walls, by slaves who are simultaneously butchers and hunters, and off the island, by mercenary Zapolit troops. This repulsion, however, does not hinder the Utopians from accumulating enormous quantities of gold and silver from their judicious commercial enterprises; neither does it keep them from eating meat, nor from being able to defend themselves with courage and valor in an all-out war of patriotic sentiment. But now we know that the utopic figure whose production takes place in the neutralized space between contrary elements is perfect for gathering up these same elements, now neutral, in a group that is at once complex, coherent, and pluralistic.

These narratives are Raphael's narratives. They can concern cultural contacts between the Old and New Worlds or commercial and military expansion in the Other (utopic) World. The narratives can be negative or positive. Raphael has become a figure from this scene and a character of the narrative with the representation. And with him comes history, submerged in literary form itself.

Historians show this type of narrative in the utopic figure by reversing its meaning and nature. We would like to elaborate this last point by closely examining a few passages from *Utopia*. How do these narratives show history in the utopic figure? What kinds of operations does this literary example use? What do these signifying practices and productions teach us about ideological censorship (involving both blackouts and coverup)? Actually, they reveal it. In order to answer some of these questions, we have chosen several narratives of acculturation, both profane and religious. There are two examples of apprenticeship—one concerning the acquisition of the classics, the other the religion of Christ—with two examples of failure. In their brief way they play the role of a lapsus. If these narratives only had a simple illustrative function, these "missed occasions" would have no meaning in the coherent whole of its figurative play. The narratives involve the monkey's and the neophyte's accidents. They alone could constitute the fable whose moral would be utopia, if the syntagmatic line of the text did not separate them and make them fulfill an analogous function in "contrary" profane and religious contexts.

Raphael revealed the wonders of Greek "literature and learning" to the Utopians. "It was wonderful to see their extreme desire for permission to master them through our instruction."[1] ... "According to my conjecture, they got hold of Greek literature more easily because it was somewhat related to their own. I suspect that their race was derived from the Greek."[2]

> When about to go on the fourth voyage, I put on board, in place of wares to sell, a fairly large package of books, having made up my mind never to return rather than to come back too soon. They received from me most of Plato's works, several of Aristotle's, as well as Theophrastus on plants, which I regret to say, was mutilated in parts. During the voyage an ape found the book, left lying carelessly about, and in wanton sport tore out and destroyed several pages in various sections. Of grammarians, they have only Lascaris....[3]

In another context, after presenting the situation of slaves, the practice of euthanasia for the terminally ill, marriage rules, laws, prohibitions and rulings, treaties and war, Raphael comes to the Utopians' religion and to the teaching of Christianity provided by his companions and himself.

> But after they had heard from us the name of Christ, His teaching, His character, His miracles, and the no less wonderful constancy of the many martyrs whose blood freely shed had drawn so many nations far and wide into their fellowship, you would not believe how readily disposed they, too, were to join it [so much so that] not a few joined our religion and were cleansed by the holy water of baptism....Even those who do not agree with the religion of Christ do not try to deter others from it. They

> do not attack any who have made it their profession. Only one of our company, while I was there, was interfered with. As soon as he was baptized, in spite of our advice to the contrary, he spoke publicly of Christ's religion with more zeal than discretion. He began to grow so warm in his preaching that not only did he prefer our worship to any other but he condemned all the rest. He proclaimed them to be profane in themselves and their followers to be impious and sacrilegious and worthy of everlasting fire. When he had long been preaching in this style, they arrested him, tried him, and convicted him not for despising their religion but for stirring up a riot among the people. His sentence after the verdict of guilty was exile.[4]

These are the two accidental occurrences concerning the Western acculturation of the Utopians on a profane and religious level. Are they simply anecdotes reinforcing the referential effect of reality for the narratives in which they occur and for the representative figure of the larger narratives they punctuate? Is this their sole signification? The second tale acquires another meaning because it is the illustration, *a contrario*, of Utopian religious tolerance. We have, however, come to suspect those image-narrations of taking part in another, deeper discourse that deconstructs the figure's representation. And would it then be possible that these two fragmentary anecdotes, in turn, inside this larger hidden narrative of the contacts between the Old and New Worlds, are the narrative elements for the deconstruction of our own global narrative of modern times. Does it then carry with it the implicit and oblique indices of its own production?

Actually, these two anecdotes, as well as the narratives in which they occur, cannot signify unless the contributions of Western culture and society find a relative contrary meaning opposed to Utopian culture and religion. Difference is thus established. We must carefully analyze the play of this difference. Just as in the dialogical structure of the text, the difference contained in the didactic discourse must be "different" from, but also reducible to, the same, in order to authorize the relation of oppositions and contrary elements. This relation, presented on the semantic axis, articulates content and gives it meaning. Recall also, however, that Utopian culture and religion are a part of the complete picture of "the rivers, the cities, the inhabitants, the traditions, the customs, the laws"[5] that Raphael has been invited to describe. We are thus led to the space of the figure, to the utopic place in the representation. But this happens to be a discursive level different from what we have heretofore encountered. It perhaps involves description, but not description of a topography, a constructed space, or of a schematic map of fictional imagination. This description comes from the topic of a secondary model, whose operations should release the meaning of the narratives and anecdotes occurring there.

The figure here is not presented in a space or scene that has been constructed by, and is limited to, a former narrative setting. It is, rather, the narrative that finds its own space of play, of operation, within the figure. This space no longer entails the imaginary or geographical architecture of the city or island, but, instead, rhetorical and logical *topoi*; it involves a philosophical and theological space of Utopian religion and culture. The actors involved will have their anthropomorphic masks removed. The text reveals a level of discursive grammar more profound than would reveal propositions of the imaginary. Here it will involve ideas and beliefs of the Utopians, while in the meantime we wait for the fictional narrative as told by the symbolic traveler to introduce the dynamic play of difference into this immobile decor. This is what we need to reflect on: figure as the description of a discursive didactic topic and its acquisition of meaning. It exchanges signification through the anecdote that is told within it. How can this "anthropomorphic" narrative find and give meaning in a "didactic" discourse whose only figural framework is the general subject, "the Utopians"? On the level of literary form, of expressive dialogical structure, this question is the same as another question, which is on the level of the form of content: what kind of articulation exists between the utopian and elementary ideologies that Raphael's narratives show?

Utopian Ideology: Primary and Derived Ideologies

We are concerned here with Utopians' ideas and beliefs. They form a system of representations and immediate evidence, which translates into a mediated domain of intellectual and affective activity, of the relations of production and the economics of social existence. They are thereby legitimated. This is Utopian ideology, one of a fictional, secondary nature that More constructs from his own ideology. It can only be a conscious "superstructure" of his own original ideology. In other words, if ideology is a system of representations, beliefs, and ideas whose systematic but "blocked" form is the unconscious, the secondary ideology Raphael-More constructs will be the fictional, symptomlike formation of the unconscious system of representation that constitutes primary ideology. This secondary formation will function as a screen for primary ideology. Screen has two meanings: it is a space for projection and a dissimulating surface. The ideological screen is a part of the utopic figure and a topical discursive element of this figure. It seems to be a very useful secondary figure because it works on the primary figure (of which it is a part): it disguises and reveals the ideological discourse in which it is caught. It is in this way that the narratives caught up in it, and especially their internal accidents, can be used to analyze its operations.

Religion Within the Limits of Simple Nature

Utopian ideology is an ideology polarized by two hierarchical terms. One regulates and corrects the other: rational wisdom and religion. The first term defines a morality of pleasure. The Utopians' "principal and chief debate is in what thing or things, one or more, they are to hold that happiness consists."[6] As a result the Utopians do not hesitate to declare pleasure as "the object by which to define either a whole or chief part of human happiness."[7] Here religion intervenes; "it is serious and strict, almost solemn and hard," because "they never have a discussion of philosophy without uniting certain principles they think reason insufficient and weak by itself for the investigation of true happiness."[8] For them happiness comes not from just any pleasure; only religion is able to determine the truth in it. "Happiness rests not in every kind of pleasure but only in good and decent pleasure. To such, as to the supreme good, our nature is drawn by virtue itself, to which the opposite school alone attributes happiness."[9] This means nothing but virtue conforming to nature. This conformity is obedience to reason, love of God, and the search for pleasure: "Reason...inflames...men to lead a life as free from care and as full of joy as possible and, because of our natural fellowship, to help all other men, too, to attain that end."[10] Religion and nature, pleasure and happiness, rational wisdom and the natural love of God, human charity: all elements are interdependent. The confrontation and regulation we first saw that would have philosophy act as religion's servant now seems to smooth it over harmoniously. Reason can understand the two religious principles: immortality of the soul and the position of God as man's destination for happiness. "Reason leads men to believe and to admit them."[11] Hence the religious sphere will include both the domain of the positive specifications of these fundamental beliefs and that of the religious institution. Utopian religion, in short, is philosophy, and philosophy is religion within the limit of simple nature.

Philosophy and Religion: The Place of Enunciation

These specifications result in one kind of tension that penetrates Utopian ideology; it outlines the presence of a third term: the nonpresent position of

More-Raphael in utopic discourse. There is a tension between philosophy and religion because the former is subordinate to the latter, but the latter is indiscernible from the former as far as its content is concerned. In order tc distinguish between them one must resort to artificial means, which are revealed as the trace of the utopic figure's history, in figure itself. When the conqueror Utopus discovers (and founds) the island, he encounters a variety of sects, which he manages to preserve in a state of neutrality and reciprocal tolerance due to a minimum common belief in the soul's immortality and the workings of providence in the world. Peace is also maintained due to certain civic and communal rituals and mutual respect. In other words, this initial tension between religion and philosophy, on the one hand, and a plural history and unitary dogma on the other, simultaneously reveals and covers up a religious viewpoint occupied by Raphael-More, the viewpoint of revealed religion. The first questioning of natural religion begins here as a preface to a philosophy of the Enlightenment. At the same time it is the figure of the second ideology of the Utopian philosophical religion: the great rupture in Western Christianity brought about by the Reformation.

Pleasure and Sociability

Two fundamental themes make their appearance in the natural religion of the Utopians: first, the tendency toward altruism and solidarity with others are inscribed into the natural search of pleasure; second, the precise enumeration of false pleasures resulting from social convention, this enumeration being equivalent to the perversity of desire. Here again we encounter two themes in a relationship of tension. How can the individual's search for pleasure not compromise the social community as a whole? How can certain experienced pleasures be banned without resorting to a revelation of the Fall? How can this ban be justified in a purely natural light? The Utopian philosophical belief echoes the theses of Aristotelian philosophy. It places "humanity" among the fundamental "drives" of mankind: "it is especially humane (and humanity is the virtue most peculiar to man) to relieve the misery of others and, by taking away all sadness from their life, restore them to enjoyment, that is, to pleasure. If so, why should not nature urge everyone to do the same for himself also?"[12] By reversing the initial premises of the problem the Utopian argument resolves this problem ipso facto.

In this wisdom of pleasure it is more important to justify one's own individual search than to allow for altruism and social solidarity. Because there is a natural pleasure in giving pleasure to others, the most "solemn and serious a follower of virtue and hater of pleasure cannot but recommend pleasure while bidding you regard as praiseworthy in humanity's name that one man should provide for another man's welfare and comfort."[13] The essential point is easy to see: humanitarian feelings, altruism, and solidarity with mankind are "initial" virtues, and therefore sources of pleasure. Society does not need to be explained on the basis of an original selfishness or infinite desire to appropriate pleasure as nature's own, ***homo homini lupus.*** On the contrary, society (or man's social tendency) is this basis; it founds and justifies the individual search for pleasure. Society has at its roots friendliness, or rather the pleasure gained from man's humanity to man. "If you not only are permitted but are obliged to win [a pleasurable life] for others as being good, why should you not do so first of all for yourself, to whom you should show no less favor than to others?"[14] Indissolubly, natural facts constitute rights and demands: laws of nature, norms of reasons, and conversely, duties and rules for individual and social ethics. These are dictated as givens, as forces of nature. From this, egoism and altruism, individualism and solidarity, personal appropriation and communal exchange, are identical because humanitarian tendencies found the individual search for pleasure, just as this latter propensity is realized in an agreeable, full, and pleasureful life offered to others. In this Utopian rewriting of certain larger themes of Classic morality, beyond the humanist euphoria of the Quattrocento coming to a close, the essential ideological relation of the bourgeois revolution can be glimpsed. Humanism is part of its superstructure: the individual, now freed from the constricts of feudal organization, has been caught up in new conditions of production. He perceives himself in a new contractual form of society. He does not define himself as an individual (with private property), but he is recognized as such because he recognizes others as proprietors and individuals. "As long as...laws are not broken, it is prudence to look after your own interests, and to look after those of the public in addition is a mark of devotion. But to deprive others of their pleasure to secure your own, this is surely an injustice."[15]

Perverted Pleasures and Libidinal Economy: The Feudal and Bourgeois

This harmonious and natural equivalence between individual pleasure and altruistic joy is opposed to the ban of false, artificial, and "pathological" pleasures. These latter pleasures are the result of desire's perversion. Desire itself conforms to social convention in its most subtle and "ideological" form: the convention of naming. "In fact, very many are the things which, though of their own nature they contain no sweetness, nay, a good part of them very much bitterness, still are, through the perverse attraction of evil desires, not only regarded as the highest pleasures but also counted among the chief reasons that make life worth living."[16] But Utopians also believe that this false idea concerning pleasure stems from the fact that men "hold that [certain things] ...are sweet to them in spite of being against nature (as though they had the power to change the nature of things as they do their names)."[17] Perversion of desire, social convention, and language are all linked together by a chain of similarities that could transfer the definition of pleasure from a natural, gentle, and agreeable thing to one resulting from one's own will, from one's rational goal. Would nature then be tricking us when desire carries us toward certain illusory pleasures? Would nature's goodness be so incomplete as to allow corruption and instability? But in nature itself isn't corruption the result of an incorrect convention by which men can consider, or *name*, as agreeable things that are not so? But isn't this convention (simultaneously social and linguistic) really the consequence, and not the cause, of desire's corruption? In short, if there are illusory pleasures that are generally accepted as pleasures but are nonetheless false and deceitful, this means that nature is imperfect or has been corrupted by the human sphere. This in turn means that nature is not at one with reason, that our tendencies are out of step with our just will, our desire is out of balance with virtue, our social feelings are in conflict with society. And in this space of rupture the dogma of original sin must be inscribed—but "invisibly." Unsaid but present in this division is Christian revelation, and implicit in it is Raphael-More's position of speech.

As my analysis of Utopian philosophy of pleasure has shown, the reverse side of this economic, ethical, and sociological critique of feudal ways of living consists in the problem of original sin, nature's corruption: this is the article of faith for revealed religion. Aristocratic feudalism is a sin against nature and against reason, just as the philosophic and religious ideology of the Utopians is the rational nature and natural reason of bourgeois existence. Nonetheless, this is true only if the critical analysis I have made allows us to see in false pleasure a certain number of conditions dictated by the "feudal mind," whose denunciation is carried by contradictory tension in philosophy and religion, morality, and pleasure, individualism and sociability. These tensions point to the place around which utopia's discourse is constructed. It is Raphael-More's position of speech as controlled by the ideology of Christian humanism. This is the ideology of the dawning bourgeoisie.

The analysis of the authentic pleasures for the soul and body in Utopian religious philosophy would similarly show us the values of bourgeois virtue. Included would be an economy of spending and forces contained in a rational conduct, the hierarchism of profits, the useful distribution of activities, and the rational employment of time. The pleasures of the body's necessary expenditures would exist in a balance between repletion and excretion, a peaceful restfulness in health. The pleasures of existence would correspond to exercising virtue and experiencing this economy of life. Just as for the list of false pleasures the critique of nobility as landed hereditary wealth revealed certain ideological tendencies in this philosophic discourse, so, too, for authentic pleasures the critique of religious or philosophic asceticism suggests in the margins of the blessed Thomas More's discourse the demands of an ideology for which the author of *Utopia* cannot totally claim responsibility. He projects it continually in the discourse about Utopia, in the very wisdom of the Other World's inhabitants:

> "But to despise the beauty of form, to impair the strength of the body, to turn nimbleness into sluggishness, to exhaust the body by fasts, to injure one's health, and to reject all the other favors of nature, unless a man neglects these advantages to himself in providing more zealously for the pleasure of other persons or of the public, in return for which sacrifice he expects a greater pleasure from God—but otherwise *to deal harshly with oneself for a vain and shadowy reputation of virtue to no man's profit* or for preparing oneself more easily...to bear adversities which may never come—this attitude they think is extreme madness."[18]

From the Utopian perspective asceticism is the negative opposite of the false pleasures of showy wealth and gratuitous, regulated behavior. The critique of asceticism in the name of reason and nature circumscribes the space of false pleasure, as well as bourgeois ideology. This critique can only be made from a Utopian viewpoint, however. Raphael-More shows this in his conclusion very clearly:

> This is their view of virtue and pleasure. They believe that human reason can attain to truer view, unless a heaven-sent religion inspire man with something more holy. Whether in this stand they are right or wrong, time does not permit us to examine—nor is it necessary. We have taken upon ourselves only to describe their principles, not to defend them.[19]

The critique here is conducted from the standpoint opposite to the one conducted concerning aristocratic pleasures. This founds its attack on two points of view: Utopian and Christian humanistic.

Thus, bourgeois ideology in its positivity can only be approached from the discourse of Utopia far from the position of speech of him who enunciates it. This is a new and remarkable example of the dialogical structure of discourse in which the enunciated phrase is separated from its enunciation, from the subject-author and origin of discourse. An *other* enunciation the subject refuses to recognize becomes the enunciation of the ideology in which it is caught. Such is the force of utopic signifying practice and its critical power. Not only does it *indicate* the enunciative position of discourse, but it is also "suspicious" of this position: it reveals what it dissimulates or disavows. Raphael-More would thus occupy the complex position of the enunciation of humanism *and* Christianity, of philosophy *and* religion, of reason *and* revelation, of nature *and* dogma. Utopia is utopian religious philosophy; it is neutral. Utopia's position of speech in enunciation is neither Christian nor humanist: it is *other.* But utopic practice in the interacting processes of secondary and primary ideologies would entail the effect of difference, the neutralizing questioning by which is indicated the unoccupied places of the ideology of enunciation within the enunciated phrase itself. The ideas and systematic ideal relations of these systems have not yet made their way into critical consciousness, eventually to subvert them practically and to overthrow them theoretically.

I have translated these complex enunciative relationships into a play of epistemologic spaces. It is a secondary model constructed from utopic discourse, from the practice that produces it, and from the ideology in which it emerges. We have included the relationships between discursive practice and figure, between primary ideology and the secondary transformation into which it is projected and dissimulated (see Figure 27).

The Monkey and the Greek Book

It is within the decor of this ideological figure of Utopian philosophy and of philosophic religion that the narratives of their profane and religious acculturation are acted out. The first tells how they learned the Greek language and were initiated into the storehouse of letters and science of Western civilization. They had such ease in this "appropriation." It would be miraculous if this discovery were not a remembering; it would be amazing if the natural qualities of the Utopian nation did not carry the traces of history and if their intellectual virtues were not really memories of a pluperfect past that Raphael's visit had reactivated. In this way utopic representation carries along with it the markings of history. Could it possibly involve an "other" history—perhaps of religious hostile sects from the continent of Abraxa when Utopus conquered it, or of an original lineage reaching back to the ancient Greeks? Perhaps it is an imaginary

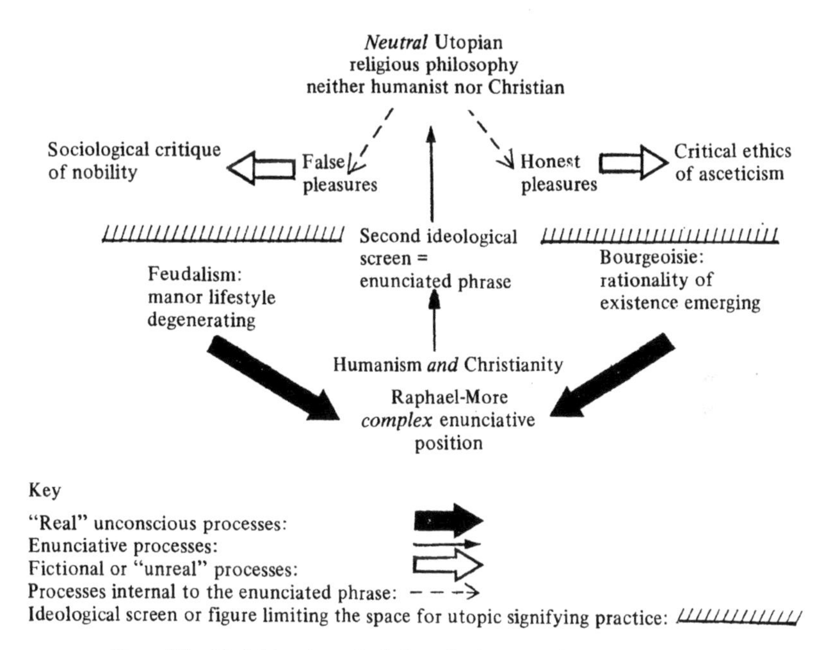

Figure 27. Model for the articulation of primary and secondary ideology

history denying the admirable wholeness of the Perfect City. Nonetheless, it must be admitted that historical temporality, or an "idea" of history, is inscribed within the representative figure. It is not surprising that the narrative must tell of the effects. The narratives of acculturation play on the figure, animate it, and within this difference of position and status of speech (and on a discursive level) they all provoke meaning.

The Book

Witness, then, how the first of these narratives has been marked by an accident: the monkey destroys a few pages of Theophrastus. Here we encounter such a perfectly accidental and insignificant event that, listening to such a *complete* relation of Utopia and its description, the reader becomes suspicious. Meanings abound once suspicion sets in. Actually, there was an echo of this interruption in the narrative a few lines earlier. Nothing could get in the way when the Utopians were learning Greek literature, *unless one counted "faulty readings" of the text.*[20] The fundamental Western problem is thus introduced into the text: the Old World confronted with the *Other*, the problem of tradition in culture. The very problem of history is raised, one involving place and institutional names. This, plus the ease with which the Utopians learned Greek, gave rise to history in Raphael's thinking. He is, recall, the painter of perfect representation.

Cumulative and progressive, all of Western knowledge is dependent on the text in which it is enclosed, unable to be uttered alone. There it has been put *in reserve, accumulated* and *conserved* in mute signs. It is contained in signs that tell us nothing, in *in*-significant signifiers (using the double meaning of this *in*-). Meaning is enclosed there, deadened. A reserve of knowledge is contained in voiceless signs: this is the true place of Western culture and even of history, because a generation's knowledge can be conserved and transmitted there. It can *last* and *grow* without limit. It is not by chance that the narrative of the Utopians' profane acculturation finishes with the rediscovery of the printing press and paper, with the *Other World*'s Gutenberg. The narrative begins, recall, with the easy and faithful imitation of letters from the original language, Greek. Here there is endless duration and growth of knowledge due to the transmission of letters and science, in servile signs, with no other end in mind than *possible faulty readings of the text.* Historical tradition (the negation of lived time in inscribed time) would be interrupted, and the very absurdity of the event affirmed, at this precise moment. Here we witness absolute and unpredictable contingency.

A faulty reading of the text is forever possible. It is both history's proof and its negation. It is its unavoidable presence, not always easy to master even in the utopic figure. This is the risk contained in appropriating a culture whose signs are simply props by which one can always grow, in appropriating knowledge that has been confided to the inert, unchangeable, and unchanged signs of writing, as Plato says in the *Phaedrus*. They can unexpectedly be found missing, however, without recourse. The conditions and means for acquisition and accumulation of culture always leave it exposed to the event's pure contingency. It can be destroyed at any moment. They can be exposed to death at any time because they are already inhabited by it. This is the absurdity of the inscribed sign, always a prey to time and death. The mortal risk of Western culture, it is a transmittable product and an object of appropriation. The monkey signifies this in his insignificance: the symbolic lapsus in the narrative of Raphael as signifying practice.

The Book's Functions

It is true that this event provides a very powerful "effect of reality," simultaneously giving credence to the narrative and to the figure in which the narrative is written. This, however, is not a characteristic outside of its solely symbolic nature. The narrative is the repetition in discourse of real history. Something actually did happen, and the most convincing sign of this resides in the event's unpredictability. It is as if the truth of the narrative, far from insisting on the likeness between the real and rational, demanded instead absurdity as the criterium of reality. But narrative constitutes, by this repetition, history in its signifying order as "narratable." Because the episode of the monkey is an ***absurd*** accident, it lends credence to the narrative, and as narrative it causes history to signify as one of narrative's moments. Because of this, history envelops utopic fiction with its "reality" beause of its accidental interruption.

The humanist library (and along with it Western culture) is more perfectly *transmitted* to Utopia because a monkey mutilates Theophrastus. It is this interruption in the transmission, this "noise," which more firmly anchors the Other World in the Old World. It more clearly affirms the cultural conquest of the other by our own identity. The ***cultural appropriation of and by the book*** is all the more secure in a narrative system if a ***book is mutilated*** by a monkey. In fact, it concerns a book of botany. A Greek book is the necessary mediator between men and the world; it performs the link between nature and mind. It is also the record of the relations between them as well as the storehouse of science. The mutilation of Theophrastus' work on plants is the figurative event for the passage between two functions of the book. A sign of this is provided by one of Raphael's reflections on giving to the Utopians one of Hippocrates' treatises and the *Ars Medica* of Galen. Raphael informs us that they highly value these works, but ambiguously. Because they do not need medicine as a therapy, they honor it in the book. It is knowledge from a disinterested point of view. Simultaneously, however, the book is no longer the transforming and mediating instrument of knowledge; direct observation takes the book's place, so that the book is but a place of conservation and transmission.

> Even though there is scarcely a nation in the whole world that needs medicine less, yet nowhere is it held in greater honor—and this for the reason that they regard the knowledge of it as one of the finest and most useful branches of philosophy. When by the help of this philosophy they explore the secrets of nature, they appear to themselves not only to get great pleasure in doing so but also to win the highest approbation of the Author and Maker of nature.[21]

Henceforth the theme of the books as a compendium of observations and experiences is related to the theme of a natural mechanism and to the *Deus Opifex*.

> They presume that, like all other artifices, He has set forth the visible mechanism of the world as a spectacle for man, whom alone He has made capable of appreciating such a wonderful thing. Therefore He prefers a careful and diligent beholder and admirer of His work to one who like an unreasoning brute beast passes by so great and so wonderful spectacle stupidly and stolidly.[22]

Nature is a spectacle to behold, the representation of an artful fabrication that God, its maker, offers to mankind. Because it is defined as an object of knowledge with reference to a subject, an attentive and interested spectator, this latter will reproduce it in the two major modes of representation at his disposition: the visibility of the painting and the readability of the book. Both emerge from an order of signs; both are articulated by signs, but each differently. The book as a representation, the representative painting as a book, both reproduce, within visibility and readability, the being and meaning of nature. The book is equivalent to the world, and the world offers itself as a painting. The painting is constructed as a presentation that is as readable as a book. This characteristic back and forth inaugurates the Quattrocento, affected by the printing press and true perspective. The narrative of acculturation is played out in the utopic figure. This is true essentially because utopia is first and foremost a book; it is a text whose hierarchical and discursive levels, the topical and topographical spaces it signifies, function interdependently to produce a figure, a representation: a visible space in and by a readable space. In utopia the spectacle to behold and the book both are articulated in an order of signs, even if the practice that produces them leaves within both markings that allow for their deconstruction. The episode of the monkey is the figurative accident of this historic moment. By mutilating an ancient work of botany the monkey obscurely symbolizes the passage from book—practical instrument to transform nature—to the scientific book-as-representation, representation of the mechanical spectacle of nature.

Simia-similis

The problem, finally, involves a monkey, the doubly negative and reverse of this other attentive and interested spectator, a man contemplating the machine of nature. The monkey plays with the book. He frolics in the signs and eats the pages, just as the Utopian reflects upon nature or admires the marvels of its craftsman, just as he assimilates the secrets of true knowledge, but in a contrary way. The monkey also carries within him a long and rich tradition: *simia-similis.* He is the caricature of identity in representation. He is the figure of figure, the double of figure: he reflects himself in a ludicrous mirror image. This "larger-than-life" but subhuman presence denounces the processes of representation whose image in the painting ironically signals how the result was arrived at: reproductive mimesis. But can imitation be imitated outside of an iconic representation? Can it be subtracted from the figurative process? How can the book's form of representation be imitated—as a silent vehicle for a group of mute signs? The monkey can be a painter or a musician. He can reproduce sounds and colors in a wild, animalistic disorder, thereby letting us know that melody and painting are but sounds and colors distributed in a certain order. This order, he could tell us, is more important for painting or for melody than referential mimesis, for which our monkey is an amusing figure.

How can the book's readability be visibly imitated? How can it be translated into figure unless it is shown by an act that is the reverse or ironic equivalent of reading. The monkey is capable of this; he is also a ravenous glutton: he exhibits the act of eating but in a playful, frolicking form. While reading the book, while acquiring "what is good to think," the monkey perceives the model, "good to eat," and acts out that model as a copy. He is the ironic master of the similar. He assimilates the book's material, literally. He swallows the sign's inertia as nourishing, not in a metaphoric but in a literal sense. Nourishing, of course, for the body and not for the soul. Thought and body, book and signs: the monkey translates metaphor into its symbolic literal quality of play and food. He substitutes the visible consumption of the signifier for the readable assimilation of signifier with its metaphoric signified. Reading the book means mutilating it, ripping up and ripping out its printed pages. It is reading as consumption, assimilation as manducation, textual mutilation. The monkey exposes the great play of signs, of grammaticality and orality, of intelligibility and castration, of the acquisition and the loss of meaning in the very act of acquiring, this during Western culture's "Renaissance."

The Critical Model

Raphael the humanist admits as much as he relates the following event to his hosts: "When about to go on the fourth voyage, I put on board, in place of wares to sell, a fairly large package of books..."[23] Noble ambitions! Instead of multicolored glass beads or mirrors and bells Raphael brings books: contact with the Other World is made through the exchange of Greek signs. These are the precious objects by which relations between Utopia and the West are inaugurated. These are just like the goods that triggered the Old World's exploitation of the New. But this also means that written signs are but baubles; they are only a deceitful instrument for barter and exchange. They set off and dissimulate another form of exploitation performed by culture and knowledge, by devaluing its "Western-ness" and decreasing the quantity of material props surviving because of the printing press. The monkey exposes this meaning of the knowledge and culture the Utopians appropriate by remembering their origin through the use of the book, just as the savage accepts the bauble. They are both objects of an exploiting commerce that dissipates in play. They are neutralized through gratuitous expenditure and annulled by mutilation and assimilation. In other words, the monkey is a negative Utopian, and the Utopian who goes "back to the school of the West," of Greece and of modernity, is a positive monkey. The monkey exposes cultural contact as positive commerce and merchandise as negative acculturation. The monkey is the symbolic operator that allows for the deconstruction and transformation of the (representative) figure. The figure moves from a "good" figure of Utopian acculturation by means of Greek and Western knowledge to a "bad" figure in ethnographic reality, describing the economic exploitation of the New World by means of the technical "commerce" of the Old World. Figure 28 attempts the transcription of this transforming operation in the space of a model.

The Fanatic Neophyte

The other accident marking these narratives of acculturation occurs at the end of this large narrative chain telling us about the contacts concerning religion between the Old and Other Worlds in the religious sphere. Here we encounter the history of Utopia's Christianization and the punishment suffered by the fanatic proselyte. The place and function of this story within the structure of the implicit narrative that runs all throughout the representative figure of Utopia are well known. The neutral semantic axis penetrates the utopic picture and organizes it according to two poles: non-Christian and nonhumanist. It neutralizes the complex semantic axis that has organized Raphael-More's narrative-descriptive discourse, both humanist and Christian. The narratives of Christianization and of the apprenticeship of Greek language and culture transform the axis of the utopic neutral into one of historical dimension. This transformation

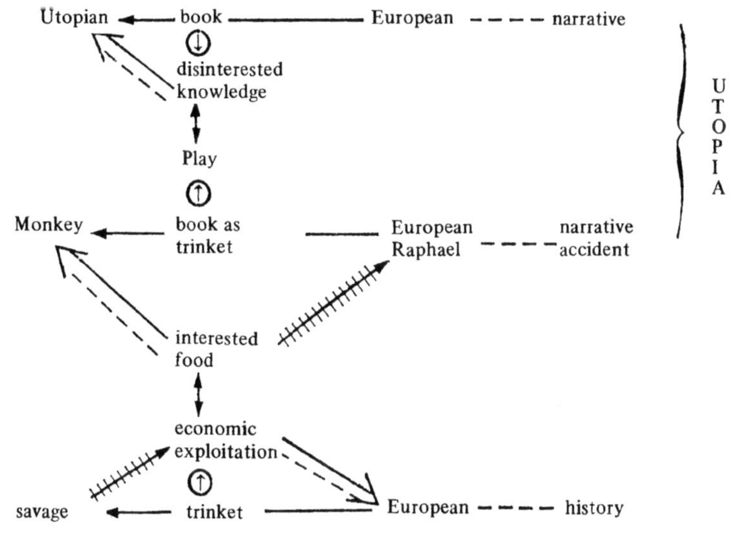

1. Solid-lined arrows show the key direction for the transmitting process of the object of exchange.
2. Solid- and dotted-lined arrows show the recipient in the transmission.
3. Segmented arrows show the loser in the transmission.
4. Circled arrows show the consequences of transmission.
5. Double arrows show mediating operator in the model.

Figure 28. Diagram of the transformation of book into merchandise (from utopia to history).

displaces and metaphorizes the end point *a quo* and the end point *ad quem* between which it is produced. My preceding analyses have demonstrated the role of the internal accident in the narrative of profane acculturation. The monkey is the symbolic operator, not only for the transformation of one of the utopic *neutral* positions into a corresponding and contradictory position of historical dimension defined in the narrative discourse, but also for the transformation of this discursive position into another corresponding and reverse position in a historical situation and praxis. This is where the very enunciation of the narrative discourse is found.

Natural Religion and Christianity

Wouldn't we find a very similar model for the accident affecting the narrative of religious acculturation? The model built earlier to account for the various operations relating to the transformation between the utopic figure and Raphael's narrative could perhaps be used in this new phase of his description: the introduction of religious space into the portrait of the perfect city. In fact, the differential correspondences between profane and religious spaces are numerous and meaningful. The Utopians easily learn Greek because this apprenticeship activates the anamnesis of their forgotten origin. Thus the difference articulating the profane culture's space into two contradictory spaces is reduced to the "historic" similarity of the origin; Raphael's library is the reason for the remembering. A large number of Utopians have adopted Christian baptism because this universal Western religion strikes them as closest to the belief they themselves "judge to be superior to others." This belief is nothing other than the reasonable and natural religion found in Utopia's history, a result of Utopus' founding activities. Utopus had prohibited proselytism; consequently the violent struggles between rival sects were quieted. These confrontations had divided up the continent's religious space. Utopus provided the one small credo for the new island community: the soul's immortality and nature's providence. This is natural religion, a deist amalgam into which several former Utopian beliefs were formed. They all believe in the existence of a supreme being who protects them; they all cal him Mithras, but "he is looked on differently by different persons." This deist amalgam surely helped them adopt the one single religion that seems the most reasonable of all others: Christianity.

Recall how easily assimilable Greek and Western knowledge was for the Utopians because of their Greek lineage and the Western *source* of their history. The same applies to the Western Christian religion: it is easily acceptable because it is so close to their own natural religion, itself the Utopian consequence of their history and of their religious and political evaluation. Here the play of differential similarities is evident; there exists the same ease of assimilation, appropriation, and acceptance of the profane and religious West, both for reasons relating to history. In the first case these reasons stretch back to a Greek origin; in the second they reach forward to the final Utopian end in the perfect city. Because of this it seems difficult to account for the Utopians' acquisition of profane Western culture without rejecting this same reason at history's origin. On the other hand, accepting their religious culture is accomplishing and finishing that history. This is a noteworthy reversal, since the acquisition of profane culture "originates" in a mythic, prehistoric time; religious acquisition is "reasoned" in a *rational*, natural, posthistorical time. The mirrorlike structure of these two narratives of acculturation *figure*, in the utopic picture, the reconciliation of the profane and the religious and the harmony of reason and belief, all under the label of a mythic "origin" of profane acculturation and of a current natural, rational order of religious sympathies. The permutation of terms and functions within the inertia of this "imaginary" representation is a "static" transformation that changes nothing. Rather, it seeks only to represent the end and negation of history in the figure. It is also, but in a diachronic form, the twofold narrative projection of the complex enunciative position of humanism and Christianity. Through the exchange of some of their properties they provide, in the narrative, the image of their synthesis. This is yet another way of ending and denying history.

Christian Unity and Utopic Scission

We move on to the narrative of Utopian Christianization. Looking very closely at what Raphael and his companions preach (and if Raphael and friends do not exactly preach, they do offer religious instruction), two phases emerge: first is "the name of Christ, His teaching, His character, His miracles," and next, the "wonderful constancy of the many martyrs whose blood freely shed had drawn so many nations far and wide into their fellowship."[24] There is on the one hand the life and teachings of Christ, on the other, the conquering and proselytism of the Church, whose actors are the suffering, dying witnesses to Christian truth. On the one side we see the *wholeness* of Christ's existence at the origin; on the other, during history's movement, the reunion of "many nations far and wide" in Catholic doctrine. Articulating these two terms there is a third, *constancy*, "the uniformity of this plurality" of martyrs, as Pascal would say. The Utopians respond energetically to this teaching of Christian doctrine. Raphael attributes this energy either to the inspiration of divine grace or to the fact that this doctrine was nearest to the belief that was the most prevalent among them. He attributes this rapid conversion, again, to the transcendental force of revealed religion, because its truth was directly revealed to the Utopians, or to Him—rational, natural and philosophical—because He and His doctrine most closely resembles the Utopian fundamental belief. He also affirms that their fundamental ways of living in common come very close to the Christian doctrine. This may have been the strong "influence" over them.[25]

The inhabitants of Utopia thus acquired a minimum Christianity through baptism, but none of the other sacraments could be administered for the lack of a priest. Nevertheless, their desire was so great to build a true Christian community that they planned to choose a candidate who might receive the sacerdotal character, even "without the dispatch of a Christian bishop."[26] More insists upon this point in his letter-preface to Peter Giles:

> ...a devout man and a theologian by profession [is] burning with an extraordinary desire to visit Utopia. He does so not from an idle and curious lust for sightseeing in new places but for the purpose of fostering and promoting our religion, begun there so felicitously. To carry out his plan properly, he has made up his mind to arrange to be sent by the pope and, what is more, to be named bishop for the Utopians. He is in no way deterred by any scruple that he must sue for this prelacy, for he considers it a holy suit which proceeds not from any consideration of honor or gain but from motives of piety.[27]

As Raphael prepares to leave Utopia, a *Christian church separate from Rome and the pope* is being created there. It plans to provide its own priests in order to enjoy the full benefits of the sacraments and of Christ's doctrine. In other words, a *scission* is proposed within the wholeness and unity of Catholicism. This unity, recall, was highly emphasized by Raphael. But instead a rupture emerges simply because Utopia is an *Other World*; in More's letter to Peter Giles, accompanied by his book, he makes another attempt at obtaining the exact location of the City No-Place. The essential otherness (by definition) of Utopia, within the most demanding affirmation of unity in history and in the doctrine, creates difference. Within the unity of religion and the reduction of difference to uniformity this otherness is a differentiating and separating force. All brothers in Christ's baptism, the inhabitants of the Other World are yet unequivocally separate for all else: others. This is how unaccomplished history, in the utopic figure, reasserts its rights through the narratives uttered there.

And then the event erupts: the accident of the intemperate proselyte. Recall that Raphael's teaching articulated the unity of the living Christ with a historic and Catholic unity in the Church accompanied by the constancy of martyrs witnessing for His doctrine. For him the plurality of the nations *spread far and wide* found *unification* in the Church of Christ. As witnesses they proclaimed their faith in the word, example, and life of Christ. They also proclaimed it through suffering, bringing about its triumph by their "wonderful constancy." Actually, the same history is repeated in the figure: a neophyte Utopian preaches Christianity in public with more zeal than discretion. He becomes so excited that he believes himself to be superior to all others. He claims that followers of other sects are impious and sacrilegious. But are not these the triumphant accents of true witnesses of the faith; doesn't he commit the same crimes for which the impious Romans condemned the early Christian martyrs? Only the punishment is different: in Rome, death; in Utopia, exile or slavery.

Utopian Projection, Critical Transformation

Utopia's overly zealous proselyte is the reproduction and transformation of the Christian martyr provided in Raphael's teaching. He is the negative term of historical Christian proselytism; he is the reverse of the historical Catholic Church's dynamic unity. Utopian law excludes him from society and expels him from the island. It is at this point, and at this point only, that Raphael tells the story of Utopus, of the number of enemy sects that existed previously on the island, and of his prohibition of all religious zealotry. He then announces the basic policies of Utopus: a plurality of beliefs, mutual tolerance among religious groups, and the central power's neutrality with regard to religion in general. Wasn't Utopus "uncertain whether God did not desire a varied and manifold worship and therefore did not inspire different people with different views?... Moreover, even if it should be the case that one single religion is true and all the rest are false, he foresaw that, provided the matter was handled reasonably and moderately, truth by its own natural force would finally emerge sooner or later and stand forth conspicuously."[28] What is the final moral of the intemperate proselyte in Utopia? Nothing but the disguised narrative of the universal Catholic Church's transformation into a laicized, religiously neutral bourgeois state through the Reform's historical mediation. It is religiously neutral because it is ideologically related to an Enlightenment philosophy, one inspired by reason and nature, itself possible only because of the split in Catholic unity.

Just as the accident with the monkey, in its very contingency, had figuratively allowed for the transformation of the *utopic* narrative of profane acculturation into another, this-time-*historical*, yet-to-be-accomplished narrative of the European commercial exploitation of the savage, so also for this new exemplary accident. The excessive neophyte emerges from an event as contingent as the previous one. The narrative relating it allows for an interpretative rereading of Raphael's religious teaching, of the narrative of religious acculturation: this narrative transforms the incident into a *historical* narrative to be accomplished, of the laicization and religious neutralization of the bourgeois state. In order to do this mediation was necessary. Certain specific processes of semantic transformation had to begin. These we remarked in the previous narrative in the form of a book, written signs and merchandise, glass objects of barter and beginning for the exploitation process. In the anecdote of the monkey the book functioned as a ware for barter. In the anecdote of the neophyte things seem symbolically less powerful. It seems incapable of such a widespread semantic polyvalence. Nonetheless, witnessing, preaching, and public profession of the doctrine all are the fundamental arguments for the Utopians' closeness to Christianity and for the neophyte's rejection from Utopia. Proof of the doctrine's truth is contained in the anecdote of the political offense. In the meantime we move from history to utopia, from a narrative with historical references to an anecdote inside a utopic figure. For if Raphael's teaching refers to the historical foundation of the Catholic Church, the incident of the neophyte is readable the first time only through the utopic picture of the island's judicial and political institutions.

Projecting the historical Christian martyr in Utopia performs his neutralization in the figure of the proselyte, more zealous than discrete. The movement from a universal and unifying single faith, Christianity, to the utopic island where people not adhering to Christianity are not shunned, and those who believe in it are not bothered, authorizes the martyr's removal.[29] Remember, martyrdom is a part of Catholic Christian teaching, itself present in the form of the recently baptized Utopians, but also present as a criminal offense. This reverse martyr irritates the law and order. Religion is thus private business. Only negatively does it involve the commonwealth or society. Utopians prefer pluralism and rupture rather than the dynamic, unifying face of a historical, Catholic, religious unity. The Other World cannot be the place for religion's universal achievement. It is rather, necessarily, its place of rupture, fictionally. This rupture is repeated in the transformation of the martyr into a neophyte. Utopia opens up religious space into a pluralism of beliefs, the mutual toleration of sects. And this for a simple reason: it can neither conceptualize nor explain, it can only produce within a figure. The coming of age of bourgeois humanism and its free development had a necessary precondition: the destruction of the feudal system and the major international focus of feudalism, the Roman Catholic Church. Before Feudalism could be destroyed piece by piece in each particular country, its central, sacred organization needed to be destroyed.[30]

Reform and Political Liberalism

Historically, this destruction is the Protestant Reform. Figuratively, Utopia brings it about in a twofold manner: first, simply transporting Roman Catholic Christianity into an Other World, a No-place, provokes the fictional rupture in its universality; second, converting the historical martyr as a witness to the negative polemics of the Utopian neophyte creates a religious utopic space made up of neutralized pockets of private beliefs. Religion is private property; the commonwealth will look after its preservation in this form. Here we encounter the utopic figure of the bourgeois state, of the social contract and its formal universality. Here again utopic signifying practice has revealed in the figure of the island, Other World (its utopic product), traces of its own production. It has shown the critical force, itself left uncriticized, whose resulting discourse exists somewhere between description and narration, history and fiction, humanism and Christianity, philosophy and religion, nature and revelation. Figure 29 transcribes this transforming operation into a model. The operation itself intervenes, not between culture and commercial exploitation, but between religion (and its institutions) and political organization:

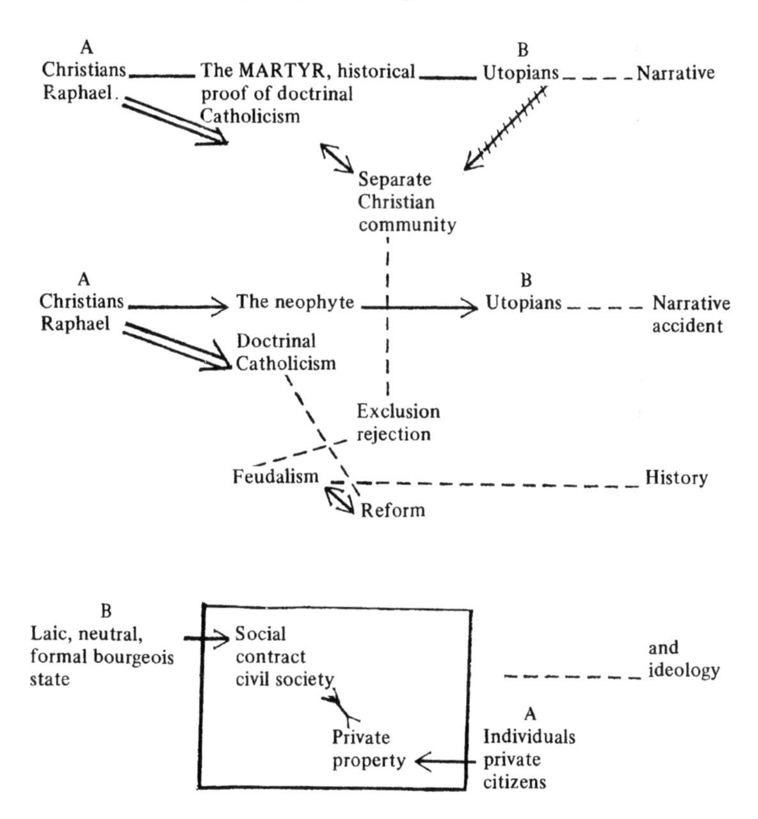

Figure 29. Transformational diagram of religious organization into a political institution (from utopia to history)

KEY

1. Solid-lined arrows ⟶ show the direction for the transmitting process of the object of exchange; here the teaching, or proselytizing discourse, and that into which it has been "transformed," the discourse of political philosophy and economy.
2. Double arrows ⟹ : the recipient in the transmission.
3. Segmented arrows ⇸ : the loser in the transmission.
4. Diverging arrows ⟷ : the oppositions of contrary elements.
5. Converging arrows >——< : the relations of conformity or of coherence.
6. Dotted lines – – – :relations corresponding within the diagram.

The model shows how the accident of the neophyte exposes the internal contradiction in Raphael's teaching and its consequences. The opposition between doctrinal Catholicism and an effective constitution (albeit fictional) of a community *separate* from Rome and the pope, not explicit in this discourse, becomes one between public and open Catholic propaganda and the exclusion into exile or slavery of its instigator. There is a rupture not so much with Rome or the pope but with society. The function of *rupture* or *separation* is the important thing, not any specific subject or term related to it. The same can be said for Catholicism and the function of doctrinal unification. Here the neophyte's adventure develops and explains the latent opposition resulting from Christian preaching in the Other World: accepting Catholic uniformity and the constitution of a separate community. By preaching the discourse of Catholicism in the Utopian community the intemperate proselyte becomes separated from that community. This movement that the narrative produces is significant for the Protestant revolution, itself an ideological reaffirmation of an original true Christianity. It is Catholicism's decisive and definitive rupture from the feudal system. I have tried to express this "signification" by the intersections of dotted lines connecting the political rejection of the neophyte and feudalism, on one side, with the doctrinal Catholicism of Raphael's discourse and the Reform, on the other.

I offer a last remark about the reversal inscribed in the diagram, before moving from the space of utopia articulated into narrative and narrative accidents to the space of history and ideology. The utopic City is the figure within fiction and *in a religious sphere* of a *political ideology* emerging *historically*. It is quite clear that the utopic figure of the religious system reaches toward the political and economic. But it also is, and remains, explicitly the representation of the religious institutions in Utopia. The reversal inscribed in the diagram aims for a spatial translation of a theoretical rupture consisting of reading within the representation the deformed projection of a political and ideological structure in the process of elaboration. In this future structure Raphael, the Christian preacher, would be in the spot where, as an individual, his beliefs, religion, and ideas emerge from his private property. On the other hand, the Utopians, or, rather, their tolerant Utopian religious institution, negatively defining the individual religious space as noninterference with others and their religious practice, would correspond to the form of an accomplished bourgeois state (at least insofar as ideology is concerned).

From Monkey to Neophyte: Correspondences

As a conclusion I would like to show how the narrative accident of the monkey in the narrative of profane acculturation and that of the neophyte in the narrative of religious acculturation rigorously correspond in a reversed structure. It seems that the reasons for this correspondence and reversal are obvious. The two narratives (whose accidents are revealing lapses) refer to the twofold position of enunciation: Raphael-More's position of speech, humanistic and Christian, philosophic and religious, rational and mystical. This double position maintains a state of tension; it is pointed out within the enunciated phrase not only by Utopian ideology or the two examples of the acculturation narratives, but also by the accidents affecting them that reveal the utopic practice's productive processes. Thus related like a monstrous Janus, the monkey and the neophyte produce the double internal and external face of the male, white, adult, civilized and Christian West in the utopic figure. The external face turns toward the rest of the world and nature, toward the "planet of the apes," toward the savage who can be an exterior or interior savage: children, madmen, women.... The internal face is like a mirror turned inward. It aims at the perfect representation of its formal and rational universality. Three centuries later Hegel will see the end of history. The state and civil society, the social contract and judicial institutions, guarantee private property and freedom of thought. Following are two tables where the specter of the neophyte and the monkey from between the lines of the utopic text confront each other:

Religious superhumanity, or mankind in excess	Profane subhumanity, or mankind by default
Preaching neophyte	Predatory monkey
in the religious world of Christianity:	in the profane world of humanism:
fanatic truth	botanical science
with excessive zealotry	by excessive playfulness
in the island of Utopia.	in coming toward the island of Utopia
Converted Utopian	anthapoid "scientist"
sets himself apart from others	imitates men
by wanting religious identity.	by creating a lack in profane signs
He sets himself apart } rupture,	he finds identity } assimilation,
and excludes himself } individualism	and confuses } exploitation.

Notes

Chapter 8

[1] More, p. 103.

[2] More, p. 104.

[3] More, pp. 104–5.

[4] More, pp. 131–133.

[5] More, pp. 56–57.

[6] More, p. 91.

[7] More, p. 91.

[8] More, p. 92.

[9] More, p. 92.

[10] More, p. 92.

[11] More, p. 92.

[12] More, p. 93.

[13] More, p. 93.

[14] More, p. 93.

[15] More, p. 94.

[16] More, p. 95.

[17] More, p. 95.

[18] More, p. 102 (my emphasis).

[19] More, p. 102 (my emphasis).

[20] More, p. 104.

[21] More, pp. 105–106.

[22] More, p. 106.

[23] More, p. 104.

[24] More, p. 131.

[25] More, pp. 131–132.

[26] More, p. 132.

[27] More, p. 6.

[28] More, pp. 133–34.

[29] More, p. 133.

[30] See F. Engels, *Socialism: Utopian and Scientific* (New York: Pathfinder Press, 1972).

VARIA UTOPICA

CHAPTER NINE

Theses on Ideology and Utopia

Thesis I.

1.0. Utopia is an ideological critique of ideology.

1.1. Utopia is a critique of dominant ideology insofar as it is a reconstruction of contemporary society by means of a displacement and a projection of its structures into a fictional discourse. It is thus different from the philosophical discourse of ideology, which is the totalizing expression of reality as it is given, and of its ideal justification. Utopia displaces and projects this reality in the form of a nonconceptual fictional totality. Reality takes the form of a figure produced in and by discourse, but this discourse functions at a level different from the level on which political, historical, and philosophic discourses function. The critical force of utopia is derived, on the one hand, from the (metaphoric) projection of reality as it is put into an unsituatable "other place"–"other" both in terms of historical time and geographic space–and on the other hand, from (metonymic) displacement. This involves the accentuation for the analogy in the expressed reality; it provides a new articulation for the analogy utopic metaphor has brought about.

From this point of view utopia disrupts the ideological discourse of historical reality through the figurative representation that constitutes utopia. Ideological discourse would hope to express historical reality by deadening and shaping it into a closed system of ideas aimed at presenting a justified and legitimated representation of it. Utopia as a figure inscribed within a fable-producing discourse *puts ideological discourse and its representations into play* in a double sense–implicitly but critically questioning them, and setting them apart in order to reflect upon the presuppositions of their internal systems. Rather than being confronted with a fixed system of ideological representation, utopia would offer the mobility of a figure acting in a dialogical stage built by a complex fable-producing discourse. From this perspective the degree of rigid coherence in the utopic figure is dependent on the figure itself, not on the connection figure-stage or figure-viewer/reader.

1.2. Utopic criticism is ideological insofar as the two operations producing the utopic figure (metaphoric projection into a no-place and a nonmoment, and metonymic displacement through a rearticulation of the analogic continuum of reality) have not been accounted for, and reflected by, a meta-discourse of the discourse that produced them. Utopic criticism is ideological insofar as utopia as discourse does not allow for the exposure of the methodology that would legitimate it. It does not produce the theory of its production. In other words, utopic discourse is ideological because it itself is not criticized and because the discursive position it necessarily implies, the operations it sets in motion in order to exist, and the historical and theoretical presuppositions that govern it are not presented in the criticism. If utopia is other than real society, and if utopic transgression is the obverse of current institutions, its (critical) negativity remains fictional. If its figurability allows for its production, it stops it, on the other hand, from reflecting upon itself in a negative social theory that would necessarily imply critically evaluating its own discursive place of production. This nonreflected place is inside current society, contemporary history, and the ideology that disguises their contradictions. Conversely, utopia is this figure produced as a fantasy or fantasm, outside of this society, history, and ideology.

Thesis 2

2.0. Distinguishing between utopia and utopic practice is the only way to arrive at a theory of utopia, the critical preface to a theory of praxis, a practice.

2.1. Utopia is a fictional construction. It is the figure of a discourse that produces it by means of specific (rhetorical and poetic) discursive operations. This figure (of a discourse) plays the role in this fable-producing discourse of an independent and relatively free representation (the utopic stage). It is here that the "other" figurability appears: the negative of contemporary social, historical reality. This latter is the absent term, as such, of the figure that refers to it. The utopic figure is a discursive object, not without reference, but with an absent referent, as its name will tell us: it is not the "without-place," "the imaginary" or "unreal place"; rather it is the no-place, the in-determined place, the neutral figure. It refers to a reality that is not said *within* the figure, that is not taken up in discourse as its signified. If it does so, it does so marginally, as the end point of a comparison and not of a referent.

In other words, utopia as figure within discourse refers to what is not of the discursive realm: it opens up onto the finality of discourse. It does not *signify* reality, but rather *indicates* it discursively. This referential indication of a real but absent term of discourse, as signification, points to the utopic practice by which the utopic figure is produced. Utopic practice is the productive force that the product (as a final, achieved figure) masks; the ideology of representation will absorb it under the auspices of social ideality, imaginary dreaming, or political project—in short, as a model whose basic criteria will be founded on whether its realization is possible or impossible. Utopic practice wedges itself in between reality and its other. It stretches along this space (transgression itself) and produces a term that neither reduces it nor neutralizes it, as both social ideality and political projects do. Rather, it dissimulates and exposes it; this is the essence of utopic figure. Pure contradiction is not resolved; transgression of a reality of norms and structures, in the institution, is not overcome; it is maintained as contradiction and transgression in a figure "other" than reality. This figure is produced by a practice that does not deny reality by changing it; instead, it only indicates it by producing the figure of its negative side. This practice would be absolutely impossible to locate in the textual form of the product if this form did not conserve, within the (nominal and discursive) signifiers, the traces of its production.

2.2. The theoretical critique of utopia attempts to produce the concept of utopic practice, first, by constructing the schema that corresponds to the traces of utopic production contained in the figure. This is the *model* of the relationships of differences between the various spaces signified by the figure or constitutive of these signifiers (the space in the text and the space of the text). Next comes the *group* of *incongruous elements* between these spaces; finally, the *topics* of ruptures within the figure. The unlocatable distance between the indication of the absent term and the signifying figure is thus thematized. As a result we arrive at a structure of the differences in the figurative product, an ensemble of signifiers and signifieds in spatial play. On a theoretical level utopic practice is the concept that corresponds to this model, group, or topic, the latter term being the place of the theoretical system's operations, construction, and revolution. Utopic practice is contained in the figure it produces, and the group of diverse operations creates the space for building its social theory and constructs the place for formulating the concept of political economy. It itself is thus not the construction of the theoretical concept, but the formation of its historical conditions of possibility. This formation is produced and contained within the utopic figure.

The figure carries with it traces of the constitution of theory and its symptoms of formation. Utopia allows for these traces and symptoms to be figured; it is their "figurability." Theory is simultaneously system and strategy. As system, it reconstructs reality within the concept; it rearticulates the given within the object of knowledge. It also criticizes our knowledge of this object. As strategy, it groups operations aimed at changing reality. It entails revolutionary practice. In short, we encounter theory as theoretical practice and practical theory. From this twofold viewpoint utopic practice's figure is nothing but a blinded figure, because the given reality of the institution is not reconstructed as "other" within the concept; rather, it is ***represented*** in its reversed and negative form. A blinded figure results because the practice or activity that produces it does not come to a consciousness of its productive operations. Utopia is the systematic figure within discourse of a strategy for spatial play: it is between the text's signifying and signified spaces.

Thesis 3

3.0. Utopic discourse makes its appearance historically only when a mode of capitalist production is formed.

3.1. Utopic discourse accompanies ideological discourse as if it were its reverse image. It negatively designates the place for the scientific theory of society. Actually, then, it appears historically only when capitalist production is formed, because it is at this specific juncture that the real conditions of possibility of a theoretical (or scientific) universality come into existence within the social domain. The theoretical concept can be formed only within a historically determined field containing its own formative conditions. "Humanity only gives itself tasks it can accomplish...the task appears only when the material conditions permit the resolution of this antagonism. With this (bourgeois) social formation the prehistory of human society is determined."[1] Theoretically, for the sciences of society and history, the epistemological rupture occurs only when the material possibilities for the existence of bourgeois conditions of production are ripe within "old feudal society," insofar as these conditions of production simultaneously create "the material conditions" allowing for the solution to the "antagonism" between the social productive forces and the conditions of production—again, insofar as a real material universality of productive forces is created within bourgeois productive conditions. However, if it is possible to describe "with scientific exactness the material revolution occurring in the economic conditions of production," it is not necessarily so for forms of the superstructure, "ideological forms where man becomes aware of this conflict (between social productive forces and conditions of production) and tries to resolve them."[2] It is only when the conflict itself produces the economic conditions for resolving it (the bourgeois model of production) that the ideological forms of awareness can be overcome and used in a scientific theory of political economy and in a scientific theory of history (or prehistory) of the human society.

3.2. Consequently, the utopic discourse appears as an ideological form of consciousness raising. The awareness of the conflict between bourgeois productive forces and feudal conditions of production becomes similar to a symptom-like formation of the material possibilities for the existence of new conditions of production in a decomposing feudal society. But this form is critical and ideological also, insofar as the utopic discourse indicates within the ideological discourse of which the critique is a part, not only contradictions between conditions of ownership (or conditions of feudal production) and bourgeois productive forces, but also (in a fictional and noncritical form) the theoretical and conceptual instruments that let us think about these contradictions scientifically. These are the theoretical scientific concepts corresponding in the superstructure to the final antagonistic phase in the process of social production.

In other words, utopic discourse is this ideological discourse that can anticipate in a theoretical way. This quality is not evident when the theory is formulated (after the new productive conditions can appear). Utopic discourse contains a sort of critical truth even within the ideology of which it is a part. It possesses this truth *historically*, between the moment of appearance of these material possibilities and the moment the theory is elaborated. Schematically, this would be between the end of the fifteenth century and the first half of the nineteenth century. There are probably analogous examples of utopic discourses in formations corresponding to the passage between economic periods in history, especially between various Asian, Classical, and feudal modes of production. These discursive forms may very well be in many ways comparable to the Classical European period or to the Enlightenment. Their distinguishing feature, however, would always be in their revelation of "topic" schemata for a scientific theory of society. As we have seen, they may be done so figuratively and according to the immanent operations already shown. We could also make a specific terminological decision and use a much wider definition of utopia. We would, of course, in this case have to carefully distinguish between its different types. Conversely, utopic discourse with its fable-producing nature and figural representation can both negatively and positively continue to exist and to be produced after the constitution of the scientific theory of society. This particular discourse would lose the anticipatory critical quality we noted and would maintain only, within ideological discourse, a watered down, symptomlike value that social theory could make use of to criticize and denounce the ideology of which it then is the simple product.

Notes

Chapter 9

[1] K. Marx, *Contribution to the Critique of Political Economy* (New York: International Publishers, 1970), Preface.

[2] Marx, *Contribution.*

CHAPTER TEN

The City's Portrait in Its Utopics

PROPOSITIONS

1. The city map represents the production of discourse about the city.
2. The deconstruction of this representation uncovers the ideology controlling it.
3. The city map is a "utopic" insofar as it reveals a plurality of places whose incongruity lets us examine the critical space of ideology.

DEFINITIONS

1. Ideology is the prepresentation of the imaginary relationship between people and their real conditions of existence.
2. The figure is a codified ideological signifier, and as such it functions by a process of concealment.
3. The discourse of the figure is the discourse producing the codes inherent in an ideology (of which this figure is a part).
4. The ideology of representation is the reflexive-intransitive form of ideology in general. It is produced by the appearance and development of capitalist forms of production (from the fifteenth century to the present).

Narrative-Description

In order to bring its textual and imaginary spaces into play utopic fiction allows two basic modes of discourse—narrative and description. The first is more immediately adapted for the diachronic and discursive manifestation of events, things, and beings. These appear as accidents, or notable incidents, and they are placed successively in a narrative syntagm of events. The listener becomes aware of them as he waits in expectation as they "come to be" in discourse. Narrative is discovery in the form of speech, which announces it, and of listening, which gathers it up. Even if these events have always been known, narrative is of the type of discourse that all that passes through it, in speech, is new. This is admitting, of course, that its discursive development, seized, as it were, in the very dynamics of its utterance, is brought about through a play between "showing" and "concealing." What is said rises up from the listener's unawareness at the moment it is said. This utterance was already "there," "unsaid," existent but unknown: such is the power of the illusion spun by referential reality. What has been shown by narrative discourse is something revealed but forever remaining partly in shadow. Narrative includes a hidden side whose nature consists always in presenting itself as the reversal of reality, its fatal correlative.

Even though description, being language, must yield to the same basic laws of narrative, it develops against the grain of narrative. As it builds, it must totally reveal its object. In order for description to do this it must mask its successive nature and present it as a redundant repetition, as if *all* were present at the same time. It is as if the object were always already visually present, fully offered to full view and potential speech. Description's time is present: a timeless present. As it marks out the perfect coexistence between the enunciating subject and the narrator's utterance, this timeless present erases his *hic et nunc* viewpoint from discourse. He is always at the exact intersection, spatially and temporally, of what is said. Discourse is thus offered as a supplement to the narrator's gaze.

Its force as language is also neutralized because of this. The act of enunciation is erased from the utterance; there is an excess of utterance concerning its reference. This latter element is both superfluous (always already there) and necessary (I can reach this original presence only when it is uttered). This is very different fron narrative, for not matter how exciting the surprise and impatient the waiting, and no matter how strong the illusion of reality, the event always appears for someone. It is the sudden *presence-for-him* of a thing, a being, a gesture; it is the meeting between an act of freedom, or destiny, and the language that tells of it. The act of utterance, the enunciation, dominates within the utterance, even if the (pro)nominal and self-referential marks are absent from it, and even if "the events seem to tell themselves."[1] Their status as events emerging into being, or "coming about," is achieved only when the narrative voice intervenes, even though this latter may be completely disguised by the enunciated expression's unfolding. This viewpoint can be either hidden or obvious: its constant displacement through successive positions marks out the diachronic eruption of the event and its discovery.

This is obvious in the utopic figure More stages at the beginning of his utopia. The narrator is present in the text as an "I," the enunciating subject, uttering a certain number of tales and narratives, as if he were absent from the description he sketches out in the discourse. However, this absence is the most laden of presences; it has a limitless power to see and know all. We have seen the formal and material meanings exhibited in the play of these two types of discourse, giving description its figural status and narrative its critical force to deconstruct representation. There utopic practice comes to see its relationship to history in the making.

Dialogue of Map and Narrative

The key, this time not of discourse but of the text, lies in this alternation between two types of speech: it is a dialogue by which the original narration achieves a sort of figurative status. This back-and-forth dialogue allows representation to present *itself*; in so doing it points out the hidden processes of its production in the pockets and narrative traces inscribed within it. By means of this articulation and relationship a discourse can carry with it a figure. *Utopia* can be a figure of discourse. Utopia is first and foremost a spatial organization designed for complete human dwelling, an activation of a sort of dwelling fantasy. Because it is mainly an architecture of places inscribed in space, the following question could be raised: Wouldn't geographic maps, and especially city maps, contain traces of a narrative discourse that would bring forth their spatial play? This, of course, would depend on the moment of history we examined and the types of narrative traces and signs we encountered. Recall that Utopia is a discourse, but it is also a figure of the discourse within discourse. How can discourse contain a figure? How can figures, which are imaginary, become text, thereby liberating a critical force that neither sign nor image possess?

On the other hand, with regard to a geographic or city map, can, and if so, how can, a discourse of that figure exist? Transposing the inhabited space of a city into a map aims at revealing its details and intricacies. We see and read it, but isn't this operation the opposite of that we witness for Utopia's island and city? Doesn't it reverse the movement from history to its schematic and monogrammatic figure in the fictional space of play, and also in the text? I tried to read this operation critically by locating the deciphering codes of history, during moments of crisis, within the text and utopic figure. Can one do the same for a map and thus uncover a *hidden* narrative by means of this operation? These operations would need to be revealed, then deciphered. Let me propose this project for two seventeenth-century maps of Paris as well as for the map placed in a painting: El Greco's portrait of Toledo. There I claim to find within the figurative and representative map texts that will produce potential narratives; they will contain in condensed versions the monograms of possible historical narratives, and the codes from which they are enunciated.

The movements I hope to disengage will be different from those we previously saw: from discourse and discursive figure to textual space, from text to historical movement, in one case, and from linear and graphic transcription to a possible discourse produced there, from discourse to a narrative of history, in the other case. They intersect at a privileged point of our critical research: a place of interference between systems of signs and of images, between representations and discourse, icon and letter, space and text. This is the utopic point.

This is perhaps why, in their own discourses, imaginary cities and ideal places like utopias are automatically proposed as possible maps in which there is a play of space to produce a text. This may also be why in their figures maps of real cities are automatically presented as *possible* discourses out of which a text can be constructed to produce a space; here we have text and space in both cases, where the difficult decoding of history takes place.

Voyages, Itinerary, and Map

In this deconstructive and productive reading of the map and the text it actually seems that we can take a short cut to get to the utopic point in these documents. There is in fact an almost direct assimilation that can be made between language and space: here the assimilation is between the notion of route and circuit and enunciated expression, between itinerary and discourse. The travel narrative would be a tracing out of unknown space with new routes; it would be a mapping by the inscription of lines on the blank page, on the virgin soil of a terra incognita. These notions also would apply for the geographic and city map. First, the map is an itinerary with successive stages—i.e., a narrative's enunciated expression with the scansion of its various narrative segments and sequences by rest areas, cities, and points of recuperation, by obstacles such as mountains and rivers to be crossed, by places where the traveler is awarded certain heroic and religious qualifications, famous sanctuaries, etc.

It has not been proven that the first medieval "maps" cannot be analyzed according to the categories put forth by structural narrative analysis. They involve legendary or magical, hagiographic or profane narratives. The moment of alienation would correspond, despite the familiar quality of the places and names, to the first phases of the itinerary because they would be moments of lack, at which point the quest for the object begins and where the narrative contract is agreed upon. This would be followed soon after in this travel syntagm by tasks and tests: according to their specific nature, they qualify, transform, glorify, etc., in order to satisfy a wish by the glory at the end. By being able to reverse the circuit on the map, we see that the nostalgic return reveals the constitution of a structural order characterized by its reversibility and by the a-chronism of relations woven by the various points of the itinerary. The scale here would be those temporal indications setting the length or "duration" of the trip: a conventional temporal measure would regulate the distance between points. The trip as an adventure narrative is thus granted its visible structure, as if this structure were dictated only by the repeated events of the voyage and by the narrative incidents. "Here the ordering comes from geography,"[2] and the map is first and foremost the itinerary of a pilgrimage, especially to the Holy Land, for the feudal and Christian West. The circuit or route is the enunciated expression performing the trip as a narrative, and the map is the geographic transcription of this expression obeying syntactic rules analogous to the latent and manifest principles of narrative discourse. Very often the basic vocabulary is the same: the toponyms referred to are the narrative's basic lexical configurations, such as cities, bridges, rivers, mountains, sanctuaries, etc. As the direct transposition of an itinerary, the map constitutes the text of a possible narrative discourse.

The System of Routes

But if the map inscribes enunciated expressions as "graphic" texts, it nonetheless radically eliminates their utterance, their enunciation. From the first it constructs the system of itineraries; it is the articulation at one fell swoop of all possible routes from one place to another. The map is the totalization of an ensemble of elements that are simply possible; it neutralizes their real formation into an itinerary. The routes within the itineraries are reduced to their text, and only to their text. In other words, they are reduced to an ensemble of elements defined by the possible positions they could occupy within the different routes. The map is thus a textual system lacking any specific process; or rather its processes are composed outside of it in a pragmatic use it always presupposes at its source and at its specific end. In this way the pilgrimage route to the Holy Land is the trace of a voyage, of an itinerary, but it is also the end-point and motivation, condensing into a single and totalizing metaphor: the Holy City.

Each point on the map would be a step in the direction of accomplishing this journey, by which is accomplished a desire triggered by a discursive process or narrative chain whose mapped text traces out its realization. Its real and symbolic trace is inscribed in the soil: the quest for the empty tomb where, as Hegel says, the sensuous completely disappears in the text of religious discourse. By examining the map of the Holy City, there is every possibility that one can reawaken this trace. The goal of the journey is the earthly projection of Heavenly Jerusalem, a perfect circle enclosing concentric circles of the *Templus Salomonis*, image of the world in its totality. Geographic space is thus the transcription of the "meta-physical," beyond this world, in the represented earth. Earthly life orients this journey and gives it direction and meaning. The inscription of the journeys and processes within a system becomes the text that holds them and articulates the mythology and ideology that gives them life. Narrative has moved into figure, and figure retains only narrative's structure.

In turn, however, figure as "geographic map" is a sort of schema that produces an entire group of possible narratives. Developing this large monogram should let us construct the code for this class, and offer this figure's latent discourse that the system inscribes and the text shows. It is obvious that the utopic moment has not yet occurred when the latent discourse is easily read in the play or tracings leading to the Holy Land in the itinerary from London to Jerusalem. If, in the toponyms and ideograms that mark out linear space, a single and obsessive meaning is given, the signifying practice of utopia's critical work has not yet begun. This is rather a moment of representation, when the mimetic and analogic operations of exchange between reality and image seek out their rules in geometry and optics, in scientific and technical mutation, and in political, social, and cultural crises.

Representations

The representative image can then try to signify the world that it imitates "exactly," and to substitute the figured sign for its reality. It would take its place completely and without residue. Next would come the moment in the discourse of representation (begun in the Renaissance), in language's signs and optic's figures, when a universal truth would be formulated: perfect adequation in signs, figures, things, and ideas. The singular cases, exceptional moments, and specific places would be excluded from this universal meaning. The signs of language, visual figures, and reason's truths would communicate in an equivalency within the great exchange of representation. Figure can then disguise, within its representative reality, the play between routes and circuits that founds and produces it. This mobile play originates figure's systems into an autonomous and closed ensemble.

From this it would seem all one would have to do is carefully examine representations in order to examine the world, to construct them in order to articulate being. The engineer, cartographer, painter, architect, playwright, and poet, all engaged in their individual activities, offer their image and meaning to the world. They extract from it its true reality within the representation they give of it. Nevertheless, this completely transparent and perfectly mimetic figure contains a play of meaning within the fullness of its analogon. The necessities of its willed absolute control, the traces of figure's hesitations and questionings, are all present. Utopic figure appears as figure of the world itself, but neutralized in its "otherly" place; it is neither panorama (of the world or city) nor map. It is not the face of the city "as the traveller discovers it from his ship's platform." It is not that image of the city lined with towers, ramparts, gables, or church-towers. It is not the flat unfolding of a bird's-eye view, omnipresent but nowhere.

The Utopic Figure of the City

With its portrait the city's utopic figure seems somewhere between geometry and panorama. It is a mapped, representative picture of the city on which place names are written: streets, recreational areas, squares, esplanades, etc. The names seem to exist only for this graphic recognition. The images of public buildings, churches, and dwellings are ordered in a way that is very different from the way a traveler would see them the very first time from his docking vessel. They are arranged from the perspective of seeing all the possible routes and circuits at once. They are arranged into a system of itineraries from the real city. The viewpoint is fixed at a totalizing point of view. One can see all. But the eye placed at this point occupies a place that is an "other" point of view: it is in fact impossible to occupy this space. It is a point of space where no man can see: a no-place not outside space but nowhere, utopic. With the panoramic view the city is seen as a horizon in the distance. The viewer is fixed to one spot on the earth and only slowly discovers, in the order of their appearance, buildings and streets. Some are hidden; others are in full view. If the city is then something hidden, waiting to be discovered, then it is easily understandable that a panorama is the semiotic transposition of a narrative circuit, one of many possible ones. "Still going toward the city, we discover the Gates of St.-Etienne, then beyond a bustling street lined by gayly painted houses. Through the gate, we reach the central square..." And there we have a potential narrative the panorama conceals in the representation of a walled city topped with roofs and steeples.

When represented geometrically the city is given as a whole, simultaneously. It is presented in its coexistence and co-presence. Free spaces are differentiated from constructed spaces. The system of streets, squares, and gardens is complemented by buildings, houses, palaces, and churches. Through the integration of these two systems the city loses its volume, its third vertical dimension. It is nothing more than a surface where there exist spaces filled and empty, black and white. The line triumphs, and all is compartmentalized. We have a vertical view, if you will. The viewpoint is not situated in one specific place, however. It is everywhere and nowhere, simultaneously. The entire surface is embraced, but each detail is present, granted a sort of regulated ubiquity, but only through the representative scale. There is no staging; simply a map. It is a surface structure that gives not a possible route, or even a system of possible routes, but articulations signaled by closed and open surface spaces. These are the original conditions of possibility for every possible route in every general "city in idea": "ideal" city, if you will, but this must not be confused with an imaginary city, an uninhabited or uninhabitable city. This "city in idea" is a figurative correlative of the descriptive discourse, transposing the ubiquitous image given by the map into signs and phrases of language by its repetitions, recurrent patterns, and condensations.

Utopic figure is simultaneously of the narrative and of the descriptive domain. This combination triggers a questioning in its very representation. This is exactly what occurs with a view from above, following the rules of linear perspective. This view is less a compromise between the horizontal and vertical than letting them play off one another. Thus we witness the internal workings of "true" representation: it reflects itself and thereby distances itself from the way the world works, all the while seeming to reproduce it exactly. A bird's-eye view gives us a "snapshot" of the city, given in its complete totality and as a system of its expressions, living in an instant of space. From the portrait of Venice by Jacopo Barbari to that of Paris at the end of the eighteenth century (called

Turgot's map) a wholly new genre comes to the fore: utopia of the city. At the same time utopia and the city are proposed in their most perfect likenesses; the city is given visibly, as it appears, and not as its idea would have it, according to a geometrical perspective from a viewpoint. Here the viewpoint gives a complete, total, and final image. Its narrative does not allow for a successive slow discovery, as in a panorama. Finally, the names written on the map trace out the texts of various routes and circuits: they are chains of enunciated expressions that create a movement with a precise direction for its reading. There are also visible signals, warnings, and indications (buildings and the like) that sketch out the lines for the city's portrait. This is how utopia takes over the representation of urban reality through its own practice. It also thereby begins a deconstruction of it by means of its ideology.

Utopic 1: This City, "Other World"

Mérian's 1615 map of Paris points to the representation of utopia by a poem:

> "This city is an Other World
> Within a flourishing world
> In powerful peoples and goods
> Of all things it abounds..."

This early seventeenth-century portrait of Paris relies on the map and the landscape. As map it seems to want to reproduce exactly a topographic image and a geographic orientation. The itinerary is recognizable through the names, and the map is made into a text and system through them. As landscape the picture offers us the representation of reality in its daily living. The viewer/spectator thus becomes the city's visitor and narrator: a carriage hurriedly makes its way to the Porte Neuve. A rider follows it at a gallop. Three herdsmen keep watch over their pigs near the Marché-aux-Chevaux, the horse market, where four horses are being inspected and tested by prospective buyers. Two horses are about to drink near the Porte de Nesle, while two bourgeois inhabitants converse in front of the Hôtel de Nesle. There two bandits hang from a gallows, not far from the garden of Queen Margarite. The incidental details have no role other than to give the impression that this representation is like reality itself; a narrative meets the eye, just as in reality, in its very unpredictable contingency. The map is thus penetrated by the landscape, which partially disperses its structure as a narrative accident and a "picturesque" detail. The landscape, however, is also infiltrated by the map, which inscribes into its representation its own written signs and graphic symbols. It takes hold of the disinterested urban landscape and issues it practical and cognitive goals. The representation has been put into play by means of signs, and the signs have been in turn affected by the contingency of the landscape: they become simple landmarks within the picture. In the incongruity of these two spaces we must try to read the secondary discourse indicated and dissimulated simultaneously.

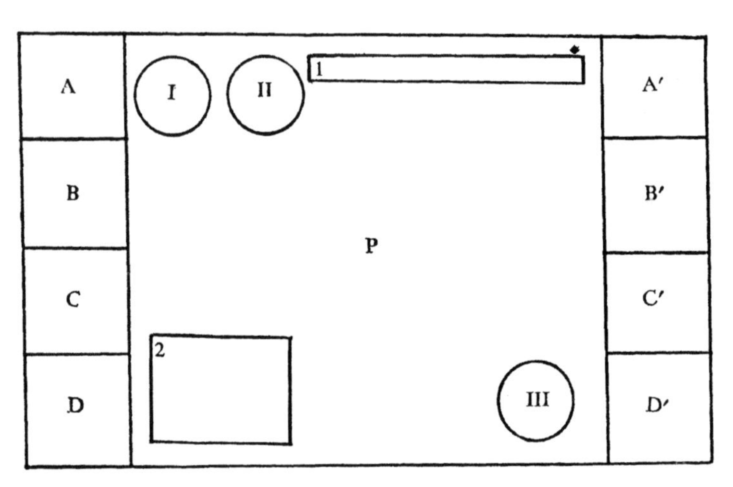

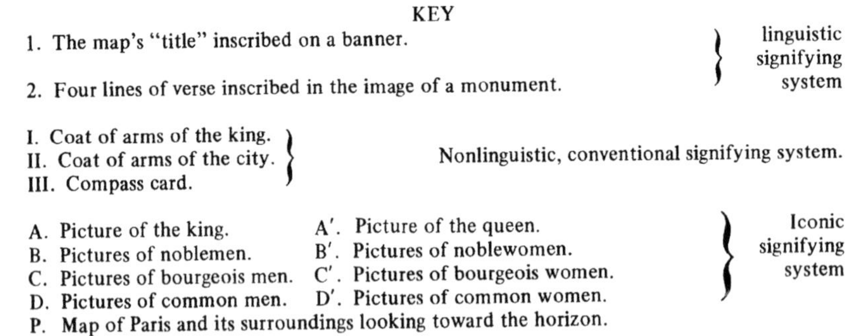

Plate 1: Diagram of Merian's map of Paris

The Picture Frame

Because of their "difference" from the landscape, the painting's surroundings will make up a code in which our urban utopic discourse will be formed. The decorative elements should limit the landscape, just as the representation's frame and codes are signifying. They define four coded dimensions within the discourse of figure. In other words, the representation's frame, in its polyvalent difference from what is represented, not only constitutes the representation as such, but also is the channel for the code in and by which this representation is represented. Not only is a space outside space constituted (u-topic), but the grammatical rules and lexical elements that determine the figurative discourse are exposed and laid down. These limit the play of represented spaces in the painting and help give the painting a meaning, and not just any meaning.

Title and Banners

The picture-portrait has its title inscribed on a banner: "Map of the Metropolis, City, Universities and Outskirts of Paris with the Description of its History." This title names the painting and makes up the upper part of its frame, one of its limits. By naming the painting the title offers on its very surface a summary of the elements of which it is composed: the metropolis as a city map—political organism—university—cultural and religious organism—outskirts—the area immediately surrounding its walls. The title simultaneously articulates its presence to the discourse that englobes it, description. It then connects this description to its history, its "present" contemporary inscription being the representation of the city: "with the Description of its History." As a signal for the painting, the title points out that this city here represented is Paris. It authorizes the exact adequation between representation and its object; the exchange between them is given in this landscape-map, but only after passing through a kind of screen, given, for the moment, as the network: "Metropolis—City—University—Outskirts—Paris—History..." The upper part of the frame includes two coats of arms, symbolic texts describing the city as the place of the king, capital of the state, and as a "bourgeois" city, a community of commodities and rights. These are new, nonlinguistic texts that articulate the representation by a second network.

Poem

The lower part of the frame is unmarked except for a monument inscribed by the poem already quoted. On its upper ledge is a decorative and emblematic arrangement of flowers and fruits. Visually, it signifies abundance and wealth, pompously granted the city and world it controls. In a way the poem in turn also lends title to the city and its represented spaces, but in a different manner. "This city..." the demonstrative refers to the representation of the city, to the figure inscribed in the painting. But it does so without individualizing it with a name. It refers only to the "portrait" the viewer directly contemplates. Recall here the text from the *Logic of Port-Royal* that defines the contract between mimetic representation and signs from language. Because there is a "visible relationship of meaning" between the representation and what is represented, I can *say* "directly and unqualifyingly," standing in front of the map of Italy, "It is Italy," or in front of Caesar's portrait, "It is Caesar."[4]

But a play of differences opens up in this perfect adequation between city and portrait. The deconstructive mechanisms of signifying practice and its utopic figure start their work. In fact, the poem, title, or signs that make up the banners are inscribed in a representation inside the representation. The main banner and its title, the monument and poem, and the coats of arms in the neutral field of laurels and Order of the Holy Ghost only duplicate the landscape-representation in a second representation whose only function is to support a text. This text points toward the city, in a certain way, and initiates our reading of it by a representative field specifying the code.

The city is another world, just as the emblems of abundance decorating the monument are of the graphic space of the poem inscribed on it. The city is signified doubly by a movement of metaphoric condensation: as one term of opposition to the world and as a world in itself. This is a different world, and difference itself becomes a world. The doggerel reproduces in the signified what the representation has provided visually. The world is the *natural* landscape of a flourishing city extending to the horizon of the panoramic portrait. Even the trees, herdsmen, villages, and castles echo it. But this landscape can be summarized and "reversed" into its contrary by offering it the stage of its representation: the Other World. The map-landscape of the city within its closed circularity reproduces the open space it inhabits and of which it is a part. But this space is also the center where wealth and substance is concentrated. And thus we encounter the third code for reading the discourse of the city as figure, the economic dimension of metaphoric-metonymic articulation. The city is thereby signified as a world different from the countryside and nature in general: utopia as city.

Pictures, Networks

The sides of the representation's frame are made up of eight rectangular inscribed medallions; both sides are connected by a twofold series, one that is sexual, the other social. On the left are men; on the right, women. From top to bottom, are the king (queen), noblemen (noblewomen), the nobility of the sword and wealthy merchants (noble wives and bourgeois women), workingmen and peasants (working- and peasant-women). In this way a sociological diagram of the city is formed following certain categories: the aristocracy, bourgeoisie, and common people, the whole crowned by the royal figure. This diagram is made up of a representation and an inscription that are completely demonstrative: "*Such is* in formal dress the King, unequaled in virtue–*Thus are gentlemen dressed* daily changing their vestments–Noblemen of the sword and wealthy merchants *are such* in the city of commerce–Peasants and workingmen dress *in this way.*" Similarly, for the women: "*See* an admirable Queen to whom France owes much–Noblewomen and ladies *are thus* in their dress–Noble wives and bourgeois women are good, *like this*, good and courteous–*Dressed in no other way* are those who carry broom and water."

By referring to the representation the inscription *indicates* only the clothing as a classificatory sign of social recognition, while simultaneously *signifying* the king and queen through virtue and admiration, noblemen and -women through their clothing, merchants and common women through their various activities. If there is ambiguity in classifying the inscriptions (especially concerning the common man), it disappears if we note the emblematic and classificatory value of the decor alongside the figures: palaces, thrones, armed guards for the king and queen. Notice the sculptured gardens for the noblemen and women; the ships, commodities, and harbor for the merchants; the saddled donkey and farmyard chickens, the cottage nestled in the countryside for the peasants. A third network–sociological and economic–is constituted on the sides of our representation of the city. Who lives in the city? What are their activities? The king and queen, the marks of virtue, are presented in their places as representatives of "good government." The court is made for show, glory, and prestige. The bourgeoisie is the source of wealth and worldly activities. The commoners, finally, are basically attached to *carrying* items into the city. The artisans and shopkeepers do not seem to appear, just as the churchmen are absent. The peasant is not cultivating the land; nature remains wild. Instead, he performs a tertiary activity: he transports goods. Notice, then, how all the productive and transforming activities have been concealed. The city is not to be read as a work-place. It is, rather, the place of virtue and glory, commerce and exchange. In other words, it is presented as a space of communication and of ethical and political transmission. It is a commercial and economic space, not a place for the production of goods or the transforming of nature.

Model

To formulate this in another way, and in so doing to conclude this section, the city as utopia plays with a number of spaces that do not overlap. In their play the city's ideological discourse can be interpreted: the representation of the imaginary relationship people have with their real conditions of existence. This representation is a result of a compromise formation between the landscape or panorama and map, the narrative (i.e., history) and description. The resulting representation would be the complete idealization of these elements. In the bird's-eye view of the city four codified dimensions cut into each other's domain, slowly narrowing and isolating themselves into articulations that are constantly shifting. The first dimension consists of the text, situated between narrative and description; the second is that of the political, between the royal space and the bourgeois community; the third becomes the economy, between the "flourishing" natural world and the "powerful" cultural center. The fourth, finally, consists of the social order, situated between virtue and glory on one side, commerce and exchange on the other. The first dimension introduces the representation's viewer-spectator into the discourse of figure. By means of the others he discovers the tensions between power and wealth, political virtue and commercial exchange. He sees how these tensions hide the labor and mask the true faces of the workers of the scene, the peasants and artisans. One can thus substitute the discourse of the utopic figure within its structure for the representation of the city in its portrait, thus indicating the codes for reading that discourse. It is this discourse that acts as the frame and limit of the representation.

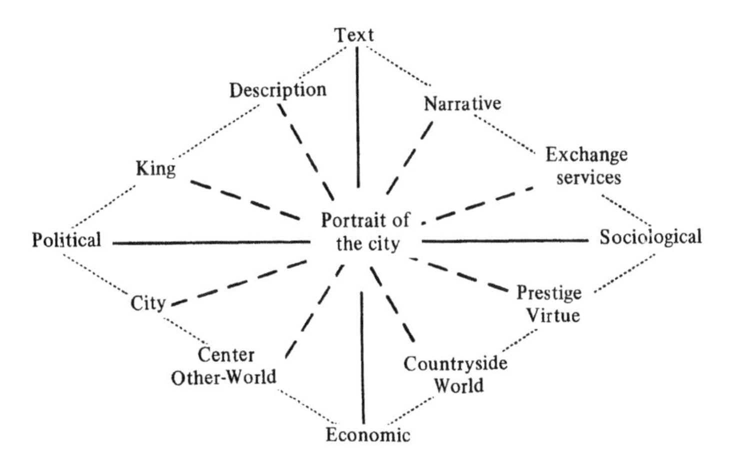

Figure 30. "Utopic" of Mérian's map of Paris (1615)

Utopic 2: The City in Its Geometric Form

The play of spaces and definitions of centers of meaning are yet stranger if we were to add to Mérian's map of Paris Gomboust's map, done some thirty years later. Both maps are of the same city, and both have the same geographic orientation. The topographic layouts are similar. However, every level of the reading code has been modified in the latter, and the political and economic discourse resulting from the map's text and in the play of figures is no longer the same. Even though the referent is identical, and even though certain of the rules governing syntax and some of the representative vocabulary do not change (west is still at the bottom so that church facades can be viewed), the discourse of figure shifts both in texture and code. Thus another city is shown to us; a different city is offered for decoding. A second text needs organizing, and another representation must be deconstructed. Just because the object of representation is the same and the two portrait-maps are similar should cover over the shifts and dispersion in the spaces set up. Here we are faced with a new urban "utopic."

First, there has been a shift in accent from narrative and panoramic to description and map. As A. Bonnardot, a nineteenth-century commentator, writes, "Here we are occupied with a map actually based on geometric principles.... It is so precise that it will have an influence on later maps for almost a

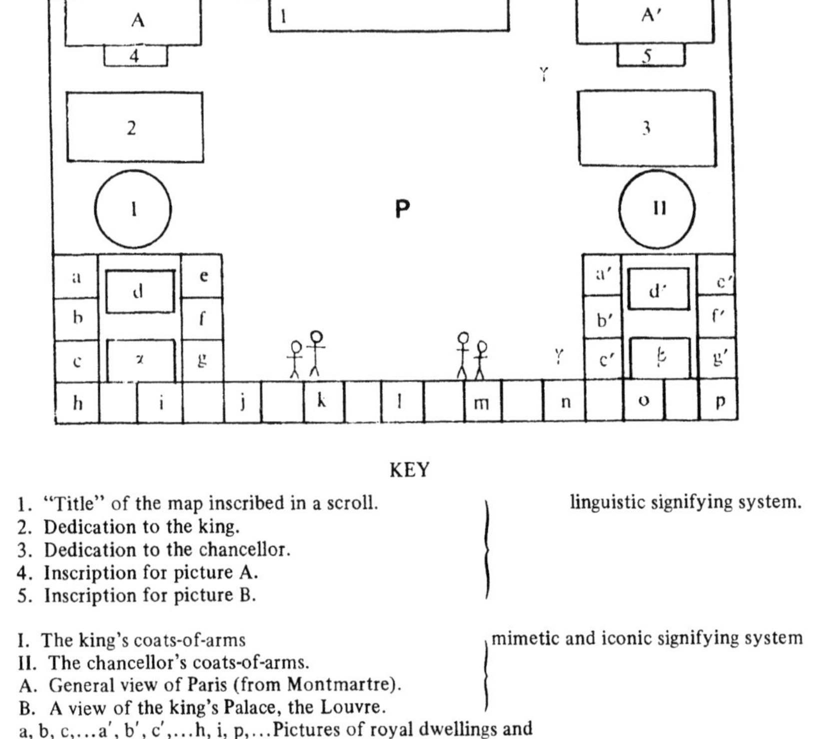

KEY

1. "Title" of the map inscribed in a scroll.
2. Dedication to the king.
3. Dedication to the chancellor.
4. Inscription for picture A.
5. Inscription for picture B.

} linguistic signifying system.

I. The king's coats-of-arms
II. The chancellor's coats-of-arms.
A. General view of Paris (from Montmartre).
B. A view of the king's Palace, the Louvre.

} mimetic and iconic signifying system

a, b, c,...a′, b′, c′,...h, i, p,...Pictures of royal dwellings and aristocratic palaces.

α, β, γ...: Scales and direction points } conventional, nonlinguistic, scientific signifying system

P. Geometric map of Paris (except for religious buildings, royal dwellings...)

Plate 2: Diagram of the map of Paris by Gomboust

century."[5] In fact, Gomboust transforms a number of techniques. He moves from the bird's-eye viewpoint to a geometric viewpoint. By giving up the pretension of *representing* the houses of Paris, remarks our scholarly commentator, Gomboust can provide an exact scale map, about 5.5 millimeters per ten *toises*. This illustrates a precise geographic geometry and a pretension to scientific exactness underlined in the dedication to the king and in the address to the readers inscribed on the surface of the map. The dedication and address are located inside the frame of the map, on the left in a sort of scroll and on the right in, again, a sort of monument:

> Here is the Map of your incomparable city of Paris that I venture to offer Your Majesty...Other maps of this same city which have been issued have been criticized as entirely false, and at least without measure or proportion. There is reason to hope that this map, composed according to the rules of geometry, will be considered not only because of the advantages that can be drawn from it in the service of Your Majesty, but also in order to prove the greatness and beauty of Paris to those in far-off lands who have believed its reputation to be beyond truth.

The poem of the microcosm, of the center and of the Other World, has been replaced by a reflection on scientific method, measurements, and calculations. In addition, there are six carefully established scales presented to the reader in a scroll both on the right and left supported by two large pedestals. These facilitate his rapid and practical orientation. The representation ceases functioning as the mimesis of a spectacle to be viewed and as the representation of an appearance. It turns into a geometric schema and analogic model whose metric rules of production are precisely put forth.

Ideological Values

Gomboust, however, does not completely abandon mimetic representation, the urban landscape or the bird's-eye view. He proposes another sort of compromise. The churches, palaces, mansions, and noteworthy dwellings are given as if from a bird's perspective, but the small islands of bourgeois and commoners' houses are symbolized by simple lines, and between the lines Gomboust provides dotted lines. In other words, figurative representation (the "landscape") is the privilege of certain constructions. Note that the privilege is accorded, essentially, to the political and to the religious. Aesthetic and aristocratic prestige, political power, and religious presence are given a representation that results from mimesis, history, or narrative discourse. Using the vocabulary we employed in our description of Mérian's portrait of the city, the rest of the city in its exchanges and services, commerce and bourgeois wealth, result from another type, a schematic geometry and learned structure. It comes from a semiological description of science. There is a redistribution of values that is different from what came before. The representation's split into two expressive levels is brought about through the articulation of sociological and political categories. The representation of the city blindly exposes its text; it reveals without further ado the two strata of different inscriptions. Their syntactical rules and utilization are different; the two spaces are complementary. Both make up the major portion of the map: the represented city.

Title, Panorama, Vanishing Point

The title itself is written on a banner in the upper center of the map—"Lutetia-Paris"—indicating the two historic poles of the city. On either side are two pictures inside the frame, but whose referents are taken from the geometric space they interrupt. The first, on the left, represents the entire map. Here the city is seen as a panorama, as opposed to the geometric view we examined in the map proper. The map has been transformed into a landscape with a particular inscription of its own: "Paris seen from Montmartre." The picture represents, in a mimetic perspective, what the map figures in a projected schema. The second, on the right, represents one of Paris' scenes, a section taken from the larger map: it is nothing other than the king's "space" when he is in Paris: "The *Galerie* of the Louvre." Considering only the visual movement controlled by perspective in the reproduction of this urban landscape, the Louvre is hidden from general view, left out among so many other roofs and chimneys. Yet it is actually the vanishing point for everyone's gaze, the focal point where everyone's contemplation converges. The whole city's visual concentration should narrow in on this space: the king's palace.

"Lutetia-Paris." The seizure of these two names takes place between the synoptic picture, which provides the referent, and this building, which gives it signification. Witness here the object designated by the name lending its title to the map, and witness the central place in this object giving meaning to both name and map. I have already noted a rupture between two inscriptive registers on the map, the mimetic space of the bird's-eye viewpoint and geometric schematic space. This rupture has been repeated and emphasized by the two pictures above. They also provide a sort of title to the map, similar to the two names we already saw. These pictures are two panoramas that provide two views from a certain perspective, a fixed and named point of view. They contain two particular views of Paris: a general view of Montmartre and a unique building on the Seine. These specific elements of perceptive visibility can be opposed to the structural visibility of the map and its geometric syntax and rational ideality. In addition, the urban landscape on the left encounters its perspective deconstruction in the picture of the king's palace on the right. The plastic screen gathering the appearances refers them to a focal point that organizes and articulates them. They disappear as they reach the eye of contemplation at the viewpoint. By this referential movement the unity of mimetic visual representation explodes in those pictures supposedly explaining it.

Monarchy, Bourgeoisie

But there is another deconstruction at work here because they clearly point out the *coded dimension, in ideology*, of the complementary spaces in the mimetic and schematic map: the opposition between essence and appearance, structure and image, geometry and mimesis. These oppositions are all related to royal power. If the viewpoint is the vanishing point, the place in which the represented figures are identically unified, and if it is also that space from which they usually develop into their variety, then the equalization of this focal power has profound meaning. The viewpoint is a royal *topos*, both a Maximum and a Minimum, God in Heaven and His representative on earth. The equivalence of those dwelling in abstract space inscribed on a geographic soil brings about a mapping of places in two-dimensional figures representing exactly the schema and the sacrifice of the viewpoint for a constantly displaced verticality. *Geometry* inserting itself into the city's map has profound political and social implications: it signals the presence of bourgeois rationality.

This opposition can also be found near the bottom of the map, indicated by the two large monuments on the left and on the right. They carry trophies, representative coats of arms and medals. First note that these two architectural elements are represented according to a precise perspective; they are seen on the reader-viewer's eye level. This is not surprising because the two bases carry the scales, which need to be read exactly. The scientific metric needs are thus underlined in mimetic representation itself. But the various panels of the two monuments present pictures in the form of painted landscapes: "Royal and noteworthy dwellings near Paris: Monceaux, Villers-Cotrait, Limours, Bois-le-Vicomte, Chantilly and Ecouen" are shown surrounding Fontainebleau Chateau on the left, while the royal coats of arms and martial trophies adorn the top. On the right are pictured Madrid, Versailles, Vincennes, Bicestre, Rueil, and Arcueil with the chateau of Saint-Germain, again while the chancellor's coats of arms and symbols of the law, of science, and of the arts decorate the upper portion of the monument. Each of these two groups corresponds to the two texts, which are spatially very closely tied to them. One is a dedication to the king; the other to the chancellor. They provide the secondary codes that help to decode the various symbols and emblems of the monuments.

Actually these landscapes, pictures of a macrocosm under the influence of royal might and the state's civil power, serve the same function as Mérian's poem for his "portrait of Paris," itself posed alongside the king's and the city's coats of arms. Here, however, the natural world and countryside in opposition to the social and cultural world of the city are represented by pictures drawn in proper linear perspective. In this representation of Paris, its geographic surroundings are nothing but the political metonymy of the city's central place: the Royal Palace. Within this perspective, representation's vanishing point is developed and explained not only in the general scene of Paris (city of the king, as Gomboust writes in his dedication), but also in those outlying areas of Paris defined by the metonymic network of royal dwellings revolving around the two secondary palaces, Saint-Germain and Fontainebleau. Let me add one last remark to this construction-deconstruction of the map: also present in this mapped inscription of power are the aristocratic powerful. Below the oak leaf frame, ten chateaux are presented, one after the other, each separated by a leafy garland. Each chateau has its toponym, and each its owner's patronym: "Anet belonging to Mounsieur de Vendosme; Dampierre belonging to Monsieur de Chevreuse; Rosny belonging to Monsieur de Sully; Nanteuil belonging to Monsieur de Schomberg," etc.

Figures of Enunciation

Closing this study of maps leads us back to problems I originally raised at the beginning concerning the relationship between narrative and description; we were concerned with the discursive narrative voyage and its story of an enunciative itinerary and textual system. This system was made up of elements in certain positions, also entertaining possible relations among themselves, all forming the totalization of a circuit. Thus emerges utopia, the representative product of a signifying practice of neutralization. It acts as the staging of figure through a play between narrative and description, and further removed by a play between the referred spaces of the text and the spaces of the text. Because of this play and this staging, figure within its representation partially liberates and affects a latent figural discourse where its own productive traces emerge, which let us deconstruct it by revealing them.

We have the marks of this spatial play and staging of the spaces of and in the text; they exist in the map or, more precisely, within the ambivalence between schema and picture. Issuing forth from behind the large decorated monuments, a number of figures appear. Standing on a hillside planted with bushes and shrubs, we see on the left a rider and his horse, followed by his servant. On the right side, a woman and her two attendants contemplate Paris. Both groups seem

Gomboust's Map of Paris (1647)

MAP of PARIS under LOUIS X

M, by Mathieu MÉRIAN – 1615

Panorama and map of Toledo by El Greco (ca. 1609)

Museum of Toledo

to be advancing toward the city. These small, insignificant figures trigger the narrative; they begin the itinerary from the plains of Grenelle through the rue de Varenne, passing by the gardens bordering the Seine that lead to the Porte de Richelieu. These are figurative, enunciative signs, gestures represented in the very representation of the organizing act. They produce the discourse for the larger figure of Paris. But what do they actually see as they follow their itinerary toward Paris? Of course they see Paris, but which Paris, which city space? The space rising in front of them is geometric; the map on the wall or unfolded on the ground can only be seen from a determined point of view. Nevertheless, they look at this same Paris from hillsides straddling the Seine, from Grenelle and the *faux-bourgs* of Montmartre.

The rider and woman are figures of the incongruity of spaces within representation. They demonstrate how the map straddles schema and mimesis, the force of a bourgeois and rational idea for a city *reduced to its map* and the power of a monarchic royal *topos as represented from one single point*. This is utopia, the city contained within its map, but whose spaces do not correspond. Rather, they interfere, producing the first statements of an ideological discourse about the city.

In addition, a meaning different from the sociological grid Mérian painted on the sides of his map emerges with Gomboust's engraved figures. Recall Mérian's order: men on one side, women on the other, and both groups socially ordered. With Gomboust we find a similarity, men on the left, women on the right, but they simply represent an enunciation that rapidly disappears in the geometric map but then reemerges in the two pictures above, "Paris Seen from Montmartre" and "The Palace of the King." Our tiny figures do not see Gomboust's map engraved by A. Bosse and sketched with the help of Petit, administrator of fortifications, correspondent of Mersenne, and Pascal's partner and collaborator. It is rather the landscape within the map that they see. From this view of Paris in general they begin the itinerary of enunciation, beginning at Montmartre and continuing on to produce a narrative of Paris, every representation new and surprising. They head toward the representation's focal point, the very principle of representation: the king's space, his palace, the Louvre. As the rider and lady present homages in the courtier's flattering manners, the narrative of the city will come to a close at the moment another, already-suspected, silent discourse opens: the monarchy's political discourse.

Attempting once again to schematize the discourse of figure and of the city's utopia in its structure, the following results help pinpoint its reading codes:

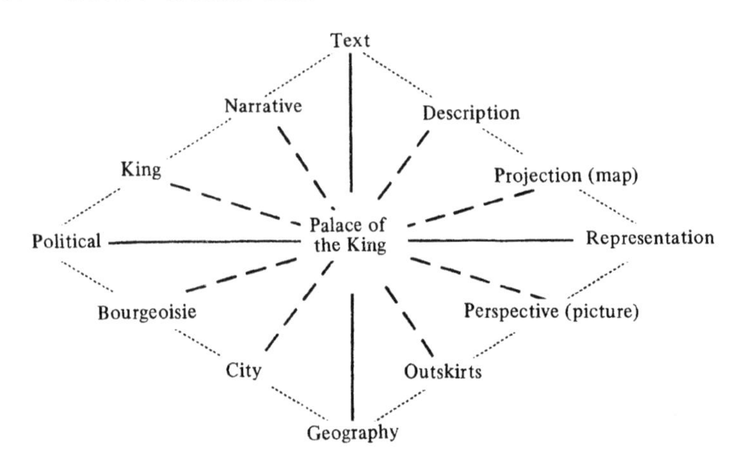

Figure 31. "Utopic" of Gomboust's map of Paris (1647)

Utopic 3: Dis-location of Toledo

A painting by El Greco representing the city of Toledo shows so clearly the play of multiple spaces characteristic of utopic production that one wonders if the very patent and obvious theme of the painting is not to represent the deconstruction of the representation and thereby to demonstrate the ideological discourse in which it is caught. It is possible that the utopic figure's critical force, within the representation, was reinforced by El Greco's "position-of-speech." It is both marginal and archaic. Being the very place of the producing discourse through its placement and by its contingent historic situation, it allows for critical theory itself by including the enunciation in the critique.

Schema and Landscape

Four spaces play off each other here in the same representation. The enunciating gesture and its reversal are commented on by the representation in a text included in the picture. Two poles are represented in the work: a panoramic "portrait" of the city and its geometric map. This map is situated at one end of the pictorial representation and becomes its perfect accomplishment. Because it is *painted* as part of the picture and as a map, it represents in a mimetic way the analogon of a map. Henceforth the deconstruction has begun. This is different from Gomboust's map of Paris, where the city is mimetically represented by its political and religious monuments and geometrically projected into a schema of streets and bourgeois houses. The two spaces are complementary and thus constitute the map of Paris. Here, rather, the urban landscape of Toledo is represented from a specific point of view situated on the other side of the ravine. The city seems like some great stretched archway of clear blue sky. This landscape has also been transposed into another space devoid of apparition and images. It appears in the surface of a map, alone capable of an exact diagram of the city's topography, lacking any point of view. This second space doubles the first. It occupies a supplemental position and places the painting's viewer-reader in an ambivalent position; he must decode the picture and contemplate written signs. His functions form a sort of chiasmus of spectacle to be viewed and text to be *deciphered.*

But note that the map is a bluff. It is actually completely a spectacle to be viewed because, in its exactness and geometric rigor, it is nothing but illusion. Geometry returns into mimesis without, however, giving up its geometrical nature. Toledo that *you see* on the slope, like a great crescent, is but the appearance of its intelligible schema, of its almost circular structure that *you think out* on a flat surface—stretched, extended, and fragile. But the schema inscribed in the map, the sheet of parchment, is in turn an image of the painting representing the landscape of Toledo—an image of an image that offers, nevertheless, the exact diagram of it. The geometric map goes back into the painting of which it is part and parcel. And yet it represents it, entirely. At this point in the analysis, El Greco's work is the structural reverse of Gomboust's; included in the geometric map of the city this time are not the two signifying "ornaments," the urban landscape and the focal point, the King's palace. Instead, the map has been put in the landscape. This reversal echoes political sway: Gomboust the bourgeois, friend of engineers and scientists, highly acclaims the rigors of scientific truth. He allows political discourse a place, but off to the edges as rhetorical figures, especially evident in the two paintings. Domenico Theotocopoulos, the Greek, gets a hand on geometry in 1609 and inserts it in trompe l'oeil; he makes the map be a part of the painting. In the most illusory of resemblances, he indicates that representation is not resemblance, as Descartes will write in the *Optics*. But *where* is Toledo, if not in the unrepresented, and unrepresentable, gap separating the whitish rectangle of the map upon which the schematic diagram is inscribed and that arched landscape and the image that appears there?

Myth and Allegory

Let me sketch out the two other spaces that play into the space of the landscape and map. They activate two domains, mythic history and rhetorical allegory, which are unlocatable within the mimetic representation and its geometric double. The picture of the city in its utopic figure can reveal and stage them through their metaphors: in the lower-left corner, a river god huddled in a sort of fetal position has tipped over an amphora containing water of the Tagus. The river had been sketched out on the map rather conventionally by a winding line; it was absent from the landscape, bubbling at the very bottom of the ravine, the top of whose cliffs the city dominates. In the painting it has produced its poetical and allegorical *topos* as an allegory or symbol, not of the king or of the city, but of an element absent from the painting but present on the map. It can only be inserted into the representation as metaphor; otherwise the authenticity of the city's image would be put into question. This metaphorical space inscribes into the landscape the risk of a figure in the unlocatable spot of the absent represented element. As he turns away from the viewer, the obscure figure counterbalances the shining presence of the figure exhibiting the map: here in the painting is this obscure figure's symbolic double.

In the sky directly above the cathedral's spire, a descending group of figures reproduces more than coats of arms, an allegory, or the city's emblems and mythic figures involved in a miraculous exploit. Here, surrounded by angels, the Virgin has come down from heaven to bring a chasuble to her faithful paladin, the Archbishop Saint Ildefonso. This legendary narrative has left the mark of its privileged moment on the city's panorama. In fact, it inaugurates the city's history by summarizing it in this unusual monogram and this emblem. What elsewhere had been inscribed in the text as a history of the city (the title of the portrait of Paris had referred to and recalled it) here is provided by a mythic vision granting Toledo its heavenly origins. This is the second metaphoric space of an originating history that the schema of the city figures elsewhere. The mythic monogram now must be added to the painting, at another level than that of the unfolded geometric diagram with its intelligible drawing. This group of figures, in its ensemble, provides the movement of religious tradition.

In this way, the heavenly cipher and poetic allegory (instead of the river) are two differentiated metaphoric spaces that isolate two legendary fragments related to the city map. These spaces are its *legendum*, allowing for the deciphering of its geometric abstraction in the signifieds, each one spelled out, of the drawing's signifiers. The river god and the Virgin carrying the chasuble are two *legenda* of the painting; they are two places in which are deposited coded elements of our reading, and a varied accomplishment in the state of dispersion. This is the distance separating the doubles in the landscape and in the map within the deconstructed unity of the same representation.

The Figures of Enunciation and Its Reversal

In order for my critical reading to come to a conclusion, or at least to the beginning of a conclusion, the enunciative marks and an enunciative reversal need to be mentioned. The representation carries these marks on its surface and even provides a commentary on them in a text written in its utopic place. The city may present itself in the representation of its landscape, but the map is shown by a human figure. We are thus informed that the map is a representation of a representation, the geometric schema of a landscape, if the city as panorama is given to us as a representation. But this double of the landscape enters into the landscape because of the figure carrying it; he is a part of the painting there, at the lower-right side, looking at the viewer, this latter raising his or her eyes up toward him. The angle his arched arms form responds formally to the arch formed by the city's landscape. It is through this figure that the spaces of the spectator-viewer and the representation talk to each other. Within the very painting, he is both an enunciative and receptive mark. He is the painter's delegate: he points out the spectator's position by showing him the map.

But it is easy to see that he does not fit into the represented space. He and his map do not belong to the landscape. He produces a new space in the painting: the place of enunciation. His space is the place of him who represents; it is neither inside nor outside the representation. Through it a second place allows for the staging of representation; here the painter is shown in the form of his delegate. In truth, he presents, in the representation, the map that represents, in schematic form, the city represented in the painting. He is the obvious exhibitor or the simultaneity of co-presences of surface areas. In the geometric formulation of the city, all is visible, nothing dissimulated. The presence of the painter echoes his negative obscure figure of the river god, this latter allegorically figuring an element present on the map but absent in the landscape. By coiling up and avoiding the spectator's eyes, he is totally enclosed within his own metaphoric space. He reverses the represented figure of enunciation. The figure of the exhibitor is thus a self-reflexive and critical abstraction for the process of representation: the painted man opens up the space in which the painting points to itself. This is the figure of the index: ***this is*** Toledo, two times in its map and in its landscape.

The Utopic Center

The representative for the enunciation is one of the poles on this "utopic" triangle of the city, simultaneously mythic and historical, rhetorical and symbolic, geometric and linguistic. In the play of interferences between these three poles that make up the city, and at their intersection, a surprising image emerges. A noble structure rests on a cloud between the city's map and the reclining god, directly underneath the Virgin in the hollow of the span of the landscape's arch. This is a fantastic, yet worldly, image. It is the reversed and symmetrical image of the holy image of the virgin. This earthly image functions not as a foundation for the city represented in the mythic tradition of the origin, but as a deconstruction of the representation. It signifies its own order through the ***reversal of what is represented*** within the painting of the urban landscape. Is not this structure the San Juan Baptista Hospital, situated, backward, in another place?

El Greco was not reluctant about providing the code for the critical productive operation or his reasons for it:

> It was necessary to include Don Juan Tavera Hospital in the form of a model [*en forma de modelo*—Barrès paraphrases this by: "that is, by presenting it as a detail, by putting it outside the ensemble"], because not only did it hide the Visagra Gates, but its cupola reached to such a height that it rose above the city. Once I had placed it as a model, and moved it, it seemed to me [preferable] to show its facade rather than its other sides. If one wants to see the rest of it, the map can be consulted. As for the story of Our Lady carrying the chasuble to Saint Ildefonso, it was for ornamental reasons [*para su ornato*] and to make the figures large, that I availed myself [I took advantage—*me he valido*], in a certain way, of the fact that it was a question of painting heavenly bodies. I treated them by taking advantage of how we see things illuminated: seen from afar and in reality very small, they seem to us large.[6]

Thus at the very center and in the utopic place of the painting, El Greco figures the deconstruction of the representation. This place is the plural space for the intersection between myth, allegory, and enunciation. El Greco points out the neutralizing work of utopic practice within the representation of the city. Indeed, the viewpoint is given by the contradiction in the scale and by the front and the back. The representation falls apart in the thing represented. In addition, the structure cannot be represented in the map on its own scale: another structure must be represented there, in the schema.

On the map we see one different from the one in the painting. A narrative route can discover it, however: El Greco's own text written about the painting. This edifice is very much in the form of a model, not only, as Barrès notes, because the painter has placed it away from the ensemble and presented it as a detail, but because it is a metaphor, the metaphoric figure *en forma de modelo* of the operation of critical reversal. The enunciative position has been reversed in the enunciative expression, the thing represented, even though it produces it and organizes it. It *shows* the shift and spacing between the map and the landscape. It *signifies* the substitution between the orders of painting and nature. The structure breaks away from "perspective's" demands as well as the "projective" demands. A "real" architectural structure is represented as an apparition. It is transformed into the "other" of the glorious mythical vapors coming down from heaven. Lastly, with the whitish mists on which the structure rests, it institutes a neutral space or the figure of neutral space situated in this blind zone of representation clouding over the perspective point of view and focal point. These two are wiped out in the temporality of *written discourse:* the painter *explains* the operation for transforming represented reality and *submits the heavenly image* to the laws of geometry and the optics of light.

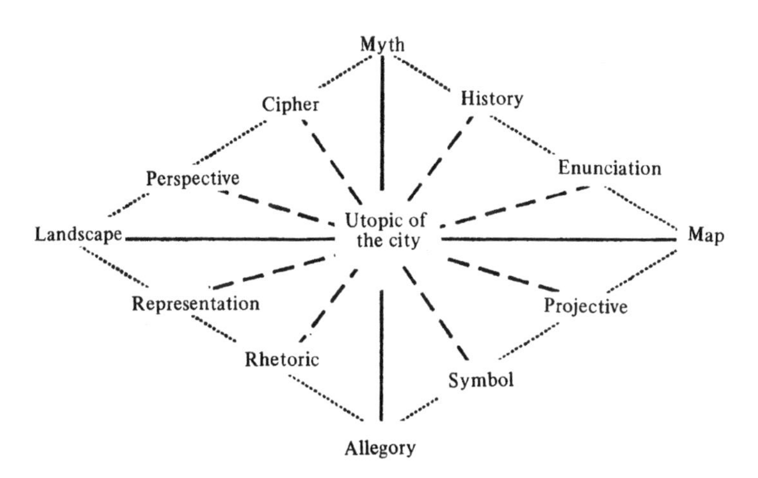

Figure 32. "Utopic" of the map and the painting of Toledo by El Greco (1609)

As a conclusion, Figure 31 is a model once removed from the previous one, based on El Greco's painting. It shows the utopic play involved in the representation of the city within the multiple spaces where it is figured.

Notes

Chapter 10

[1] Emile Benveniste, *Problèmes de linguistique générale* (Paris: Gallimard, 1966), pp. 237 ff.

[2] H. Lavedan, *Les Représentations des villes dans l'art du Moyen Age* (Paris: Van Oest, 1942), p. 15.

[3] Hegel, *Lectures on the Philosophy of World History* (New York: Cambridge University Press, 1975).

[4] *Logique de Port-Royal*, Chapter XIV, Part 2 (Paris: Flammarion, 1970), p. 205. Cf. Louis Marin, *Etudes sémiologiques*, pp. 164–65.

[5] A. Bonnardot, *Etudes archéologiques sur les anciens plans de Paris* (Paris: 1856), p. 292.

[6] M. Barrès, *Greco ou le secret de Tolède* (Paris: Plon, 1923), pp. 114–16.

CHAPTER ELEVEN

Utopia of the Map

"Of Exactitude in Science.

> *...In that Empire, the craft of Cartography attained such Perfection that the Map of a Single province covered the space of an entire City, and the Map of the Empire itself an entire Province. In the course of Time, these Extensive maps were found somehow wanting, and so the College of Cartographers evolved a Map of the Empire that was of the same Scale as the Empire and that coincided with it point for point. Less attentive to the Study of Cartography, succeeding Generations came to judge a map of such Magnitude cumbersome, and, not without Irreverence, they abandoned it to the Rigors of Sun and Rain. In the western Deserts, tattered Fragments of the Map are still to be found, Sheltering an occasional Beast or beggar; in the whole Nation, no other relic is left of the* Discipline of Geography."
>
> (*–Suarez Miranda.* Viajes de Varones Prudentes, *Lib. IV, Cap. XIV, Lerida 1658*). Quoted by Jorge Luis Borgès.[1]

1. We will confront the parable directly: there is movement from map as analogic model of its object, and which reduces its object according to a predictable measured scale to map as a "double" of the Empire, its "other." This movement goes from representation to the utopia of representation; at the same time the represented object is converted to its simulacrum, unlocatable because it is the map in its complete correspondence to the Empire, yet different from it. Rather, the Empire is different from the map, because it remains, whereas the map is discarded. This gap is very strictly the place of the neutral. The practice of this difference is utopic. This is so because maps of a city, country, or continent—no matter what the scale, how reduced, or what has been erased or included—always implicitly functions as a double. They are diagramatic repre-

sentations and schemata whose syntax (its rules of reduction and selection) is explicit, but forgotten in nature once our gaze settles on it in its multiple circuitry: "As we perceive the thing signified from its sign, it is clear that we do not mean that this sign is really other than what it signifies. We simply mean that it is other as a sign and figure. Thus we say directly and unqualifyingly...of a map of Italy that it is Italy."[2] The expression commented on in 1683 by the logicians of Port-Royal, and the gap between the meaning of the figure and the "expression" of the thing itself, are the themes of the parable "quoted" by J. L. Borgès.

2. The forgetfulness that moves in between speech and the intention that brings it to life is nothing else than the trace or wake of passage of the force contained in the neutralization the map carries along with it. The perfect map conserved the mark of difference within the exposition of its rules. The map of hubris is infinite reproduction. This does not mean numerically or distributively indefinite, as with the printing press Raphael described, which teaches the Utopian people the secrets of the West, but, rather, infinite in a qualitative way. The map beyond measure is so perfectly measured that it is no longer an analogon of the country, its equivalent, but is, rather, its double and "other." It inverts the *measure* of sizes, which nevertheless produces it, into the fiction of *simulacra.* Double: therefore indistinguishable from the space and places it doubles. Nevertheless double: therefore different, "other," from them.

3. One of the keys to the parable concerns history: the map cannot resist it. The desecrating movement of time reveals the useless passion involved in this creation of simulacra, no matter how exact or scientific it is. The science of models is a mythic procedure; it provides a society with the illusion that it can affect its future, that it can reproduce its origin or even *itself.* The utopic *work* is not only contained in constructing that double or representation in order to enable a city or society—some bit of reality, even—to see itself as different from itself or other than the way it perceives itself. It carries with it a reversed, negative image. This is the result of an impious decision because countless generations have played out this founding origin and immobile beginning in the map's double. It is also, however, an effect of time. With and in time, abandoned, the double makes its appearance as the double of..., and therefore different. It stops being the imperceptible duplicate and is seen to have been produced at a specific time—in fact, at that specific time when it corresponded exactly to

reality. The utopic figure's goal is thus to imprint on a dynamic world the history of the traces of its production. With these traces the world can be thought. As they were being set down, the traces of the passage of time did not reveal their value.

4. At first the extensive map was nothing but a simple sketch executed by the College of Cartographers. Even when it had come to be the indiscernible double of the Empire itself, it was still different, or utopic, in its figurative representation. Standing before the map of the Empire, when its subjects *said*, "This is the Empire," they really *meant*, "This is a figure of it." And this is why they lived both in the Empire and in the map, as a representation: the image of their own homeland that was offered to them by the elite of the Empire was both within measure and unusual. The utopic figure of the Empire is, in this sense, a product of the ideology of representation; the Port-Royal text provides its perfect logical and grammatical expression. The contradictory movement of history displaces the utopic map, which henceforth becomes the figure of its difference, far off and long ago, marginal, different, subhuman and antisocial, in ruins. "In the western Deserts, tattered Fragments of the Map are still to be found, Sheltering an occasional Beast or beggar." Here the utopic figure has been set in motion, the result of historic contradiction. The ideological representation that was formerly locked in its identity has been freed.

5. Let me examine Borgès' text as the producer of the map's utopia, as the trigger that reveals the utopic work in the representation. Borgès repeats the cartographic operation. Through this repetition in a textual maneuver, he releases its neutralizing force, and at the very place of this force's production he points to himself. Borgès' text is quoted from another text; in fact, Borgès' text *is completely quotation.* Borgès' own discourse is missing; no frame exists to indicate, *through difference*, its obvious status as a quotation. J. L. Borgès and Suarez Miranda, the Argentine writer and Spanish narrator, become one in text just as the map coincides with the empire, point for point. But Miranda is Borgès' other, just as the map was other than the empire. It is impossible to define the distance separating them; yet they cannot be distinguished without the gap separating a simulacrum from its object. What is Borgès' enunciating position? From what spot is he speaking? How can the discourse on the extended map be uttered? It must be done from a nonplace, neither imaginary nor unreal. Can the fact that Suarez Miranda does not exist, and never did exist,

be proven? Can it ever be shown that he never wrote *Viajes de Varones Prudentes* or that this work includes no chapter XIV in Book IV? We cannot affirm, however, that Borgès "imagined" this Spanish writer or his book or its publication date or, for that matter, this small textual fragment. In truth, no other text exists: it is Borgès; it is Miranda. The texts are two, and both provide the ultimate framework for the other, the white page on which it is written. Borgès' text only exists in the neutralization of Miranda's text, just as this latter acquires textual consistency only with respect to the degree zero of writing that quotation really is. What we are really reading here is the reverse side of Borgès' text. The one side can be read through the presence of an absent text on the other. This absence is the enunciative position, the place of the author and the origin. Now it is clear why the extended map in the story told to us seemed like the mythic repetition, even in the most exact scientific environment, of the founding origin. This is a useless passion: both a Sartrian definition of God, and that of "author."

6. "Of Exactitude in Science" demonstrates for us exactly the utopia of the text in which it is expressed. In its singularity this text may reveal the crucial experience of the utopia of every text, a play of levels and surfaces joining together and breaking apart to articulate "possible meaning"; there is play in the movement because each image is but coincidental, point aligning with point, between a surface of identities making any difference between the Empire and its Map indiscernible. This is how the text's utopic figure works. Soon, however, as the impious succeeding generations show us, wear begins to appear in the image; levels and surfaces play, incongruous spaces line up and separate, spaces full of meaning and empty of definition come into contact: this also is utopic practice as it produces the text.

7. The capital letters mark out the immeasurable distance between the map and the empire. The empire deserves an E only in its ideal institutional existence, as map. Time is measured only through the Rigors of Sun and Rain, through time's deconstructive effect on the map and its damaging power. The same is true for succeeding Generations. Capitals seize meaning's signifying force in order to create monumental solemnity and tradition. Representation has sucked on reality. As a vampire, the blood of things has been absorbed by their doubles. They exist and have meaning only with respect to the map. They signify only through it, even when it is absent: "in the whole Nation, no other relic is left

of the Discipline of Geography." On the other hand, the "reality" of writing, the presence of the text, is both contested and constituted.

Notes

Chapter 11

[1] Jorge Luis Borgès, *A Universal History of Infamy* (New York: E. P. Dutton, 1972), p. 141.

[2] *Logique de Port-Royal*, p. 205.

CHAPTER TWELVE

Utopic Degeneration: Disneyland

PROPOSITION:

A degenerate utopia is ideology changed into the form of a myth.

REFERENCES:

1. Ideology is the representation of the imaginary relationship individuals maintain with their real conditions of existence.
2. Utopia is an ideological place; utopia is a sort of ideological discourse.
3. Utopia is an ideological place where ideology is put into play; it is a stage for ideological representation.
4. Myth is a narrative that resolves formally a fundamental social contradiction.

COMMENTARY:

In trying to analyze Disneyland as a utopic space, two goals are intended. First, I mean to show the permanence of some patterns of spatial organization that can be qualified as utopic. Not only can they be found in architectural schemata and related works, but they are also in works that fill a specific function with regard to reality, history, and social relations. The patterns I am seeking can all be classed, theoretically and speculatively, as expressions of utopic practice. All contain a neutralizing critical impact, and within ideology the neutralization defines the specific space for building and elaborating social theory. These patterns and functions appear in the topography of ***a real space*** in California, and by the visitor's real use of it. From this vantage point the eventual tour that visitors commence when they come to Disneyland can be viewed as the narrative that characterizes utopia. The map of Disneyland visitors buy in order to know how to go from one place to another can play the role of the description; it performs the part of the representational picture which also characterizes utopia. But this real example is more interesting from another point of view: I would like to show how a utopic structure and utopic functions degenerate, how the utopic representation can be entirely caught in a dominant system of ideas and values and, thus, be changed into a myth or a collective fantasy.

Disneyland is the representation realized in a geographical space of the imaginary relationship that the dominant groups of American society maintain with their real conditions of existence, with the *real* history of the United States, and with the space outside of its borders. Disneyland is a fantasmatic projection of the history of the American nation, of the way in which this history was conceived with regard to other peoples and to the natural world. Disneyland is an immense and displaced metaphor of the system of representations and values unique to American society.

This function has an obvious ideological function. It alienates the visitor by a distorted and fantasmatic representation of daily life, by a fascinating image of the past and the future, of what is estranged and what is familiar: comfort, welfare, consumption, scientific and technological progress, superpower, and morality. These are values obtained by violence and exploitation; here they are projected under the auspices of law and order.

All ideological pressures are brought to the fore here. All the forms and aspects of capitalist alienation and of modern imperialism are represented. Disneyland is the representation of the makeup of contemporary American ideology. Because this place is a stage and place of projection where we can view and test out the ideology of the dominant groups in American society, we might assume that this world built by Walt Disney fulfills the critical function for ideology we noted for utopic production in general.

This is not the case, however, because this "stage" where ideology is put into play and where its critical function comes to operate is really not a stage. The visitors to Disneyland are on stage themselves; they are actors in the performance in which they act. They are captured, like a rat in a maze, and are alienated by their part without being aware of performing a part. In this way, then, Disneyland does not "work" like a projection of ideological representation. Disney's utopia really is not a utopia. Only when a meta-discourse analyzes its map does it become one. Then we can look at the semantic structures. We can examine how the visitors' tour becomes a narrative, how their itinerary becomes a narrative, how their itinerary becomes "lexical," revealing a reading for the picture as a whole. The divergent systems then emerge, pitted one against the other, and their correlations can be examined. Thus the backstage workings are revealed, and their ideological meanings and repercussions can be pinpointed. It is at this point that a degenerate utopia, changed into text and image, can start to produce. It should tell us what we have known since the development of a theory of political economy and ideology.

In other words, the visitors to Disneyland are put in the place of the ceremonial storyteller. They recite the mythic narrative of the antagonistic origins of society. They go through the contradictions while they visit the complex; they are led from the pirates' cave to an atomic submarine, from Sleeping Beauty's castle to a rocketship. These sets reverse daily life's determinism only to reaffirm it, but legitimated and justified. Their path through the park is the narrative, recounted umpteen times, of the deceptive harmonization of contrary elements, of the fictional solution to conflicting tensions. By "acting out" Disney's utopia, the visitor "realizes" the ideology of America's dominant groups as the mythic founding narrative for their own society.

The Limit

One of the most notable features of the utopic figure is its limit: the utopic discourse inscribes the utopic representation in the imaginary space of a map, but at the same time it makes its inscription in a geographical map impossible. There is an insuperable gap between our world and utopia. This separation is usually indicated by a narrative mark in the signifier. We have seen this, for example, in the manuscript that turns out to be the ship's log of a captain who has visited a utopia. The first pages, which contain the blessed island's precise location, have been removed, however. Another example might be the narrator who has suffered a blow knocking him unconscious, only to wake up once on the marvelous island. As well, a servant could have a violent coughing fit just as our narrator reveals the island's coordinates. A voyage to the Perfect City begins only given this sole condition: this empty abyss must commence the tour. In other words, this signifying mark in the text indicates the image-producing operation in the discourse by signaling its condition of possibility. It corresponds to the semiotic transposition brought about by the frame, using a signifier/signified as a detour.

This gap is a neutral space, the place of the limit between reality (the world with its geographic and historical networks) and utopia. It reveals the work of neutralization in utopic practice. Utopia is not only a distant country on the edge of the world; it is also the Other World, the world as "other," and the "other" as world. Utopia is the reverse image of this world, its photographic negative. Utopia is thus the product of a process by which a specific system complete with spatial and temporal coordinates is changed into another system with its own coordinates, structures, and grammatical rules. This limit is thus an index and zero-point; it is also the bridge to the "other."

Outer Limit

In Disneyland the neutral space of the limit is displayed by three areas, each having a precise semiotic function. Each of them repeats in its function the representation's frame: the outer limit of the parking area, the intermediary limit of ticket booths, and the inner limit of the route made by the Santa Fe and Disneyland Railway. The first area is an open, unlimited space, weakly structured by the expandable geometrical "net" of the parking lot. There the visitors leave their car; they abandon what brought them to this suburb of Los Angeles. With this gesture we encounter what is tantamount to a shipwreck or a loss of consciousness; this is equivalent to the break in former utopic narratives. Now the visitors are really no more than a possible performance of a certain number of trajectories in the utopic text. They will be an acting narrator and an acted-out discourse within this contemporary "utopia." They are an "anthropomorphized" surface element in the inscribed text. As they journey, they reactivate signs and markings according to detailed syntactic rules Disneyland's guide pronounces. Given the enormous importance of the private car in the United States, especially in California, the parking lot takes on an even stronger meaning beyond its useful function. The fact of leaving one's car is an overdetermined sign of codical change; for pragmatic utility, for the visitor's adjustment to a certain system of signs and behavior, the system of playful symbols, the free field of consumption for nothing, the *passeist* and aleatory tour *in* the show.

Intermediary Limit

The second area is linear and discontinuous. It is made of ticket booths toward which the visitors are driven in small buses that wind their way through the parking lot. One must go through these booths in order to enter into Disneyland, because a monetary substitution takes place there. A simple substitution between money and tickets does not occur. The visitors buy Disneyland money, with which they can take part in "utopian" life: they do not purchase goods with "real" money. Rather, the visitors acquire the signs, or at least the signifiers, of the "utopian" vocabulary. As a result, they will lend meaning to the visitor's varied tours through the amusement park. This, then, is the second exchange and the second shipwreck: the limit neutralizes for a second time. After leaving behind the car, the visitors abandon their money in order to reach the Other World by another way, and by discursive signs other than those of monetary exchange. The first of these new signs that the visitors "pronounce" gives them the right of passage in return. They begin to utter the "utopian" discourse, to take their tour in Disneyland. The amount of the exchange of real money for utopian signs determines the importance of their visit, the semantic volume of their tour, the number and nature of its entertainments—in other words, it indirectly determines the number of syntactic rules that can be set working to coordinate the different signifying units. For example, for several dollars the visitors receive ten "utopian signs"—one A, one B, two C, three D, three E—and are able to give utterance to the following series of potential narratives:

either/or {
Horse-Drawn Street Cars
Main Street Vehicles
Main Street Fire Engine
Sleeping Beauty's Castle
King Arthur's Carousel

either/or {
Main Street Cinema
Swiss Family Tree House
Alice in Wonderland
Mark Twain Steamboat
Casey Jr. Circus Train

either/or {
It's a Small World
Mad Tea Party
Autopia
Shooting Gallery
etc.

either/or {
Rocket Jets
Indian War Canoes
Space Mountain
etc.

either/or {
Pirates of the Caribbean
Submarine Voyage
Haunted Mansion
etc.

either/or {
Enchanged Tihi Room
Matterhorn Bobsleds
Jungle Cruise

Inner Limit

The inner limit is circular, linear, continuous, and articulated. It is the embankment of the Santa Fe and Disneyland Railway with its stations. The visitors cross this final limit through two tunnels leading them into the Other World. This last limit is not a border for the visitors, or the "performers," since they do not necessarily use the train to go into Disneyland, but it is a limit for the utopian space that is encircled and enclosed by it. One neither enters nor leaves Disneyland by means of it. This limit belongs to the picture, to the representation, or to the map more than it appears as a limit to the travelers and the tour they take on the land. The outer world is completely neutralized through the inscription of this "nowhere."

This pure limit, bridgeless except for the two tunnels, is nonetheless broken by a train of the future: the Monorail. Itself enclosing nothing because it is held up by great pylons, it connects Disneyland Hotel with another area within Disneyland, Tomorrowland. Both a limit and its transgression are given. The past shuts in the "utopian island," the locomotive and winning the West. But the advanced technology of the future breaks the limit to join the blessed and happy island to reality. Technical progress is transgression defined by the rule it breaks. On the very last limit of "Utopia" in this first quick description of its figure and narrative route, the endless tension of neutralization within differentiating space between reality and utopia is clear; it is really a tension between the limit and passing beyond the limit.

Utopia is not only a different world and a world of difference, it is also the difference of the world, the "other" of the world. Neutralizing both the car and money and transforming them into "utopic" equivalencies illustrates this. Instead of driving a car, you are transported in nineteenth-century or twenty-first-century vehicles. Money is exchanged for "utopian monetary signs," which work less for exchange than for conversion into specific enunciative narrative routes. These routes can be produced on or through the limit I just described as the first mark of the figure of Disneyland. The railway line is semiotically the signifying result of the two neutralizing forms of space the narrator-visitor has traversed: the open, weak, and indefinite structure of the parking lot is opposed to the limited, discontinuous, highly structured ticket booths. This opposition is reconciled by the circular line that closes off a highly structured, continuously closed space, but allows entry every so often. This reconciliation illustrates the ambivalence in this kind of neutralization; there exist both a tension in contradiction and possible harmony in the contrary elements. The monorail's transgression should also underscore this ambivalence and even add a temporal dimension to it. The possible synthesis in a complete state of harmony for these contrary spatial elements (surface/line, continuous/discontinuous, open/closed, isotropic/anisotropic, etc.) can be historically determined; it is overdetermined by a tension between past and future, between nineteenth and twenty-first century. The articulation of space is thus supported by a historical opposition that the visitor will pronounce as he journeys through various narrative routes. This overdetermination constitutes the very "framework of his discourse." This is the latent but insistent injunction of an imposed signified: it obliterates the present by enforcing the double pole of the origin and of the end, of the past conquest of the West and the future conquest of "Space."

Access to the Center

Disneyland is a centered space. Main Street USA leads the visitor to the center. But this route toward the center plaza is also the way toward Fantasyland, one of the four districts of Disneyland. So the most obvious axis of Disney's utopia leads the visitor not only from the circular limit or perimeter to the core of the closed space, but also from reality to fantasy. This fantasy is the trademark, the sign, the symbolic image of Disney's utopia.

Fantasyland is made up of images, characters, and animals of the tales illustrated by Disney in his animated films, magazines, books, and other products. This district is constituted by images; of particular significance is the fact that these images are realized, are made living by their transformation into real materials, wood, stone plaster, etc., and through their animation by men and women disguised as movie or storybook characters. Image is duplicated by reality in two opposite senses: on the one hand, it becomes real, but on the other, reality is changed into image. The support for the figure has become the figure. The "Horseman" of Dürer's engraving has not only emerged as the "horseman described," goal of the attempt to make a portrait; it is in reality the horseman. However, going the other way, reality is transformed into an image. The figured element is nothing but its support. The Horseman, Death or the Devil, has no other reality than its figure: it is a being grasped by the "imaginary."

Thus, the visitor who has left reality outside finds it again, but as a real "imaginary": a fixed, stereotyped, powerful fantasy. The utopian place to which

Main Street USA leads is the fantasmatic return of reality, its hallucinatory presence. This coming back of reality as a fantasy, as a hallucinatory wish-fulfillment, is in fact mediated by a complete system of representations designed by Walt Disney and constituting a rhetorical and iconic code and vocabulary that have been perfectly mastered by the narrator-visitor. So this coming back appears to be brought about through a secondary process that is not only the stuff of images and representations molded by wish, but which constitutes the very actuality of the fantasy where wish is caught in its snare.

But this brings about a rather violent effect on the imaginary by fantasy. The other side of reality is presented (Fantasyland is Disney's privileged place for this), but it emerges in the form of banal, routine images of Disney's films. They are the bankrupt signs of an imagination homogenized by the mass media. The snare I mentioned is the collective, totalitarian form taken by the "imaginary" of a society, blocked by its specular self-image. One of the essential functions of the utopic image is to make apparent a wish in a *free* image of itself, in an image that can play in opposition to the fantasy, which is an inert, blocked, and recurrent image. Disneyland is on the side of the fantasy and not on that of a free or utopic representation.

The Practical Function of the Center

Main Street USA is the way of access to the center, to begin the visitors' tour, to narrate their story, to perform their speech. From the center they can articulate the successive sequences of his narrative by means of the signs they have received in exchange for their money at the entrance. If we consider Disneyland as a text, Main Street USA is the channel of transmission of the story narrated by the visitors in making their tour. It allows them to communicate. Its function is phatic: it is the most primitive function of the communication, since it only permits communication to take place without communicating anything. Thus, Disneyland can be viewed as thousands and thousands of narratives uttered by visitors. Its text is constituted by this plurality of "lexies," to write like Barthes, which are exchanged endlessly by the visitors according to the codes (vocabulary and syntax) imposed by the makers of Disneyland.

Semantic Plurality

Now this semiotic function, the condition of possibility of all the messages, all the tours, all the stories told by the visitors, is taken into account structurally in a "lexie" belonging to a superior level, in the diagrammatic scheme of all the possible tours, an open and yet finite totality, the Disneyland map. When we look at this map, we acknowledge a feature that we do not perceive when we recite the story in passing from the entrance to the center: the fact that Main Street USA is not only a street, but a "district," a land that separates and links Frontierland and Adventureland, on the one hand, and Tomorrowland on the other. For the narrator-visitor Main Street USA is an axis that allows him or her to begin to tell a story. For the spectator it is a place on the map that articulates two worlds; this place makes him look at the relations and at the difference between these worlds, without realizing how they are joined. This district is what allows the various other places to exist on the map. With it visibility is *inscribed* into the map. It was at first seen as an *aleatory moment* and *choice to be made.* As *Main Street USA* becomes part of the visitors' way, the first narrative they compose, we see how it is *the* first way and founding narrative for their own utopia. It transforms reality into its other; fantasy becomes reality, and reality becomes fantasy. Between narrative and description, narration and the map, reality and the imaginary, the functional plurality of Main Street–USA, no less–presents its semiotic polyvalence, the analysis of which I shall undertake.

We can sum up this analysis in the following terms: Main Street USA is a universal operator that articulates and builds up the text of Disneyland on all of its levels. We have discovered three functions of this operator: (1) *phatic*–it allows all the possible stories to be narrated; (2) *referential*–through it, reality becomes a fantasy and an image, a reality; (3) *integrative*–it is the space that divides Disneyland into two parts, left and right, and that relates these two parts to each other. It is at the same time a condition by which the space takes on meaning for the viewer and a condition by which the space can be narrated by the visitor (the actor).

Semantic Polyvalence

These three functions are filled up by a semantic content. Main Street USA is the place where the visitor can buy, in a nineteenth-century American decor, actual and real commodities with his real, actual money. Locus of exchange of meanings and symbols in the imaginary land of Disney, Main Street USA is also the real place of exchange of money and commodity.

It is the locus of the societal truth–consumption–that is the truth for all of Disneyland. With Main Street USA we have a part of the whole that is as good as the whole, that is equivalent to the whole. The fact that this place is also an evocation of the past is an attempt to reconcile or to exchange, in the space occupied by Main Street USA, the past and the present—that is, an ideal past and a real present.

Actually, it is here on Main Street USA that reality reemerges in a mediated system of collective representations and figures, transformed to the mold of forgotten memories: Disney's special children's world. Recall that the whole operation was built by a cartoon film-maker. But as the cartoons become real, they also deform and disguise reality here on Main Street USA. In USA Today the visitors see themselves and their contemporaries in the shopwindows. Money regains its power; there is nothing utopian here. In Fantasyland they also see their image, but, as it were, transformed by differences in scale, and by formal modifications obeying an imaginary system of representations the society holds in common.

On Main Street private citizens are left to their own devices in their confrontation with their own environment, that of their everyday world. The outside has been placed inside and has thereby gained in evocative power; it has been seized by the trappings of the utopian scene. It has been carefully placed within a framework of brightly pained nineteenth-century houses. Main Street USA actually belongs to one of the particular areas of the western side of Disneyland, Frontierland, because of its decor. It thus also promotes a feeling of historically "winning" the West in heroic fashion. Given the merchandise in the shop windows, however, it seems rather to belong to an area on the eastern side, Tomorrowland, where the most advanced technological products of American science are displayed.

Another additional proof of Disney's utopian operation can be found in the name "Main Street USA" itself. "USA": through America's self-contained potential the reconciliation of opposites is performed, but within representation, of course. The past and future, time and space, the playfulness and serious determination to be found on the market, the real and imaginary—all are brought together. Utopia is perfectly present, but remember, only as a representation. Its harmony exists only on a stage. As a result, the work of utopic fiction is embedded and immobilized in an ideological figure. It therefore loses its critical force. The ideology that holds it restricts its play so that it no longer represents the true conflicts men and women imagine themselves having.

Disneyland's Worlds: From the Narrative to the System of Readings

Let us now leave the narrator-visitors and their enunciation to the hazards of their possible tours. The syntax of their "discourse-tour" is defined first by their passing through the limits and by their journey to the center. The visitors have learned the codes of the language of Disneyland and have thus been given the possibilities to tell their individual story, to utter their own "speech." Yet their freedom, the freedom of their own individual narrative, is constrained not only by these codes but also by the representation of an imaginary history contained in a stereotyped system of representations. In order to utter their own story, the visitor is forced to borrow these representations. They are manipulated by the system, even when they seem to choose their tour freely.

These remarks allow me to substitute the analysis of the map for a possible narrative and for its performative narration. The analysis or description of the map would involve not an itinerary in time (which is always a narrative) but of a picture, the parts of which coexist in the space of the analogue-model. Methodologically, we assume that the narrative tours constitute a total system and that the map is the structure of this total system.

The pictorial map includes a left and right, depending on the visitors' place in front of it. The map determines their bearings and gives them a second view; they, of course, occupy the privileged viewpoint. This viewpoint charges the utopic figure as it is ideologically fixed in the narrator's imagination. There is a substitution, however, which determines the price paid for the triggering of the narrative to begin. The visitors—here spectators—***are necessarily outside the pictorial map***; they are also excluded from Disney's utopia in its neutralizing power. He is rather in a "secondary" space that perfectly coincides with utopic space. The map forms the analogue-model of that space. Charging the system—setting it in motion and putting it into play—consists in substituting the paradigmatic model for the possible routes and varied syntagmatic readings. The structure is equivalent to its performance, language to speech, the system of paradigms to the aleatory succession of syntagms. The total analogon can be substituted for the articulation of narrative units and brief "discourse-tours."

It may be that this substitution is necessary in order for the analytic meta-discourse to function. We must remember, however, not to jumble together the narrative processes by which people readily live, thus consuming their town and their house and textual system that gives them the signs, symbols, and syntactic rules through which they display and perform narrative processes. An architectural set is at the same time a set of places, routes, and pathways and a visible, "specular" totality. Viewed from this perspective, Disneyland displaces the spatial habitability into its "spectacular" representation. It reduces the dynamic organization of the places, the aleatory unity of a possible tour, to a univocal scheme allowing the same redundant behavior. We are thus justified in viewing the map of Disneyland as an analogue-model that assimilates the possible narratives of its space.

The Map of Disneyland

On the left of the map are two districts: Frontierland and Adventureland. Between them is New Orleans Square. Frontierland is the representation of scenes of the final conquest of the West. Here narratives of how the West was won illustrate the ever-increasing American appropriation of land and resources. The frontier has no limit: it is itself transgression. The "semantic" content of this utopic discourse informs us what we had already suspected was constitutive of its general code; the frontier is both closure and transgression. The limit is a pretext for transgression. It is quite amazing that most of the stories in Frontierland involve rides of conquest or exploitation, from Mike Fink's boats and Tom Sawyer's Island rafts to mule-train mines of precious metals and steamboats on the Mississippi. These all involve penetration into and victory over the lands of the first inhabitants, the Indians.

Adventureland is the representation of scenes of wildlife in exotic countries, viewed during a boat trip on a tropical river. If Frontierland signifies the temporal distance of the past history of the American nation, Adventureland signifies the spatial distance of the outside geographical world, the world of natural savagery. It represents the next possible fields of action, because adventure is also a frontier; the primitive cannibals rising on the riverbanks seem to repeat the gestures that the Indians made in Frontierland. These latter, of course, have already been beaten. These two districts represent the distances of history and geography, the distance represented inside America in the first, and the distance represented outside in the second. They are both assimilated because they are shown on the same stage, so to speak; they are thereby neutralized.

We can quickly understand why the map's right side is occupied by a single district. Tomorrowland consists principally of representations of the Future-as-Space, Einsteinian Time-Space, which realizes the harmonious synthesis of the two-dimensional world represented on the left part as time and space, time as historical, national past and space as strange, exotic primitivism. Tomorrowland is space as time, the universe captured by the American science and technology of today. Tomorrowland also has an excentric center, the Carousel of Progress, a gift of the General Electric Corporation.

Models

We can construct two models that are secondary representations of the map. Figure 33 is a truly analogous diagram, and Figure 34 is a semantic structure articulating more precisely the oppositions.

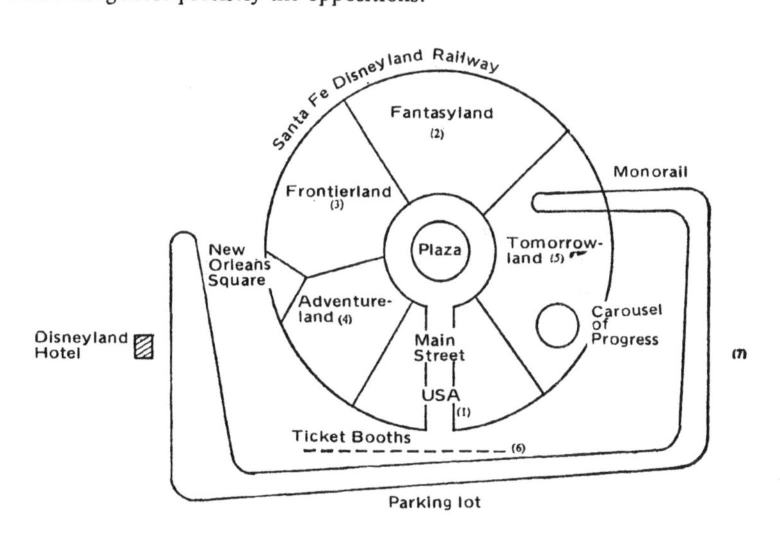

Figure 33. Map-diagram of Disneyland

Consideration of the center of these two models elicits the following remarks: first, the center in the map is not the center in the semantic structure; in other words, the structure is not a simplified map. In the structure the center is the sign of the numerous semiotic functions of Main Street USA as a route to the

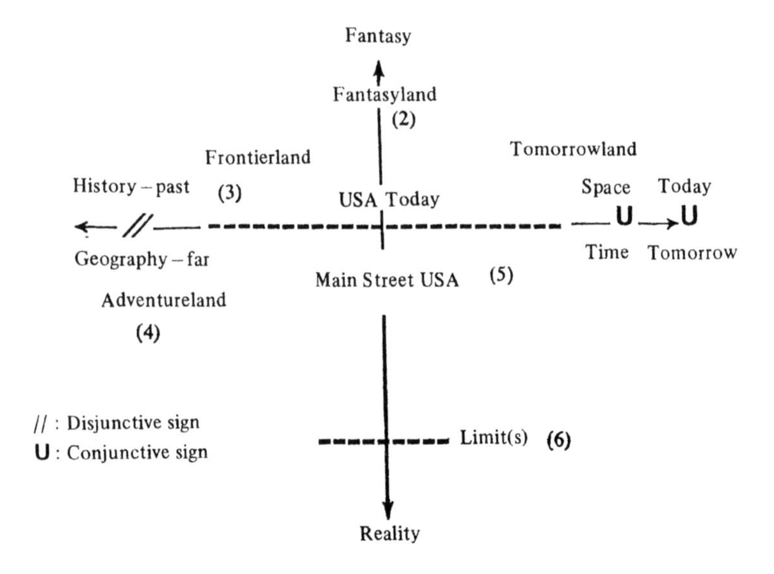

Figure 34. Semantic Structure of the Map

mapped center, an axis exchanging a scientific and technological conjunction of space and time for historico-geographical distance.

Second, in the semantic structure Main Street USA appears to be on different levels, formal and material, semiotic and semantic, a place of exchange and labor: the exchange of commodities and objects of consumption but also of significations and symbols. The center of the structure functions at once inside and outside the structure. Inside it is determined rigorously by the two main correlations of which it is made up, reality and fantasy: historico-geographical distance and space-time.

But it is not only an intersecting point of these two semantic axes; somehow it produces them as well. Through it the contrary poles of the correlations exchange their meaning: reality becomes fantasmatic and fantasy, actuality. The remoteness of exotic places and of the American national past becomes the universal space-time of science and technology, and this universality becomes American. In the semiotic theory of the narrative the center is the representation of the dialectical mediation from which springs the narrative solution: it is the image of the inventions determined by the story on its different levels.

It is not without significance that in this case this image, this representation, is named "USA" and is conjugated in the present tense. The ultimate meaning of the center is the conversion of history into ideology, a conversion by which the utopian space itself is caught in that ideology. It is no less significant, as I bring these particular remarks to a close, that in this structural center of the map another one can also find the existence of an element already noted in the organization of representative pictorial space from the quattrocento to the Impressionists. This central element carries out the conversion of the painting's semantic figures and semiotic functions. Their polyvalence allows for the conversion of time into space and narrative into symbol. The visual, spectacular nature of Disneyland and its center has already convinced us that they are a space for the representation of representation. As such, Disney's utopia should obey the general laws of representation. This representational mediation makes it clear that in the utopian place commodities are significations and significations are commodities. By the selling of up-to-date consumer goods in the setting of a nineteenth-century street, between the adult reality and the childlike fantasy, Walt Disney's utopia converts the commodities into signification. Reciprocally, what is bought there are *signs*, but these signs are *commodities*.

The Excentric Centers

The districts on the right and left of the diagram have secondary centers, themselves connected in a meaningful way. New Orleans Square on the left and the Carousel of Progress on the right both are metaphorico-metonymic elements of the subsets of which they are a part. The first brings together two attractions (recall that the left side of the map is composed of two distant districts semantically and topographically separated in geography and history): the Pirates of the Caribbean and the Haunted Mansion, an idea taken from one of Poe's tales. The second attraction shows a series of domestic scenes from the nineteenth century to the present, and already now the future, whose moral proves the progressive satisfaction of human needs by technology and science. Space and time are reconciled. The people from the past become those of tomorrow; the modest "original" farm is slowly transformed into a duplex somewhere between two heavens, one of stellar space, the other situated under the magical lights of the city. These attractions, two among many, seem to condense in them the signification of the worlds of which they are a part.

The Fantasy of Primitive Accumulation

The attraction Pirates of the Caribbean reveals all of its semantic content only in its narration. So the visitor must begin to speak again in order to recite the underground tour, for the syntagmatic organization of his ride displays a primary and essential level of meaning. The first sequence of the narrative discourse is a place where skulls and skeletons are lying on heaps of gold and silver, diamonds and pearls. Next the visitor goes through a naval battle in his little boat; then he sees from off-shore the pirates attack a town. In the last sequence the spoils are piled up in the pirate ships, the visitor is cheered by pirates feasting and reveling, and the tour is concluded. The narrative unfolds its moments in a reverse chronological order; the first scene in the tour-narrative is the last scene in the "real" story. And this inversion has an ethical meaning: crime does not pay. The morality of the fable is presented before the reading of the story in order to constrain the comprehension of the fable by a preexisting moral code. The potential force of the narrative, its unpredictability, is neutralized by the moral code that makes up all of the representation. Similar remarks could be made for the Haunted Mansion.

Moral Economy and Economic Morals

But if we introduce the story into the structural scheme of the map, and especially if we do so by relating it to the structural center, another meaning appears beneath the moral signification. The center, you remember, is a place of exchange of actual products and commodities of today: it is a marketplace and a place of consumption. Correlated to the excentric center of the left part, Main Street USA signifies to the visitor that life is an endless exchange and a constant consumption and, reciprocally, that the feudal accumulation of riches, the Spanish hoarding of treasure, the Old World conception of gold and money, are not only morally criminal, but they are, economically, signs and symptoms of death. The treasure buried in the ground is a dead thing, a corpse. The commodity produced and sold is a living good because it can be consumed.

The Myth of Technological Progress

I do not want to overemphasize this point; but in Tomorrowland, on the right side of the map, the same meaning is made obvious by another excentric center, the Carousel of Progress. Here, the visitor becomes a spectator, immobilized and passive, seated in front of a circular and moving stage that shows successive scenes taken from family life in the nineteenth century, in the beginning of the twentieth century, today, and tomorrow. It is the *same* family that is presented in these different historical periods; the story of this "permanent" family is told to visitors, who no longer narrate their own story. History is neutralized; the scenes only change in relation to the increasing quantity of electric implements, the increasing sophistication of the utensil-dominated human environment. The individual is shown to be progressively mastered, dominated by utensility. The scenic symbols of wealth are constructed by the number and variety of the means and tools of consumption—that is, by the quantity and variation of the technical and scientific mediations of consumption. The circular motion of the stage expresses this endless technological progress as well as its necessity, its fate. And the specific organization of the space of representation symbolizes the passive satisfaction of endlessly increasing needs. There is absolutely no reference made to money and even less to its deathlike accumulation. Here the wealth that is shown to the visitor is of a different order than monetary signs or precious metals. Rather, it is exhibited by the growing complexity of the utensil world increasingly filling up the human environment. It demonstrates, actually, the utensil's mastery of mankind. Men and women adapt perfectly to this environment and "act" mechanically. The signs of wealth are made up of the utensils' wide applicability and diversity, and not of consumption, as we saw on Main Street USA. These utensils, rather, represent the means for consumption, the chronological and scientific mediation for consumption.

The excentric centers, I mentioned, are metaphorico-metonymic elements of a whole. We will be able to demonstrate more clearly one very important relation structuring Disney's utopia due to the meaning-effects they produce as subgroups of larger ensembles. This relation governs in a complex way machines and living creatures, technology and culture, and, finally, nature and culture.

Machines and Living Creatures

The left side of the map illustrates both the culture supplied by Americans to nineteenth-century America and the one produced at the same time by adult, civilized, male, white people in exotic and remote countries. The living beings of Adventureland and Frontierland (and, even more so, the pirates and New Orleans Square ghosts) are only reproductions of reality. The cave in the Pirates of the Caribbean is the Platonic cave in which simulacra walk about. The difference, however, resides in the fact that visitors observe themselves and not their own shadows. This is actually no real difference, however, because they are only quasi-living. They seem real, but just as in Plato, the puppets' masters are hiding.

Nothing is true, however. All that is living is an artifact. "Nature" is a simulacrum. Nature is a wild, primitive, savage world, but this world is only the appearance taken on by the machine in the utopian play. This monster is a *thauma*, a Daedalian wonder. There is, however, a certain truth that must be separated from all the artifacts and automatic movement. What is signified by the left part of the map is the assumption that *the machine is the truth, the actuality of the living.* Mechanism and mechanistic concept of the world, which we noted in More's original utopia, are at work in Disney's degenerate utopia; in More this idea coincided with the emergence of industrial capitalism. It is also true, however, that instead of this mechanism being presented to the Utopians as knowledge so that they may admire God the Creator and Artisan, here it is a dissimulated and disguised apparatus that can be taken for its contrary, natural life.

The Reduced Model

On the right side of the map the underlying truth of the left side becomes obvious. In Tomorrowland machines are everywhere: from the atomic submarine to the moon rocket. The concealed meaning of the left side is now revealed thanks to the mediating center, Main Street USA. But these machines are neither true nor false; they are not, as in the left part, false reproductions. Instead, they are scaled-down models of the actual machines. We have false duplicates of living beings and concealed mechanistic springs on the left, obvious machines and true models on the right. Real nature is an appearance, and the reduced model of the machine is reality. Disney's utopia performs an operation of exchange between biological nature and mechanistic technology. Appearance and reality crisscross, and both are neutralized.

The utopic force of the neutral wears out in such an environment. The ideology of representation and machine is all-pervading, and man is twice removed from nature and science. Nature, which he sees, is a representation, the reverse side of which is a machine. Machines that he uses and with which he sometimes plays are the reduced models of a machinery that seizes him and plays with him.

We find the same function of the reduced models, but on a different plane, in Fantasyland. This district is constituted by the real-realized images of the tales animated by Walt Disney. Fantasyland is the return of reality in a regressive and hallucinatory form. This imaginary *real* is a reproduction of the scenes the visitor has seen in the pirates' cave and in the haunted mansion, but it is a regressive reproduction on a tiny, child-size scale. We find the same fantasies of death, superpower, violence, destruction, and annihilation, but as reduced models of the attractions of the left side. Reduced models like those of Tomorrowland, but reduced models of death, strangeness, exoticism in the imaginary; they are the opposite of the reduced models of the right side, which show life, consumption, and techniques in their images. The realm of the living in life-size is the realm of natural appearance in its historical past, geographic, anthropological remoteness. Here, also, the realm of the machine as a reduced model is the cultural truth of the American way of life, here and now, looking at itself as a universal way of living.

The function of Disney's utopia is to represent the exchange of the first and second realms of natural life and scientific technology and to express the ideology of this exchange on the stage and in the decor of utopia.

Disneyland's ideological exchange can be illustrated by an elaboration of the semantic structure of the map (see Figure 35).

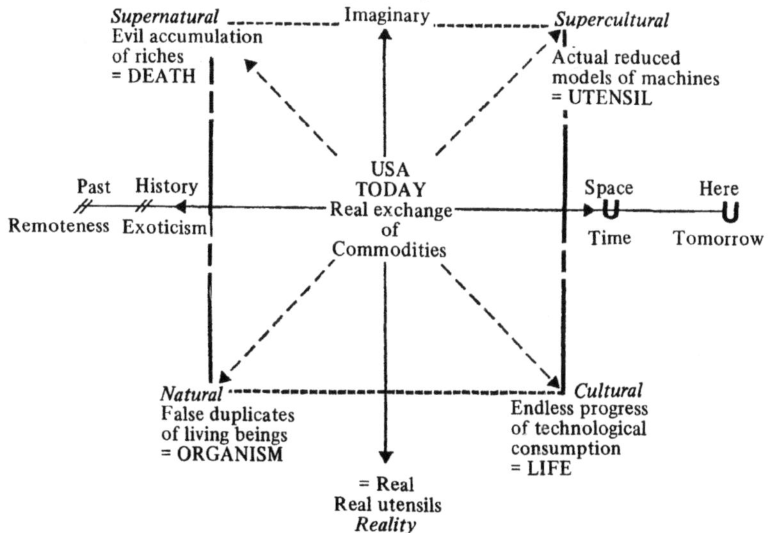

Figure 35. Semantic structure of the ideological representation in Disneyland

CHAPTER THIRTEEN

About Xenakis: The Utopia of Verticality[1]

I will concern myself here with but one text.[2] It will not lead us to Xenakis the musician; rather, we will meet Xenakis the poet-mathematician of architecture, and we hope also to encounter a poetic practice he encourages, called "utopia." I will also concern myself with a city that has been built after a model in the form of a text. There are sketches illustrating it, but actually no schemata or maps reproducing it completely. They tend to offer a glimpse of it in a future voyage for a wandering explorer of an *other* planet—ours.

In turn, this city and text will then serve as pretexts for another journey into figure that Xenakis' pages offer, as if in the filigree of their writing. Our journey will displace the lines and give play to the forms; I will then disfigure the structures contained therein and "test" the model representing this city presented there.

Myths: Decentralization and Orthogonism

Xenakis comes to utopia through his critique of a twofold myth that to him seems to animate all international urban politics. This myth can be found at the crossroads of two tendencies: decentralization and its conceptual utensil, orthogonism. Setting this course toward the Other World because of a critical rupture is the path Thomas More also chose—and was the first to invent. As with *Utopia*, despite appearances, the resulting work accompanying this criticism of the contemporary world will not be the answer to it. Utopia is not a proposal designed to replace something else, even if technical data are provided and seem to finalize his ideas. His projects are not realizable because they *cannot* and *should not* be realizable without losing their strength. Many utopian thinkers make the mistake of believing this. The Vertical Cosmic City will not be an effect of Xenakis' critique of myth or a consequence of his questioning. It will emerge in the very contradiction every myth opens up in society's foundation;

industrial society is no exception. The City will be born, like all true utopias, in the space of contradictory elements, not as the solution of their synthesis, but as the product of the force of difference opposing them.

Reread Xenakis' text. His theme? The present type of urban concentration cannot be endured; it is suffocating and anarchic. Response: the dispersion and decentralization of city centers is the universal solution.[3]

The nature of myth, or what in modern times we call ideological formation, involves setting up a contradiction whose elements have no other function but to be elements of an antithetic couple they form. The antitheme of decentralization is nothing but the flip side of the theme of concentration. Mythic activity or ideological practice will essentially want to displace the contradiction so as to soften its oppositional nature: satellite, suburban, and bedroom communities repeat in their own way the same problems of concentration they sought to avoid or avert.[4] Myth's nature is the contradiction of a theme and an antitheme, lacking any thesis or antithesis that would place them in any true contradiction. The myth is the simple and inert articulation of the situation and response made in terms of contrariety. It is the displaced repetition of this articulation, an unconscious reading determined in advance on the surface of social dynamics. Myth is a reading itself caught in this surface of appearances.

The Critical Thesis

This moment of myth or ideology for a modern society recalls the passage from Book One in *Utopia*, where Cardinal Morton's guests try to come up with ways to stamp out England's increasing crime. Actually, they do not make any new attempts; they just repeat the same contradictions of the theme, "Theft is increasing at an alarming rate," and the antitheme: "Its suppression must become increasingly stiffer." This continues until Raphael, the traveler from Utopia and teller of tall tales, turns the tables by denouncing social misery and its source, the increase in sheep grazing land for commercial profit. But it is also at this moment that the cause-effect analysis ceases; a brusque shift of attention (and discontinuity in the discourse) leads us into the blessed land of the Polylerites.[5] The analogy between the arguments is quite amazing: in place of an ideological statement of mythic contradiction, Xenakis substitutes a theoretical formulation of society in its physical nature: "As contemporary observers," we see that centralization has developed "like a strong, blind, irreversible force....It even seems that a simple but terrible law can be extracted from this observation: the large centers grow more than the small ones following a logarithmic curve."[6] Then he reverses the theme of urban concentration: "Centralization favors expansion and all sorts of progress," the amount and wealth of information, and exchanges. Statistically, this rapid increase provides the "possibility for the appearance of the exceptional event";[7] this means the maximum amount of determinable possible meaning given the constraints controlling that appearance and the combinatory of elements for "social language."[8] Centralization is the necessary condition for the increase in social and cultural complexity of a particular society. The proposed thesis thus leads to a *denunciation*, not of urban concentration, but of the asphyxia brought about by old-fashioned communications systems, badly organized time, etc. He then attempts to provide the structural reasons supporting the overall phenomenon; from here he looks at how the current answers fail to alleviate the situation. If the clogged communications network (at every level), the density of information (no matter what kind), and the appearance of a maximum of possible meanings result from an irreversible force, concentration, the problem will not be helped by decentralization. If "gas vapors poisoning the atmosphere and long waiting lines" are not inevitable, then the problem, again, will not necessarily be helped by decentralization. "Torture and hanging thieves will not reduce crime," wrote More. But by eliminating the enclosure movement and offering work to peasants thrown off their land, a beginning would be made. Pellmell decentralization and preaching the breakup of the living complexity of Paris by creating other centers repeating its inconveniences will not solve the problems of urban concentration. Xenakis instead proposes to concentrate on the general problem of the communications system and of the exchange of information in great urban concentrations. Just as the problem of theft in sixteenth-century England was not a question of penal justice, laws, or punishment, so here the communications problem does not involve plane geometry or a combination of straight lines and right angles.[10]

This is the first phase of utopic discourse: a *critique* takes hold of a mythic, or ideological, contradiction, then reverses it by neutralizing, and then exacerbating, the contradiction. Xenakis deadens the elements contained in the mythico-ideological proposition by presenting the thesis of urban concentration to its fullest. He reinforces the contradiction by uncovering the ideological representation of the city and the political means for its transformation. Contemporary urbanism puts "a simple and poor plane geometry" to work. This view is a stifling, suffocating image of urban concentration and ground-level planning; it is an opinion as "old as the centuries," yet it remains the panacea for contemporary problems of human "habitation."[11] Within the space of an open, forced contradiction and the work of differentiation, the utopic figure emerges. It is completely unified. More says as much through Raphael: "In truth, no system of laws is comparable to the one I marked down while I was travelling among the people called Polylerites."

Utopic Figure

"If concentration is a vital necessity for humanity, current ideas about urban planning and architecture must be *completely* changed and replaced by others," writes Xenakis. In order to do this, "we must uncover the face of concentration, and formalize its structure."[12] This is a perfect definition of the utopic figure as distinct from ideological representation. It is both image and model, concrete and abstract, visible and intelligible; it is a schema of the imagination and a poetic project, by itself, an operation capable of producing conceptual syntheses. In other words, the utopic figure allows practical activity and its science, real transformation and conceptual mastery, to appear, all on the level of the image and in the realm of the visible. Xenakis rightly declares, "Confronted with the tragedy of contemporary urban planning and architecture, we must construct a clear foundation and attempt the formalization of these two 'sciences.'"[13] He is also correct in suspending the scientific status of these two sciences by putting the word in quotes. But as momentary and deferred sciences, urban planning and architecture are entirely shot through with ideology and myth, with the rigid contradiction of representational images formed into a system and preconceived "ideas" about the city and space. The utopic figure of Xenakis' Cosmic City both sets into play ideological representation through the use of contradictory fiction and also sketches out future science. This is the figurative anticipation, not of the City, for Xenakis is neither a prophet nor an astrologer, but of the theory of the City. Within the sketch of the urban face can be glimpsed the future project of scientific urban planning. The utopic City is not an idea to be made real or the project of a City. It is the fiction of the conditions of possibility of urban architecture within the domain of the imaginary. That is why these conditions will be found exposed and manifest not on the level of figure like the Cosmic City, formed by utopic practice, but rather in the analytic rewriting and work another discourse performs on this figure and on the phrases produced by it.

Vertical No-place

The first feature of the City Xenakis sketches out contains the straightforward translation of the semantic structure of the word, "u-topia": no-place. This no-place does not mean the unreal or the imaginary. Rather it signifies the indeterminability of place, the place of the neutral, of difference and of the force of differentiation. It is a place neither here nor there. It is the presence of a lack whose space is that by which and around which space is organized. In fact, the first operation of the productive utopic practice of figure (axiom 2) will consist in separating the ground from the City, in creating a state of "independence with respect to the surface and the landscape."[14] The connection between place and ground had previously always seemed necessary due to the fact that place is first and foremost a marking and a name in space. It is a sort of road sign opening up the land: topography and geography. By creating the Vertical Cosmic City, Xenakis does more than simply introduce a third dimension into urban studies and architectural thought; he clarifies an early gesture of these fields' unwritten dogma. He makes a u-topia, a no-place, out of the City by separating space from all places—the ground. In other words, the fundamental, founding act of the City is the u-topic act by definition. The "no" of place, it constitutes the refusal of topography and geography. It is the "no" of space, as well, understood as a connected system of said and inscribed places, flat and extensive. The same radical feature can be found in the theoretical underpinnings of the Philips Pavillon: "Since the early Greeks, architecture has never been a truly spatial phenomenon. It was instead founded on the basis of two dimensions: it is essentially flat. The square, rectangular, trapezoidal and circular figures of temples and dwellings, palaces, churches and theaters are flat. The third dimension can be added by a translation parallel to the plumb-line."[15] By using the vertical as a "new volumetric element" in a construction or city, urban and architectural reality can become u-topia by a very simple operation. In one fell swoop, architecture enters into the utopic dimension of reality, the "other" of reality; it is thereby introduced into the pure difference of topography.

Gaze-Light

The second feature of the Vertical City's appearance involves the viewpoint, the place of the gaze (axiom 1). Its twofold form includes its "ether," light, and its operation, sight.[16] The City must be in the light, and light in the City. There will be no obstacles to block it: the City will exist in the immediacy of an absolute presence. This presence has one function: to "view space directly." This is the supreme view of visibility; light is also vision and intuition, simultaneously origin and *telos* of a never-ending movement. The Vertical City will be the City of Light and Vision. "Because of this, the width of the City must be relatively slight..." The implication contained in these two axioms carries important consequences.

Let me return to topography and geography, to the arts of inscribing and tying together places in a surface; to the "sciences" that organize and create meaning out of space through networks of names and signs, these latter originally being the traces and markings of people's movements: the path and its direction, the stream and its flow, the mountain and its obstacle. The map is originally a net of itineraries and a system of potential routings all present at the same time, co-present. These paths are the opposite of a trip and its surprises and events. They are also the reverse side of a narrative unfolding in surprise and expectation, of a story limited by its characters' viewpoints. With a map and its surface presentation, the viewpoint is no longer affected by surprise or the expectation of the unusual. The gaze is everywhere present, and all points of view are the viewpoint, similar to Leibniz's God. All points of view are negated by its ubiquitous vision, everywhere present for everyone and every detail. All routes and journeys are equivalent and *reversible.* Vertically situated with reference to the map, the dominating gaze is in complete possession of all places. It is itself not a part of their system, but rather at the transcendent center organizing them into a system so as to render the elements interchangeable. This visual utopia also contains within its position the totalitarian menace characterizing its fictions.[17]

Utopia and the Planner

Xenakis' project for the fiction of the Vertical City reveals his desire to place the inhabitants' viewpoint in the "no-place" position of the planner. He would then take over this indeterminate and determining place, the planner's, in its neutral and neutralizing power. But this is only the first step. It is certainly true that positioning oneself in the vertical, high summit of a monument, even if in effigy, signifies power. But if power exerts itself also by symbols, it precedes them. Power creates symbols or appropriates them.[18] Power, however, is curiously absent from Xenakis' utopic operation, even though he seems to have determined its fundamental nature.

The map is a utopia because of the determining place of the planner's gaze. It is also an "objectification" of reality due to two syntactic operations characterizing it: projecting reality onto a surface and reducing it to a flat analogic model. In other words, the utopic operation becomes clear because of the relationship between the planner's gaze and the representation of reality; it neutralizes the reality of the landscape and of the perceiving world. The utopic operation triggers its derealization and reification. Things of the world are transformed into analogic signs representing them; they take their place and substitute for them in the discourse referring to them. It entails an operation of doubling the real in its signs (*derealization*, because the real has meaning and value only insofar as it can become the object of a signifying duplication) and of substituting signs for the real (*reification*, because signs, all equivalent in the representative function, have become things, albeit perfectly interchangeable). This complex operation presumes the perfect coextensivity of representation and of what it represents; it assumes the coalescence and isology of the signifier and the signified in the sign system. The map as a representation has historical origins: it originates during the Renaissance and is tied to the emergence of the structures of capitalist production. It is one element of the ideology of the representation characterizing them, and also is made up of the codes specific to it.

That is why the utopic figure of the City or of the space making up the map is ideological. It is in fact an exemplary product of ideology. This is clear if we were to examine city maps from the fifteenth century to the nineteenth centuries—for example, the one of Venice by Jacopo Barbari or that of Paris, called the Turgot map. In these perfect illustrations of geography and topography a completely different system of signs crisscrosses them, but is also somewhat controlled by their own syntactic rules. The specific example of the bird's-eye viewpoint is made up of two heterogeneous *topoi*: the mimetic theatrical representation and the geometric schema. These two processes exchange their particular mode of representation. One has the poetic effect of reality; the other a utilitarian scientific goal. Each plays upon the other. This utopic figure, then, even while belonging to the ideology of representation expressing it, deploys a critical movement affecting this same ideology through the use of several incoherent "*topoi*" to whom its system belongs.

The Shell of Light

Xenakis' utopic operation consists in seizing the map and placing it in the vertical "no-place" of the planner's gaze. The map itself becomes the view, the gaze. There is no longer any point of view in the Vertical City, and it is not the third dimension of a map. With this operation the map converts to its third dimension by becoming a vertical surface, but without any thickness. The surface and ground disappear as an element of human habitation and topographic anchoring. Freed from this referential subjection, the ground returns to other technological or perhaps natural functions[19] as a definitively neutralized environment of Cosmic Cities (axiom 8).

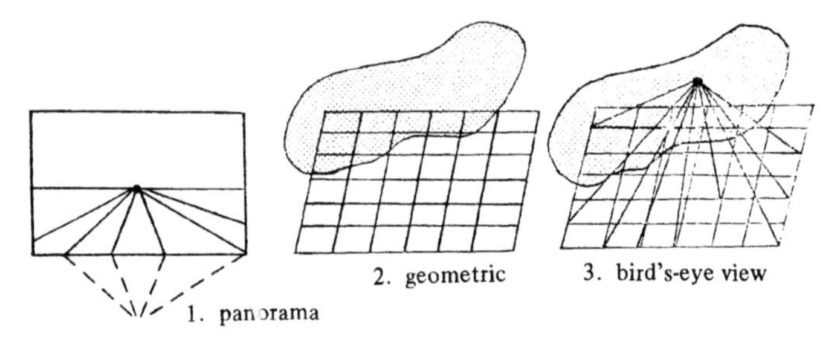

Figure 36. Diagrams of Three Constitutive "*topoi*"

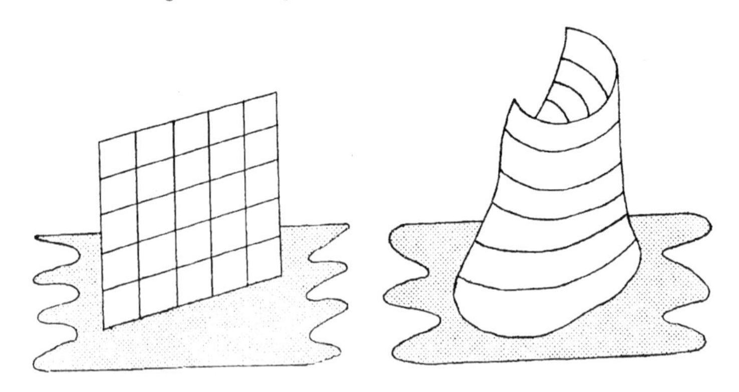

Figure 37. The Third Vertical Dimension and Its Warping in the Cosmic City

In other words, the play between the two previous *topoi* we have seen, the mimetic and geometric journal together in the "Classical" bird's-eye view in which the ideology of representation is exhibited and reflected in the varied sign system, is radically criticized. The subject viewed (the landscape, for example) no longer is controlled by the viewpoint of mimesis, organizing it into a legitimate perspective. It simultaneously becomes schema and gaze, while the map, far from being a neutralizing view, is lifted and straightened; it becomes a place from where the world and the universe can be contemplated.

I will briefly comment on one more critical element: the vertical map is warped. It is not simply the same shape, in the vertical plane, as the third "abstract" dimension. This warping signifies the tension of a "volumetric" architecture, freed from the map and from the so-called avant-garde city planner's "short-sightedness."[20] At the same time, it is easy to see why the ruling powers would not be able to find the symbol of their violence in the form and structure of this vertical construction. *This shaped and modeled form using shell-like and warped surfaces is not the third dimension of a surface; it would thus not be able to dominate it.* The form is itself surface. The map is destroyed. The third dimension is for Xenakis the symbol of power in what he calls an "architecture of translation";[21] here it is neutralized. The Shell of Light has become the pure no-place of great collective concentration.

Power of Indetermination

Xenakis comes to this most important point by indeterminate calculation. In axioms 6 and 7 the Cosmic City receives its skeletal structure.[22] The utopic play animating the figure involves heterogeneous *topoi*, all unified in a "beautiful totality"; but this is disguised by its perfect coherence. The resulting play, which causes signification and exhibits utopia's productive practice, is an interference between spaces and places; it is a mobility displacing figure in its internal architecture. Because of this play the preliminaries for the future *science* of architecture are sketched out; in addition, a certain *freedom* is elaborated and the possibilities for a dynamics of *life* are given birth. Utopic freedom is not evident in the obvious outward appearance of the figure or in the surface of the society fiction forms. It is carried out inside figurative production and dissimulated by the images in which it is expressed and fixed. It must be given its freedom again through a productive rereading which unmasks its passage—displacing it, but also destroying it. It becomes fixed in this passage.

Xenakis' cosmic community unfolds a double space of play in the city's vertical. Various groups of all sorts mix in this conglomeration, and because of this hubbub architectural elements of the city are given an essential mobility. Looking closely, however, we see that the movements making up the play are very tightly defined by a calculus whose rules and secrets are held by institutions: "In the beginning, the arrangement of collectivities should be a statistically perfect mixture.... There will be absolutely no specialized subgroup of any kind. The mixing should be complete, and stochastically calculated by specialized population bureaux."[23] The results of these calculations may lead to the despecialization of a certain group or of a certain place; the operation, however, was carried out by specialized bureaux. These specialized bureaux, however, are institutions, scientific groups wielding power and capable of decisions, and therefore excluded from the overall vertical space shared by all. In the no-place of the Cosmic City, then, there actually is a place of power. The Shell of Light withholds a small fold into which light cannot enter, and instead of the gaze, orders emerge. There is a demographic and social strategy determining the play of movement for the surface's internal limits. And thus this spatial play belongs to figure and its activities—just as in many utopias they rigorously obey rules and systematic norms defining the figure's workings.

Utopic Power

Even with the surface play finely determined in figure's outward manifestation, there are nonetheless essential divergent elements of dispersion; it is through these activities that utopic practice is expressed. One of these has been present everywhere in the description of the Cosmic City; the structure and form of the City allow for neither the symbol nor the place of power. All the same, this drive to eliminate *privileged* places, where pockets of power in this perfect cosmic democracy could develop, does produce a rather unusual place all the same. It has no determined position, whether it be in the discourse or in the image, but it is a determining place all the same. This present absence—an organizing lack—has its function to pronounce the neutralization of privileged places. It does so in discourse and in the images; the internal architecture of the city depends on it. Hints of this came when we witnessed the erection and warping of the ground plan into a vertical surface of Gaze and Light.

Very simply, *the function of power is to eliminate places of power.* All institutional risks are removed: "Workers and young people will live in the same areas as government officials or the elderly, to the benefit of all."[24] The function of power is to reaffirm utopia as a permanent revolution: the utopic place has the very specific role of getting rid of all specializations, privileges, and special places. It is to keep the utopic City within a vertical volumetrics and a homogeneous ability to view all. This special place mentioned by Xenakis seems to emerge from a lapsus on his part: "*There will be absolutely no specialized sub-group of any kind.* The mixing...should be stochastically calculated by *specialized population bureaux.*"[25] The "contradictory" distance between the nonexistent subgroup and the population bureau defines the space of utopic play: this space is a place of neutralization, becoming "no-place." The social *topos* is *utopic.* This then results in the mobile architecture of interchangeable places which can, once and only once the critical reading has been made, signify the operation by which places come together without being inscribed in a topography. They are surrounded by a flowing line that does not perform a closure. These places allow for a dynamics of space within the architecture of collective space. That is the pure operation of the utopic production.

If we take into account the fact that these statistical calculations are made from mixtures of groups, the function of power consists in not only denying its own placement, but also in *"in-determining" determinisms* of tradition, of the past and past groupings found on a traditional map. The power of in-determination. The City holds the power of *il-locution*: again, a utopic power. Just as Xenakis had put the map in the place of utopia and "utopified" the city, so also the power structure within the City acts as an indeterminate power because of the dissimulated play of diverging spaces it brings about.

This is a difficult dynamics it brings about. Xenakis translates the movements with various expressions. "The heterogeneization of the city will follow as a result, by itself, vibrantly."[26] This implies that the initial gesture consisted in building—or at least seeming to build—a historical starting point, homogeneous, from which reverse entropy would naturally introduce differentiation into life so that it would become "the collective garment, population's biological receptacle and utensil (axiom 8)."[27] Xenakis is obliged to include the form of time, or history, in the figure of the City. But time and history also must submit to the form and structure of the City. Utopias have often "figured" this problem through an annual repeating holiday or festival. The cycle and rhythm would be the scansion of an immobile temporality by identifying with difference, the reciprocal of a differentiation of the identical. This is one way to try and get at the nameless force of the neutral. Xenakis, however, tries to consider it in another way. He dynamizes the "complexification" of the homogeneous. But this heterogeneizating force—life—is but another name for the power of indetermination that has strictly calculated the perfect statistical mixture at the "origin." In other words, by using statistics, Xenakis hopes to get at what he names, in "Toward a Philosophy of Music," the "thrust" of the question by boldly uniting Pythagoras and Parmenides: it is the very brunt of utopic practice. "Consideration *of what is* directly leads us into the construction, *ex nihilo*, of the very basic givens of musical composition and *especially to the rejection of every given that has not been rigorously brought into question (elegchos, dizesis).*"[28]

Universal Space and the Urban Message

The second offshoot of the City's heterotopic spaces is provided in axiom 12: "The City's great altitude...will also benefit by going above the clouds, usually passing by from between 0 to 2-3,000 meters. The population will thus be put into contact with the huge open spaces of the sky and stars."[29] The City has freed itself from the ground and the earth, from the space of topography and geography, all through the raising of the map to the vertical dimension and by a warped shell-like structure. Once it has become light and view, a sort of biological garment for the population, the surface has neutralized the flat human "habitation" of traditional, earthly, two-dimensional dwellings. We have already seen the utopic implications of this. Freedom and indetermination: Why? In order to open toward planetary space and contacts which, to Xenakis in 1964, seem to be "*absolute communication.* The planetary and cosmic era has begun; the City will need to face the cosmos and its human colonies, instead of crawling about on the ground."[30] The City has become pure message. It has freed itself from earthly ties to make contact with the universe. Without a transmitter or receiver, and lacking reference because it operates both it and its code, the City is both carrier and message in the great spaces between the World and the Universe.

At the beginning of the sixteenth century More's *Utopia* had been discovered between England and America, the Old and New Worlds. It made the attempt at describing and comprehending the pure difference between the too-well-known horrors of Western and Christian historical space and the surprises of the unknown geography of America. Now, near the end of the twentieth century, Xenakis' utopia has been built *ex nihilo* between the World and the Universe, the Earth and the Cosmos. It attempts to figure the contradiction and differentiation between the ground, where men crawl around in their cities, and the sky, an uninhabited, empty vertical space. More's utopia seems to be the finely worked and working figure of a historical situation of crisis: the end of feudalism, the birth of the bourgeoisie as the ruling class and of capitalism through its productive relations. Of what unheard-of future can Xenakis' utopia be the figure? For what urban or architectural science does it provide the conditions? By setting the social organism, the City, and mankind's collective garment *into play* between the horizontal and the vertical, Xenakis the architect has perhaps written the poem for a technology and science of another era. He also provided the negative of the age in which we live. Utopia, figure and practice, discourse and fictional power, neutralizing and anticipatory, is both one and the other.

Notes

Chapter 13

[1] The chapter develops further an article first published in *Arc*, November, 1972, about Xenakis. I would like to thank this journal's editors, especially Bernard Pingaud, for authorizing the republication of these remarks.

[2] "La Ville cosmique" was first published by Françoise Choay in her book *Urbanisme, utopies et réalités* (Paris: Le Seuil, 1965). The text was then reprinted in Iannis Xenakis' *Musique et architecture* (Paris: Médiations, 1971), pp. 151–160.

[3] Xenakis, p. 151.

[4] Xenakis, p. 154.

[5] See Chapter VII, above.

[6] Xenakis, p. 152.

[7] Xenakis, p. 152.

[8] Cf. G.-G. Granger, *Essai d'une philosophie du style*, (Paris: A. Colin, 1968), pp. 121 ff.

[9] Xenakis, p. 153.

[10] Xenakis, p. 153.

[11] Xenakis, p. 154.

[12] Xenakis, p. 154.

[13] Xenakis, p. 151.

[14] Xenakis, p. 155.

[15] Xenakis, "Le pavillon Philips à l'aube d'une architecture," op. cit., p. 123.

[16] Xenakis, "La Ville Cosmique," p. 155.

[17] See above, Chapter 10.

[18] See the works of Henry Lefebvre, especially *Le Droit à la ville* (Paris: Anthropos, 1968) and *La Révolution urbaine* (Paris: Gallimard, 1970), pp. 33-34, 55-57, 118 ff.

[19] Thus automatic and scientific agriculture uses electronic governing and decision-making techniques. The "classic farmer and his manual work [plus, I would add, his dwellings, his chores and his inscriptions on the earth] will disappear" (axiom 5, Xenakis, p. 155).

[20] Xenakis, p. 154.

[21] Xenakis, pp. 125-26.

[22] Xenakis, p. 155.

[23] Xenakis, pp. 155-156.

[24] Xenakis, p. 156.

[25] Xenakis, p. 156.

[26] Xenakis, p. 156.

[27] Xenakis, p. 156.

[28] Xenakis, "Vers une philosophie de la musique," p. 81.

[29] Xenakis, "La Ville Cosmique," p. 157.

[30] Xenakis, p. 157.

CHAPTER FOURTEEN

Utopia is Not a Political Project, *or* "Citizen Cabet's Plans for Emigration" (1848)[1]

"I. Citizen Cabet, of Paris, appeals to all communists: 'Because we have been persecuted, slandered and abused by the government, priests and the bourgeoisie – even by revolutionary republicans, and because provisions and supplies are kept from us in order to bring about our physical and moral deterioration, let us leave France and go to Icarie'; he is hoping that twenty to thirty thousand communists will be ready to follow him in order to found a communist colony in another part of the world. Cabet has not yet declared where he wants to emigrate. It will, however, probably be in the Free States of North America, perhaps in Texas or maybe California, just recently conquered by the Americans, where he hopes to found his Icarie.

Clearly we joyfully recognize, along with all communists, that Cabet has strugged with untiring effort and has admirably pursued the cause. He has successfully fought for suffering humanity. By watching out for conspiracies, he has immensely aided the proletariat. But when in my opinion he goes down the wrong path, none of these deeds can convince me to be silent. I hold citizen Cabet in high esteem, but I will struggle against his emigration projects, convinced that if the emigration takes place it will be at the greatest detriment to the principle of communism, and that the governments involved will emerge victorious and Cabet's last days will be bothered by bitter disillusions."

With Cabet's appeal to the French communists the utopic figure turns into a political project, Icarie. It entails a plan to move to another place, thereby tactically responding to bourgeois maneuvers at the height of the class struggle. Marx criticizes this transformation, however. He complains less of utopia than of its foundation. Cabet "has immensely aided the proletariat," writes Marx; "he has successfully fought for suffering humanity." How? He served by writing a book eight years earlier, *The Travel Adventures of Lord William Cansdall in Icarie.*[2]

Not only is utopia not "realizable," but it cannot be realized without destroying itself. Included in its functioning is the notion of not indicating the means for its construction; it cannot even signify the goal or propose the erection of the Perfect City. Utopia is not tomorrow, in time. It is *nowhere*, neither tomorrow nor yesterday. It does not have its foundations in hope. Cabet makes this mistake, too: he "is hoping that twenty to thirty thousand communists will be ready to follow him." Hope takes control of the future by applying the rational strategy of a project, except for believing in the positivity of chance. Utopia does come from expectation, however. It is constantly based on surprise before the future contained in every moment of the present. Utopia is the attempt to read and construct the traces and signs of the future into a text, traces and signs we meet and come up against. Utopia is the latent thrust of what occurs, of what is said, of what is done to bring on the future and the unexpected in the flow of unexpected speech. In this way, utopia is the form the unexpected takes. It is the narrative figure or pictorial form produced by history in the process of being made.[3]

Having become a project and political response, utopia can only be the source for bitter disillusions because it misunderstands the "other," the "other" it is precisely supposed to reveal and display as "other." Once the utopic figure has moved to the field of action, waiting to be completed, it masks to what in spite of itself it gave birth. It reveals its own discourse as displaced traces within its own lines of text and in the empty margins of its pages. The utopic figure is only the product of a signifying practice. The resulting representation can thus only disguise the thrust of the "other" when it stops being the object of reading and it takes on the role of a program and strategy in a political discourse. It is no longer readable; it pretends to be realizable.

"II. My reasons are the following: I believe that even in a country where the most shameful corruption is commonplace, and even when the people are exploited and oppressed in the most vulgar way, and when law and justice no longer have value, when society begins finding solutions in anarchy (as is currently the case in France), we must resolve ourselves to stay in that country. We must enlighten the people and inspire a new courage for those who are weakening. A foundation for a new social organization must be laid; we must stand up against the rogues! If those honest people who struggle for a better future leave, they will leave the arena completely open to the obscurants and the rogues. Europe would certainly fall. Europe is that part

of the world where communal wealth can be put forward first and most easily, simply for statistical and economic reasons. Instead, fire and brimstone will descend upon suffering humanity for centuries to come."

Utopia is not an absence of history. Its no-place is not an elsewhere in another part of the globe. Its foundation over *there* does not vacate someplace *here*. "If those honest poeple who struggle for a better future leave, they will leave the arena completely open to the obscurants and the rogues. Europe would certainly fall." In the same way that utopia is not realizable, or is realizable only by denying itself, its place is not elsewhere. It is here and now, as "other"; here and now, as different. Utopia has nothing to do with occupying another land or its use by the communists, because communal wealth will occur in this very land, now, but as "other." It is its reversal. Marx relies on statistics and the economy in maintaining that Europe is the privileged place for utopia; Europe will be the first place to host the revolution. The oldest place is also where the new can take place. The "other" of this earth--communal wealth--will not emerge in another land, as if attack strategies were necessary and utopic practice would carry them out. Neutralization in and by utopia signifies revolution in and by history. This entails the creation of the text and practice of figure within the empty spaces at play utopia has traced out.

"I am convinced that Cabet's project to found an Icarie, a colony in America based on the principles of communal property, cannot yet be brought to fruition. This is so for the following reasons:

(1) All those wanting to follow Cabet may very well be ardent communists, but they are nonetheless too infected with the errors of their education and the prejudices of today's society to be able to get rid of them in Icarie;

(2) That would necessarily provoke arguments in the colony. This friction would be exploited by external society, powerful and hostile, as well as by spies from European governments. They would fan the flames of discordance leading to the complete downfall of communist society;

(3) The majority of the emigrants are artisans. The type of work there demands hearty farm-workers to plow and plant. An artisan is perhaps not as easily transformed into a farmer as one might believe;

(4) The sacrifices and illnesses due to the change of climate would cause many to be discouraged and leave. For the moment, many are in the heat of enthusiasm, and only see the pleasant side of it. But when the harsh reality

is made clear to them, and all sorts of sacrifices are demanded of them, their enthusiasm will wane. When all the little comforts even the poorest worker can procure in Europe disappear, they will quickly become discouraged;

(5) For communists – and surely Icarians – who realize the principle of personal freedom, a community of communal property without a transition period, actually a democratic transition period where personal property is slowly transformed into social property, is as impossible as is harvesting grain without having planted."

Utopia is not a political project. If it were, it would then definitely be "utopic." Marx's five objections to Cabet's plan for emigration to Icarie stem from this. All of the objections are in some sense related to the major problem of transition, moving from current society to one of communal wealth. How can utopia be achieved on its own grounds? How can the separation be eliminated, the neutralizing space be done away with? In an instant, outside time. The enthusaistic communists who have decided to leave with Cabet "are nevertheless too infected with the errors of their education and the prejudices of today's society to be able to get rid of them in Icarie." Can the trip between Europe and the Other World (also the New World) eliminate centuries of European, Christian, and bourgeois education? Can coming to Icarie also mean the arrival of the new man? Marx feels the length of the trip is not sufficient to bring about this death and birth.

Utopic neutralization is of a different sort; it does not rely on historical reality, the contradictions of which will continue to affect and upset the Icarian colony. The space in which it will be born cannot be another space separated from worldly societies by an unbridgeable *no man's land.* No map would show it; no chart would find it. "Harsh reality" is there, imminent. This is the space that cannot be eliminated, the space demanding long cultural and technical traditions; the climate is different and harder. Living at the origin – and at the founding moment – is impossible. History cannot turn around. After space comes the rude reality of time, Utopia is not accomplished; it is always already accomplished as a whole, in harmony and in equilibrium. All of its parts come from the presence of a visible figure. Narratives secretly work to deconstruct it. But, finally, the idea of communal wealth, a fundamental idea for utopia, must side with history and perserverance. Communism is the progressive result of work to alter and transform society. It is, in fact, the "ideal communist idea." When utopia becomes a political project or a platform for action, its content becomes a daydream or a fantasy, even a trap in reality. It was to represent the world, but the world turns out wrong, bittersweet: the taste of either the origin or the end of the world.

> *"III. The failure of a project like Cabet's does not endanger communist principles. Neither will it stop the practical introduction of communist principles into a society forever. It would encourage thousands of discouraged communists to leave our cause, however. The proletariat would probably suffer in misery that much longer as a consequence. Finally,*
>
> *IV. a few hundred or thousand people cannot establish and continue a communal living situation without it taking on an absolutely exclusive and sectarian nature, such as the community in America founded by Rapp. Our desire, and I hope that of the Icarians also, would not tend toward that type of community.*
>
> *In addition, I haven't yet mentioned the probable persecution the Icarians would probably–no, certainly–suffer from the outside. Everyone wanting to accompany Mr. Cabet to America should begin by reading a document relating the persecutions that the Mormons–a religious and communist sect–were and are still forced to suffer there."*

Marx's problem centers on the "practical introduction" of the communist principle to real universal humanity, the world's proletariat. By wanting to bring about Icarie, Cabet reverses the unbound force of neutralization and utopic practice's freedom. He does away with the productive polyvalence of the fiction and the generative quality of the figurative matrix. Instead, he turns it into its contrary. It becomes a closed and separated individual element. Utopic figure's neutralizing force, because it is figure, dissolves as it becomes a *sectarian split*. This is an unwelcome negation. Neither space nor time is brought under control. Neither the voyage (geographic distancing) nor the presence of the founding gesture (the instantaneity of the origin) is controlled. Utopia has no other route in realized utopia than to produce the distance and totality itself: it rejects the exterior outside of itself. It repels every element that the schema of the imagination, now turned into an abstract rational idea, cannot assimilate into reality. *The universalist-internationalist dynamics for the practical introduction of the communist principle* (the concept corresponding to the ambivalent schema of utopic fiction) is paralyzed and becomes a *static sectarian ideology*. It thus must suffer the aftershocks of the regulating force it developed in order to stay alive: persecutor-persecuted. "Everyone wanting to accompany Mr. Cabet to America should begin by reading a document relating the persecutions that the Mormons—a religious and communist sect—were and are still forced to suffer there." The paradox of this example is glaring, because a century later the Mormons are one of the wealthiest capitalist communities of the United States. Obviously, socialism cannot remain utopic if utopia is not necessarily socialist.

> *"These are the reasons I consider Cabet's project to emigrate dangerous. Therefore I cry out to the communists of every country: Brothers, stay at the battlefront of Europe. Work and struggle here, because only Europe has all the elements to set up communal wealth. This type of community will be established here, or nowhere."*

The conclusion is clear: "Work and struggle here..." Utopia is not realizable. Realizing it is not its function. This is why Marx can say, "only Europe has all the elements to set up communal wealth." In other words, revolutionary theory is the scientific revelation of the workings of a capitalist society and the practical critique of this society as it works (strategic and tactical considerations). *Socialist praxis is utopia*, or, more exactly, the explicit correlate of utopic signifying practice.[4] Marx suggests this in his powerful last phrase: "This type of community [i.e., utopia] will be established here, or nowhere." It is nowhere else than here (all the conditions already exist for it); it is neither elsewhere nor tomorrow. Utopia is already here now, but it is here as the "other" of this historical place and present, aging Europe. As utopic practice, revolutionary theory discovers in the here and now of a historical situation what is its reverse, or "other," side, its negative. It discerns the thrust of what is yet to come but is also already there, completely. "Only Europe has all the elements to set up communal wealth"—the "other" side of the present, such as the future already completely present in the situation the revolutionary movement puts into practice.

This discovery is a theoretical and scientific discovery. What the utopic communist theory had shown as lacking in its own system it makes into a concept. In this way revolution is revolutionary theory. But also, political projects have nothing more to do with founding or bringing to fruition utopias. Revolution *brings into existence*: theory as practice. This is why, after exposing why he feels Cabet's emigration plans are dangerous, Marx *cries out*. He internationally implores communists to struggle in Europe in the name of a future communal wealth already there. Because the revolutionary movement is theory, utopic practice can become the critique of present society. Utopic practice stops producing figures in which it is condensed and through which it passes, moving on different levels of society. It instead becomes revolutionary practice: a universal scientific theory and concrete practice. It is revolutionary *praxis*: utopic practice coming to the awareness of its own process, a critical consciousness seeing itself in its own figures and emerging spaces for concepts and in their production. These are the historical forces transforming the world.

Utopics—spatial play. Here is one that can be done in everyone's presence.

First, a sheet of paper should be folded four or eight times. With a pair of scissors, it must be cut into arbitrarily, creating various slits and shapes. Once unfolded, surprising lacelike forms will be discovered, perfectly regular and harmoniously organized. Now, the various sections should be realigned and parts of them crumpled, if need be, so that no holes remain. Other pieces of paper can be used to fill in the gaps.

Once this has been accomplished and the sheet of paper again resembles a continuous surface, the players will be asked:

(1) to reconstitute the holes, following the crumples;

(2) to reconstitute the cut-out and missing pieces, including those that might have been used, as well as their arrangement;

(3) to rewrite the first move of the game.

The whole question centers on whom or what in this example is symbolized by the passive voice: this is the problem of utopia.

Notes

Chapter 14

[1] Karl Marx, *La Revue communiste*, 1858, No. 1. I thank Madam M. Cranaki for bringing this interesting text to my attention.

[2] Cabet, *Voyage en Icarie* (Paris: 1840).

[3] See E. Bloch, *Das Prinzip Hoffnung* (Frankfurt: Suhrkamp Verlag, 1959). See also *Spüren* (Frankfurt: Suhrkamp Verlag, 1960) and Fredric Jameson's comments in *Marxism and Form* (Princeton: Princeton University Press, 1971), pp. 116 ff.

[4] See L. Segag, *Marxisme et structuralisme* (Paris: Payot, 1967).